"A wonderful story that kept surprising me as I read. Real conflicts and deep emotions make the powerful story come to life."

—*Rendezvous*

"Engaging...starring two scarred souls and a wonderful supporting cast...Fans will enjoy."

—*Midwest Book Review*

THE ROAD HOME

"A terrific story...a book you will want to keep to read again and again."

—RomRevToday.com

"The characters...stay with you long after the last page is read."

—Bookloons.com

BACK ROADS

"Accomplished and very satisfying...Add Crandall to your list of authors to watch."

—Bookloons.com

"An amazingly assured debut novel...expertly drawn."
—TheRomanceReadersConnection.com

"A definite all-nighter. Very highly recommended."
—RomRevToday.com

Books by Susan Crandall

A Kiss in Winter
On Blue Falls Pond
Promises to Keep
Magnolia Sky
The Road Home
Back Roads

PITCH
BLACK

SUSAN
CRANDALL

FOREVER

NEW YORK   BOSTON

Book design by Stratford Publishing Services, a TexTech business

Forever
Hachette Book Group USA
237 Park Avenue
New York, NY 10017
Visit our Web site at www.HachetteBookGroupUSA.com

Forever is an imprint of Grand Central Publishing.

The Forever name and logo is a trademark of Hachette Book Group USA, Inc.

Printed in the United States of America

First Printing: June 2008

10 9 8 7 6 5 4 3 2 1

This book was finished in the midst of wedding preparations,
so I'd like to dedicate it to Reid and Melissa Crandall.
May your marriage be happy and fulfilling and
your love forever constant.

Acknowledgments

As always, a huge thank-you to those who helped me shape this book, who didn't let me get off easy, and whom I couldn't do this without. To Alicia, Brenda, Garthia, Pam, Sherry, and Vicky, I appreciate the constant support, as well as reading those last two hundred pages with lightning speed. To Karen White, thanks for all of the hand-holding, and for being both a great sounding board and a wonderful friend.

To my loving family for their unflagging support; especially my husband, Bill, who understands when I have to write during the hours most people are sleeping.

PITCH
BLACK

Prologue

Cheryl McPherson never saw him coming. One second she was standing at the top of the stairs with a basket full of dirty laundry, the next she was in a free fall. The shove was hard enough that she sailed over the first five steps. As if in slow motion, clothes drifted past her vision; soiled socks, her husband's favorite blue shirt, her son's Little League uniform with bright grass stains on the knees. When her shoulder slammed into the sixth step, the sound of snapping bones was accompanied by a white-hot pain that shot from the point of impact down the length of her spine. By the time the pain fully registered, she'd tumbled down two more steps and another bone had broken with an audible crack. Pain swelled in a riptide that tore at all of her senses.

She landed at the bottom with her cheek pressed against the cold marble floor, her heartbeat matching the rhythm of her pulsing pain.

The plastic laundry basket came to a bouncing halt against her right shin.

She'd known this day would come. She'd allowed it to happen. Love had twisted into something ugly and unrecognizable.

Unable to move, unable to utter more than a weak moan, she stared ahead, looking down the long expanse of white marble toward the kitchen; where the telephone was, where she could call for help.

Drag yourself. Move! Move before he comes down the stairs.

But it was too late. His shoes appeared on the tile between her and that faraway telephone.

She only had time to blink; then the blow came....

Chapter 1

IT COULD HAVE BEEN THE THUNDER. Or perhaps the gust of wind that shook the house as if it was a misbehaving child. Something had jerked Madison Wade awake, with her breath locked in her chest and her heart racing. Perhaps it had been Mrs. Quigley's tomcat romancing the Persian that spent her mornings on the sunporch next door. But it didn't feel like any of those things. It felt heavy... dark, and stifling. She hadn't suffered from this kind of anxious awakening for months, not since she'd moved to Tennessee.

She forced herself to draw a deep breath and release it slowly. Everything was fine. Her son—she'd finally grown accustomed to thinking of Ethan as such—was far away from the dangers in Philadelphia, safe from the people and circumstances that had threatened to pull him under. Things were good.

She glanced toward the window. No rain pattered against the pane. Although the new day did not creep as softly as it usually did upon Buckeye, the approaching storm seemed respectful and subdued, as was accorded by the early hour. That was one of her father's idyllic boyhood stories that had proven true—one of the few truths that had ever passed his lips—here the days rolled gently one into the other. They were not announced with brittle light and a blare of car horns, or the sharp banging of Dumpsters dropped noisily to the ground. Here in Buckeye people respected the quiet of early morning. The day fell gently, as if delivered by a feather drifting from an awakening sky.

She arose and looked outside. The view from almost every window in this house was spectacular, contrasting in every way from the gray cityscape she had inhabited most of her life. Even after the passage of four months, she couldn't help but pause each morning and take in the seemingly endless reach of the verdant wilderness. The setting was the main reason she had chosen this particular house. She wanted everything in Ethan's life to be new, untouched by the cruel bleakness of his childhood.

Clouds hung low over the rolling green mountains; the valleys and draws cradled thick blue-gray mist. Had she sent warm enough clothes with Ethan? The nights could be chilly up there, even though it was only September.

She shook her head. When had she turned into such a sap? Ethan would really let her have it if he knew. That was part of what made the two of them work—love and honesty without the pretty bows and wrapping paper. It was a deal they'd struck early on; no bullshit.

Besides, her stewing was ridiculous. When she'd first taken Ethan in as a foster child at thirteen, he had spent more nights sleeping in the elements than any child should. He'd reminded her of this before he'd left—when he'd caught her surreptitiously checking his supplies, looking at the tag for the weather rating of his sleeping bag, and throwing in extra batteries for his flashlight—he was fifteen now. Which he said translated into something like twenty in regular suburban-kid years. "*Besides,*" he'd said, "*it's a whole lot safer sleeping on a mountain with a few bears than it was sleeping on the streets in Philadelphia.*"

She'd looked into his wide blue eyes and nearly cried. Crying...now that would have sent him into orbit.

Luckily, these days his past was just a distant echo that she occasionally saw in the depths of his eyes. He was safe and loved; her responsibility...her son. The adoption had been finalized the week before they'd moved to Buckeye.

Thunder rumbled again in the distance. She hoped the boys made it back down the mountain before the rain hit. With the threatening weather, surely Mr. McPherson would pack up and head back early.

Jordan Gray's stepfather took groups of boys camping once a month. The first two times Ethan had been invited, she'd managed an excuse—although she couldn't say *why* she'd been so reluctant to let him go. This time he'd called her on it. Honesty...without the pretty packaging. He went.

She should have been happy that Ethan, a newcomer, had been asked. It was a great opportunity for him to bond with other boys of his own age. Of course, those were logical arguments, not the illogical fears of a mother who wasn't truly comfortable with her new role as such. She attributed her heightened worry to her vast and intimate knowledge of how dangerous this world could be; up until a few months ago, she'd made her living writing about missing children, gang violence, and Internet predators.

Madison turned from the window and chafed her hands over her chilly arms. She'd lived alone throughout her adulthood, preferring a solitary life, relying on the only person she knew she could count on—herself. Dedication to her work had filled her days; she'd never felt lonely. But now, as she stood in her bedroom listening to the wind, she suddenly realized how starkly empty the house felt without Ethan.

Get a grip. He's only been gone since yesterday morning. She'd always thrived on independence and respected it in others. Never in her wildest dreams had she thought she'd be inclined to stew and worry while her child was off living his life. What had she known?

Certainly not how quickly a person became used to hearing overgrown feet thudding on the floor overhead; or how not finding a dirty cereal bowl in the sink made a person's chest feel hollow.

As much as she didn't want to admit it, she was glad she'd agreed to have breakfast with Gabe Wyatt this morning. It wasn't a date; she didn't date. Not now that she was the working mother of a teenage son. Both her and Ethan's lives had been in enough upheaval without adding the complication of a new romance.

But Gabe's friendship was becoming difficult to keep at that casual level. He'd subtly insinuated himself into her life, often serving as a sounding board concerning adolescent male behavior (being an only child, her only firsthand experience with the teenage male before Ethan had been her own pubescent dating). Gabe had also done his best to help her learn which toes were the most delicate in this new small town. Since she was editor of the local daily paper, more often than not those lessons went unheeded. They were appreciated nonetheless.

Up until yesterday, she'd managed to resist his repeated invitations to dinner and movies—no easy feat. From the very first time she'd heard him speak, his smooth Southern voice had had a nearly hypnotic effect on her Yankee heart. She now understood the power of those so-called "whisperers"—people who could calm animals with only their voices. It was certain Gabe Wyatt's voice called to something primal deep inside her. She had no business getting involved. But he kept asking in that voice. . . .

When the invitation had been breakfast, she'd justified that breakfast was different. Colleagues and friends met for breakfast. Breakfast was innocent, noncommittal. Breakfast wasn't a date.

She glanced at the clock. If she didn't hurry, she was going to be late.

At seven-thirty she turned onto High Street. With a gust of wind, the first fat drops of rain hit her windshield. Gabe's Jeep Cherokee with SHERIFF printed plainly on the sides and back gate was parked at the curb in front of the Smoky Ridge Café. She parked next to it.

She felt more relaxed just seeing he was here.

Relaxed. Relaxed—not bubbling with joy.

She tamped down that ripple of pure pleasure and wondered when she had started lying to herself—something as foreign to her as these hills had been on her first day here. She'd always been as pragmatic in her personal relationships as she was in her work. She wasn't sure what to think of this new aspect of herself.

She stopped asking herself questions she didn't really want to answer and hopped out of the car. The second she closed the door, the clouds cut loose. Holding her purse over her head, she made a dash for the café.

The door swung open just as she reached it. Gabe held the door and hurried her inside. For a long moment, he just stood there grinning at her.

"What?" she asked. "Never seen a drowned rat before?"

"Mermaid." The warmth of his voice poured over her, banishing the chill. "I was thinking you look like a mermaid."

"You Southern boys, always let your good manners get ahead of your good sense," she said, breaking eye contact.

"You Yankee women, never can gracefully accept innocent Southern flattery."

She looked up at him with a half-grin. "Thanks."

"For the compliment?" he asked. "Or for calling you on your Yankee ways?"

"Oh"—she feigned a surprised look—"I thought they were both compliments."

He rolled his eyes. "Here we go again."

"You started it." She walked toward an empty booth, her heart fluttering in a most *un*pragmatic way.

Gabe slid into the booth beside her and picked up a menu.

She gave him a sideways look and cleared her throat.

"Yes?" He turned innocent green eyes her way.

"Are we expecting someone else?"

"Not that I know of."

She pointed across the table. "Then get your ass over on the other side of the booth before people start talking."

With a heavy sigh, he moved.

Madison looked around the crowded café and saw knowing grins, raised eyebrows, and a few lips pursed in disapproval. The damage had already been done.

She leaned across the table and said in a hushed voice, "Everyone thinks we spent the night together."

Gabe glanced around, then grinned at her and whispered back, "Of course they don't. What man in his right mind would be out of your bed at this early hour on a Sunday morning?"

Tilting her head, trying to appear sweet and Southern, she drawled, "Why, Gabriel Wyatt, I declare, I should slap your face for such a shamefully inappropriate remark."

He gave her a wink. "Now that's how to take a compliment."

Madison made a point of *not* lingering over coffee after breakfast. Lingering was too date-like.

"I really need to get home. Ethan will be back from camping," she said, wiping her lips with a paper napkin. Now she was lying to other people as well as to herself; Ethan wasn't due home until around noon. But she couldn't stay here listening to Gabe's voice and looking into his moss-green eyes any longer. Not when her own mind had begun to follow the pattern of the other patrons; several times now she'd caught herself wondering what it would be like to spend the night in Gabe Wyatt's bed.

She reached for the check; the cash register was by the front door and Gabe paying was one step closer to this being a date.

Gabe put his hand firmly on top of hers. "Apparently you still have a lot to learn about living in the South."

She liked the way his calloused palm felt against the back of her hand—too much.

"All right then." She pulled her hand from beneath his. "I'll just use my money to buy myself something frilly that smells of gardenias."

He laughed. "Now you're talkin'."

With a dramatic huff, she got out of the booth.

He was still chuckling as he followed her to the front.

He paid, then she thanked him, painfully aware of dozens of eyes on them.

"My pleasure. How about dinner Saturday?"

His gaze held hers as his voice worked its magic. "I...I—"

"I'll take that as a yes." He opened the door and pushed her out into the rain before she could say anything else.

ONCE HOME, MADISON OPENED HER LAPTOP and began working on the duties of her new career. If someone had told her four years ago that she'd be content working at a newspaper with a circulation of less than ten thousand, editing stories about the mayor's plan for parking meters and the debate over replacing the bridge on the north side of town, she'd have laughed in their face. But here she was, miles beyond content. All because of Ethan.

And perhaps—a little voice whispered, trying to keep her honest—a little because of a certain smooth-talking Southern sheriff, too.

She'd never before let a man railroad her into a date like that. Really, she had to stop reacting to that voice....

"Enough of that foolishness," she muttered. She'd just cancel...later. Right now, if she finished proofing these articles for the *Buckeye Daily Herald*, she could do some research for a freelance article she was contemplating.

She opened the file her reporter had e-mailed her and started to read.

The work did not hold her attention. She caught herself watching the clock instead of concentrating on the article in front of her. If she hadn't been so stubborn and hurried off after breakfast with Gabe, she wouldn't have this long lonely stretch of time before Ethan came home.

She thought about how they would spend the rest of the day after he returned. Since it was cool and rainy, maybe she would take him to Augustino's for pizza. She imagined the blast of warm moist air, redolent of yeast and spices, that always hit her when she opened the door to the little restaurant. Her mouth watered. She'd thought she'd miss national chains and five-star restaurants when she moved to this little town. Again, what had she known?

At twelve-fifteen, she started making trips to look out the rain-streaked front window for the approach of Mr. McPherson's white van.

At one o'clock she called Jordan Gray's mother.

"Hello, Mrs. McPherson, this is Madison Wade. I was wondering, have you heard anything from the boys?"

"Please, call me Kate."

"Of course, Kate." She'd only met Kate McPherson in person once; usually it was a wave from the car as they picked the boys up at each other's houses. "Is Jordan back?"

Kate didn't sound in the least concerned when she said, "No, but don't you worry now, hon. Steve gets carried away up there. He's probably showing the boys thunderstorm survival skills or something."

"Oh, well, okay then, that's good to know."

"Keep in mind, with this rain and all, it could take 'em longer to get down the mountain. It's not like hopping on the bus in the city, you know."

"Yes, I suppose that's right." This wasn't the first time she'd had to be reminded that time moved differently here than in Philadelphia.

Kate said, "I promise I'll give y'all a call if I hear from them. But really, don't worry."

"Thank you."

After hanging up, Madison made herself a cup of tea and tried to stop thinking of Ethan with a broken leg after a misstep on the muddy slope of the mountain.

At two-thirty she picked up the telephone again. After only a moment's hesitation, she dialed Gabriel Wyatt's cell phone.

He picked up on the first ring. "Sheriff Wyatt."

"Hi, Gabe, it's Madison. Do you have a minute?"

"Well hello, Maddie. If you're calling to cancel our date, no, I don't." His teasing knocked the sharp edge off her tension. She didn't even take him to task over calling her Maddie—only her father called her Maddie, the placating bastard.

On Gabe's smooth Southern tongue, the nickname seemed to lose the capacity to annoy.

"I'm calling about Ethan," she said.

"Oh?"

"Well, it's probably nothing. . . ."

"Get on then and say it."

"He's not home from camping with Mr. McPherson yet."

"If you can trust anyone with your son on that mountain, it's Steve McPherson. He spends more time up there than he does here in town."

"Yes, but...two hours—"

"Is nothing when you're hauling camping gear and teenage boys off a mountain in the rain."

"You think so?"

"I do. But if it'd make you feel better, I suppose I could drive up to the trailhead where Steve parks his van and check things out."

"I hate to impose...."

"No problem." After a short pause he added, "How about if I pick you up and you can keep me company?"

It would make her feel better to be doing something proactive, rather than sitting around imagining all sorts of horrible things. And, she rationalized, it'd give her a chance to cancel their date.

"What if they show up here?" she asked.

"Does Ethan have a key?"

"Yes."

"Leave him a note. He can call your cell phone if he gets home. Besides, it's a two-lane road; we're sure to spot them going the other way."

She hesitated.

"Maddie," he sighed. "The boy survived alone on those Yankee city streets. An hour alone in your cozy little house shouldn't be a huge challenge."

"You're right." She heard the lack of conviction in her own voice. "Of course, you're right. I'll check back to make sure Jordan's mom hasn't heard anything."

"I'll be there in fifteen minutes."

"Okay." She started to hang up, then said, "Gabe!"

"Yeah?"

"I know I'm probably being silly. Thank you for humoring me."

"Believe me, it's my pleasure to humor you."

She heard him chuckling as he hung up.

SHEETS OF RAIN SLASHED against Gabe's SUV. Gusts of wind buffeted the heavy vehicle as if it was made of cardboard. Although the wipers thumped back and forth on high speed, looking through the windshield was like trying to focus through textured glass. Madison found herself leaning forward, straining to see where the winding narrow unpaved road gave way to rocky, tree-filled ditches on each side. Her cold hand blanched white as she gripped the passenger door handle.

Gabe's Jeep was several years old and took the bumps about as gracefully as a log wagon. More than once, the tires momentarily slipped on the muddy incline.

Driving in the mountains on a clear day made her insides pucker; she'd be nauseous driving in this weather, and she wasn't doing much better as a passenger. Daring to take her eyes away from the road long enough for a quick glance at Gabe, she saw he had a relaxed grip on the wheel. His face bore no sign of strain; in fact, he was smiling.

"You look like you're enjoying yourself," she said.

He turned to face her fully, his smile widening. "I am."

"Hey!" She pointed ahead. "Keep your eyes on the road, mister!"

With a chuckle, he obeyed and said, "How can a guy not have a good time with a woman bossing him around like that?"

"I just want to come back down off this mountain whole and unbroken. Smile at me later."

He turned that innocent-yet-oh-so-suggestive smile her way again. "It'll be my pleasure."

"The road," she ordered. "Mule trail" would have been a more appropriate term. It had narrowed so much that the undergrowth was nearly scraping the sides of the car.

A few seconds later, he slowed. The Jeep bounced through the shallow ditch and he pulled through a break in the vegetation that Madison hadn't even seen. They stopped in a small, relatively flat area that was a quagmire of mud and flattened weeds. Gabe called it a cove. The mountain took a serious thrust upward from this spot.

"There's Steve's van," he said.

It was the only vehicle there. "I see he's the only one crazy enough to still be out in this weather."

"Never seen Steve McPherson daunted by a little weather."

She glanced at the steep path that headed into the woods and up the mountain. "We should go up after them—something might be wrong."

"Now *that* would be crazy. You don't just take off in this terrain with no preparation, no one knowing where you are, especially in this weather." He pointed to her feet. "You don't even have on decent shoes."

She looked down. "I'll have you know these boots were the envy of all of my co-workers in Philly."

With a crooked, knowing grin he said, "No doubt. They're sexy as hell. But those heels are guaranteed to cause a broken ankle within the first hundred yards."

Again, she felt oddly out of her depth. How could she be so unprepared for a safer, simpler life?

"Can we call a park ranger or something?"

He shook his head. "This isn't park land—even so, a call for a search is premature. Steve knows what he's doing. Maybe he's waiting it out. Some of the trail is pretty steep."

"Does he always camp in the same place?"

"Same general area. He knows that helps...just in case we have to go looking for him."

"I feel so stupid. I didn't ask half of the questions I should have before I let Ethan go. Jordan's mom said her husband takes Jordan all of the time. I just assumed..." She shook her head at her own naiveté. The rain drummed on the Jeep's roof. She shivered. "I had no idea it was so—rough. I had in mind the kinds of camping areas I've seen in small state parks—you know, easy access, lots of people around, permits required. Nothing like this."

He patted her hand. "See why a couple of hours late doesn't alarm anyone?"

Madison left her hand beneath his and nodded, keeping her eyes on the inclining trail that was quickly swallowed by dark woods. In contrast to her feelings as she'd viewed it from the warmth and safety of her home, the thick forest suddenly seemed more menacing than tranquil. And Gabe's logical argument for the group's delayed return didn't quell her rising panic. Something had felt off since she'd awakened this morning.

Gabe suggested, "We can wait here until they come back."

"Oh, I don't know." She bit her lip. "I mean, how much razzing will Ethan get if his mom's waiting for him?" And how would she explain herself to him and keep with their no-bullshit pact?

"Maybe it's not Ethan's mom who's waiting. Maybe it's Sheriff Wyatt fulfilling his county duties."

"Oh sure," she said. "The only way that's going to work is if I hide in the backseat and they don't see me."

"Works for me." He hooked a thumb over his shoulder.

"Climb over and you can duck down at the first sign of them."

Turning sideways in the seat, she said, "I'm not going to climb over—"

"Too late. There they are."

The instant she laid eyes on the four boys emerging from the forest, the bottom dropped out of her stomach. "Something's wrong."

Gabe was already out of the car and striding toward the boys. He moved so quickly, he left the driver's door standing open.

With her heart in her throat, she threw open her door and jumped out. Cold rain slapped her in the face. With her second step, her foot twisted on a rock. Pain sliced her ankle and shot up her leg, but she didn't break stride as she ran toward Ethan.

The boys looked like the final scene in a slasher film. None of them had on jackets. In defiance of the downpour, dark smears of mud refused to let go of their clothes and skin. *Fishbelly white*. It was a term used by her grandfather. She'd never realized what it meant until now. Their lips, darkened by the cold, contrasted grotesquely with the pasty, translucent whiteness of their faces.

Jordan's arms were slung around the necks of Ethan and another boy. Jordan's head hung low, his steps dragged in a shuffle.

By the time she caught up with Gabe, he was scooping Jordan into his arms. She looked beyond the boys; no one followed on the trail. "Where's Mr. McPherson?"

Relieved of their burden, Ethan and the other boy swayed weakly, but didn't take another step forward.

Jordan, very small for his age to begin with, looked

frighteningly frail in Gabe's arms. His lower lip was slightly swollen, oddly blue-purple against his translucent skin. Inanimate as death, the boy didn't even blink the rain out of his eyes.

The fourth boy, a kid built like a future linebacker, sat heavily on the ground, heedless of the muddy brown puddle he landed in. He buried his face in his grimy hands and sobbed. It was a sound teetering between relief and devastation.

Madison wrapped her arms around Ethan, their unspoken ban on sappiness be damned. "Where is Mr. McPherson?"

Ethan pulled back and looked up at her with hollow eyes. "Dead."

Chapter 2

A CHILL BEYOND THAT of the wind-driven rain reached deep into Madison's heart, strangling her lungs with an icy grip. Dead? Steve McPherson was dead. Her gaze cut from Ethan to Gabe. He apparently hadn't heard Ethan's choked response. He was a few steps away, trying to open a door on McPherson's van while still cradling Jordan.

Dear God. "What happened?"

"An accident." The wind tried to gobble up Ethan's words, but his face blazed with fierce conviction. This was a side of him she hadn't seen of late; that slight jutting of chin and rigidity of shoulders, the stance of a child used to being dismissed, disbelieved, and disregarded.

"What kind of accident—"

"It's locked," Gabe called.

Madison looked up, squinting against the rain.

"I'm putting him in my car." Gabe started toward the Jeep. "He's like ice. Bring the others."

The linebacker in the puddle made no move to get up. He'd wrapped his arms around his knees and was rocking back and forth.

Madison put an arm around Ethan and the boy standing next to him. "Get in the car." She set them in motion toward the Jeep. Then she knelt before the boy sitting in the puddle. She was already chilled, but the cold of the wet ground quickly made her knees ache. This boy had to be near numb.

"Come on," she said. "Let's get you out of the rain."

The boy didn't respond, keeping his face buried in his arms. Rain ran in a stream off his hair, splattering into the puddle between his feet.

He was much too big for her to heft up off the ground. She laid a hand on his arm. "It's warm in the Jeep. The other boys are already over there."

Slowly the boy raised his eyes to meet hers. He looked bewildered. It took a moment for his gaze to register her presence.

"I'm Ethan's mom," she said, leaning closer. "Let's go. The sheriff'll get you boys home."

"Wh-wh-what about...?" His gaze moved upward, toward the trail.

"Sheriff Wyatt will take care of him, too."

"We just left him." The boy squeezed his eyes closed, his mouth screwed into a tight frown and his chin trembled. "We just left him there...."

"What's your name?"

The boy ran his forearm across his runny nose. "J.D."

"It's okay, J.D. You did what you had to do. You did what Mr. McPherson would have wanted you to do." She put her hands under his elbows. "Let's go to the car."

He faltered as he got to his feet. Struggling to keep her own feet beneath her on the soggy ground, Madison managed to steady him until he was able to move forward.

Ethan and the other boy were already in the backseat. She guided J.D. to the front passenger seat, which was soaked with rain, but the heat was blowing full force.

"Just sit here for a minute." She closed the door and went around to where Gabe had the rear hatch open. He'd laid Jordan in the cargo compartment and covered him with his own coat.

He was rubbing Jordan's hands and saying, "Jordan? Come on, buddy, look at me. You're going to be all right. Come on, Jordan."

Jordan's eyes remained unfocused and he only moved when Gabe physically moved him.

Ethan was on his knees, leaning over the backseat, his worried gaze fixed on his friend. "He stopped talking hours ago. The last time we stopped to rest he wouldn't even look at me."

Madison leaned close to Gabe's ear. "Ethan said Steve McPherson's dead."

Gabe stopped rubbing. His gaze snapped to Madison's face. "Christ! How?"

"An accident," she said softly, then glanced meaningfully toward Jordan. "I don't know more than that."

"Was Jordan injured, too?" Gabe asked Ethan.

"No." He paused. "At least—not that— No."

"And you're certain about Mr. McPherson...beyond any doubt?"

Ethan nodded gravely. "*Very* sure. It...it happened late last night."

No one seemed willing to say outright in front of an

already traumatized Jordan that his stepdad was lying alone and dead on the mountain. Even though, from the looks of the boy, he wasn't hearing anything at all.

"Where is he?" Gabe asked.

Ethan said, "Near the bottom of a waterfall."

"Harp Falls or Black Rock Falls?"

"Black Rock, the tall one."

Before Gabe could ask another question, Jordan began to shake.

"What's wrong with him?" Panic sharpened Ethan's tone. "Why is he doing that?"

"Shock. We've got to get him to the hospital." Gabe turned to Madison. "You drive. I'll stay back here with Jordan."

"No way. I'll stay with Jordan." She climbed into the back of the Jeep, lifting Jordan's head and shoulders into her lap. She pulled the hem of her sweater from beneath her jacket and dried the boy's face. "Shouldn't you call someone to go after...?"

"I can't from here; no radio. I will as soon as we get out of this dead area."

The Jeep lurched when Gabe put it in gear, then rocked and bucked over the uneven ground as he turned it around.

"Ethan. Sit," Gabe said.

Madison looked up.

Ethan was still hanging over the backseat. "M, is he gonna be okay?"

"We need to get him to a hospital," she said. "Sit down and fasten your seat belt."

ONCE THEY REACHED AN AREA where the radio repeaters would transmit a signal to dispatch, Gabe got the ball rolling for a recovery team. He gave the location of the body, then said, "I want Carter in charge."

Beth, the dispatcher, acknowledged, then asked, "Anything else?"

Gabe thought of Jordan's mental condition and the quietness of the other boys. "Just have him secure the scene, photograph, and let the ME begin her investigation. I don't want the body moved or anything disturbed until I get there. Tell Carter that unless we get real lucky, he's not going to have radio up there."

"Will do."

"And call Bobby Gray and Kate McPherson and have them meet us at the hospital." He hoped Jordan seeing his parents would ease him out of his disconnected state. Divorced or not, Kate and Bobby had remained friends; Kate was going to need Bobby there when she got the news of Steve's death.

Gabe signed off and looked over at J.D. Henry. The boy's head rested against the window, his eyes closed. Every exhaled breath increased the circumference of fog on the glass.

"J.D.?"

After a few seconds, J.D. opened his eyes, but stared straight ahead.

"What happened up there?" Gabe asked.

J.D. blinked sluggishly. "Mr. McP died."

"How?"

A look of revulsion contorted J.D.'s face. "He had this big gash in his head." He put his hand on the side of his own head. "There was blood all over."

"Ethan said it happened last night."

J.D. nodded. "Just before dark."

"Can you tell me how it happened?"

"I guess he fell."

"You weren't there?"

J.D. shook his head. "Colin and I were in camp. We didn't know anything until Ethan started yelling for help."

"Where were they?"

"Clear down by the creek, near the waterfall."

"What did you see when you got there?"

"Jordan was running around yelling and crying. Ethan was kneeling beside Mr. McP on the ground." J.D. swallowed convulsively. "He didn't even look like a person—" He groaned and grabbed for the door handle. "Stop! I'm gonna puke!"

Gabe stopped.

J.D. released his seat belt, opened the door, and hung his head out.

Gabe looked in the rearview mirror. Colin had his eyes closed and didn't open them. Ethan had his arm over the back of the seat, his hand on Madison's shoulder. His attention focused on Jordan.

When J.D. pulled himself back into the car, he was still ashen. Gabe handed him a bottle of water. "Rinse and spit. Don't drink."

J.D. silently did as he was told.

Gabe decided to hold the rest of his questions for now.

BY PULLING INTO THE AMBULANCE BAY AT THE HOSPITAL, Gabe managed to get the boys into the ER without Kate and Bobby seeing Jordan. He wanted to break the news of Steve's accident and prepare them for Jordan's detached state. After the boys were all in the hands of health professionals, and the other parents had been notified, he went to the emergency waiting room to get Jordan's parents.

The instant Gabe set eyes on Kate, it became clear she was going to need Bobby even more than he'd imagined. She sat folded in on herself, looking as small and frightened as a child. Jordan had taken after her; fair and slight of build, with a fragile temperament. Bobby's tall, dark, and athletic genes had to be buried somewhere very deep in the boy's DNA.

When Bobby saw Gabe, he sprang out of his chair. "Where's Jordan? Is he okay?"

"He's being attended to. He's suffering from exposure and exhaustion, a couple of bruises and scrapes, but he's not badly injured."

Kate closed her eyes for a second. When she opened them, her pleading gaze fastened on Gabe and she asked in a raspy whisper, "And Steve?"

"Come with me, please."

Bobby shot a panicky look at Gabe before he silently helped Kate to her feet and across the tile floor toward the double doors to the ER. Gabe felt the pitying eyes of everyone in the waiting room follow them. Bad news traveled fast in a town the size of Buckeye, but not this fast. Even without details, the bystanders had to know news from the sheriff in the ER probably wasn't good.

Once away from the public area, Gabe directed them into a small conference room. It held four teal-colored vinyl chairs, a small round table with two six-month-old magazines and a box of tissues, and an X-ray viewing box. He directed the couple to sit.

"There was an accident on the mountain. Steve suffered a fall...I'm sorry, Kate, but he's still up there. I've sent a recovery team and am headed back up there myself as soon as I get a few more answers here."

"He's going to be all right though, isn't he?" Desperate hope colored her voice.

"I haven't received a report yet. We'll know more in a few hours."

She recoiled as if he'd physically struck her. "You think he's dead!"

"I didn't say that." *Not until I have official confirmation.*

It appeared she wasn't breathing.

Gabe knelt in front of her. "Kate. Kate, look at me."

Her stunned gaze shifted to him.

"Now take a breath."

She drew a shuddery breath.

"Good. Now, Jordan's safe, he's not injured, but he's in shock." That was the only word he could think to describe the weird, detached state that seemed to have latched onto her son. "The four boys walked down off the mountain in the storm. Jordan has been through a lot. He'll need you two to be there for him." He glanced at Bobby, who nodded and put a hand on Kate's shoulder.

"How...how did he fall?" Kate's voice slid below a whisper.

"We're still sorting things out. What's important right now is taking care of Jordan. I wanted you to have time to collect yourselves before you see him."

Tears slid down her cheeks as she gave a jerky nod.

Bobby slid his hand across her shoulders and pulled her close. She leaned into him in a way that sparked a flash of memory. When Gabe had been a freshman in high school and Bobby and Kate had been seniors, a friend of Kate's had been killed in an automobile accident. The news had come during a basketball game. Kate had collapsed. Bobby, the lead scorer and team captain, left the basketball floor, picked her up, and carried her out of the gym. Not for the first time, Gabe wondered how two people who had spent their entire lives as best friends could have a marriage that ended in divorce. What did it take to hold a marriage together these days?

That thought brought another. "Do you want me to call anyone for you? Is Todd on his way here?"

A thin whine came from deep in Kate's throat. "He's at work...at the video store. He'll be so upset...."

Bobby said to Gabe, "I'll call him."

"I'll give y'all a few minutes." Gabe left the room before Kate got herself together enough to ask why, if Steve was injured, one of the boys hadn't stayed with him.

Jesus, sometimes Gabe hated the fact that the size of this community meant he was familiar with almost everyone. Not for the first time, he longed for the anonymity of breaking bad news to people he didn't know.

AS HE MADE HIS WAY to Ethan's ER cubicle, Gabe considered the stress this unfortunate incident would put on Ethan and Madison. They were new here and the transition from city to small town—*Southern* small town at that—had been a little rocky for both of them. For the first few weeks, Ethan hadn't seemed able to shake the edgy posture of someone waiting for trouble. He had moved through their community looking as if he was expecting someone to come up and knock him off his feet. Only recently had Gabe noticed the wary rigidity of the boy's body beginning to relax. And when Ethan began to relax, so did his mother.

Gabe paused just outside the treatment room, looking at Madison through a gap in the curtain. Her skin looked washed out under the harsh fluorescent lighting. He didn't know if her lack of color was from the cold or worry.

Her dark hair had begun to curl as it dried, giving her a softer, more feminine look than her usual straight style. He wanted to tell her she should wear her hair that way all of the time, but then, it really wasn't his place. Not that he hadn't been doing everything in his power to maneuver himself into that place.

Ever since he'd laid eyes on her at a county commissioners meeting, asking the kinds of questions that only an outsider would even think of asking, Gabe had been trying to coax her closer. It was a bit like trying to tame a wild animal—although more along the lines of a cougar than a soft-eyed doe. Like a mountain cat, he could see the hunger in her eyes, yet she kept her distance, wary of what he offered in his open hand.

Madison Wade was a strong, confident woman and she'd been determined not to open her life to complications. He had to wait until that hunger overcame caution. But just to speed things along, he'd made certain he was close enough for her to smell the meat as often as possible.

He'd just begun to convince her that she didn't have to choose between being a mother and being a woman. He hoped this experience wouldn't make her shy away again.

He parted the curtain, stepped inside, and said to Ethan, "You're looking better."

Ethan was in a dry hospital gown and wrapped in

warmed blankets. Unlike Madison, the color was barely beginning to return to his skin.

"How's Jordan?" Ethan asked. "Has he said anything?"

"The doctor is with him now. His parents are here. Maybe that will help him."

"I need to see him."

Madison put a hand on Ethan's shoulder. "He's with the doctor."

"M, it's important. I *have* to see him."

Gabe said, "I'll make sure the nurses take you to see him as soon as the doctor says it's okay, how's that?"

Ethan looked grim, but nodded.

"How are *you* feeling?" Gabe asked.

Ethan lifted a shoulder. "Okay." He paused. "Is someone going after Mr. McPherson?"

"Yes. Tell me what happened up there." Gabe sat down in a chair next to Madison. He rested his elbows on his knees and clasped his hands together to keep from reaching to comfort her in front of Ethan.

"We didn't want to leave him there like that—honest. That's why it was so late before we came back down; Colin and J.D. and I argued about it for a long time. It seemed wrong...but Jordan had totally freaked out. No way could he make it back to the van on his own, and he needed help more than any of us. We sat with Mr. McP all night, you know, to keep the animals away. But nobody..." Ethan pressed his lips together.

"Nobody what?"

Ethan's gaze moved from one thing in the room to another, never coming close to landing on Gabe's face. "Nobody wanted to stay up there alone with a dead person. So we left him."

Madison stood beside the bed and put a hand on Ethan's shoulder. "You didn't have a choice. Jordan needed help."

"Ethan, how did Mr. McPherson get hurt?"

"He must have fallen and hit his head on a rock."

"None of you boys were with him at the time?"

Ethan visibly swallowed and shook his head. "Me and Jordan were picking up firewood. Colin and J.D. were in camp."

"What was Mr. McPherson supposed to be doing?"

"I dunno. Like I said, me and Jordan were out getting firewood."

"How did you find him?"

"We heard something, a weird sort of yelp, and went looking. We found him near the bottom of the waterfall."

"Was he conscious?"

Ethan shook his head.

"How far is he from where you were camped?"

"I'm not sure. I mean, you could hear the waterfall at the campsite—not real loud; it sounded like rain on trees."

"How did Colin and J.D. get there?"

"Jordan, he was going nuts...I mean, crying and stuff. I couldn't leave him, so I ran partway back and just started yelling."

A nurse came in. "Excuse me, I need to take his temperature again."

Gabe got up. "I'll get out of the way here."

Madison followed him outside the curtain. She wrapped her arms around her middle. "I hate it that they had to go through that. Poor Jordan..." She shook her head.

"Just keep reassuring them that they did the right thing by getting Jordan back."

She nodded.

He looked down at her jeans. They were still wet, and mud covered the hem and knees. "You should change out of those wet clothes. I'm sure someone has an extra pair of scrubs around here."

"One of the nurses has already gone to get me some." She glanced down at her ruined boots, then lifted a foot. "Guess you were right. I didn't even make it twenty yards in these things."

"Think they're salvageable?" He raised a brow. "I was looking forward to taking you dancing in them."

She gave him a half-smile. "Maybe."

It lifted his heart to see some of the tension leave her face.

A young nurse came up and handed a set of blue scrubs to Madison. "You can change in the third door on the right."

"Thank you."

Gabe stopped the nurse before she walked away. "As soon as Jordan Gray is able to see anyone, will you have someone get Ethan? He's desperate to see his friend."

"Sure thing." The nurse departed in the direction of the trauma room that housed Jordan.

Gabe turned to Madison. "Listen, I have to get back up there. Do you have someone who can pick you up and take you home?"

"Of course. I don't think they'll keep Ethan too much longer."

Gabe looked into her eyes, probing for the inner woman. "He calls you M?"

She gave him a crooked smile and a little color returned to her cheeks. "Yeah. It took him a while to call me any-thing at all after the adoption. Finally, he started with M.

He says it's like the character in James Bond." She looked down. "I guess at fourteen, starting to call me Mom was a little odd for him."

Gabe brushed her cheek with the knuckle of his index finger. "James Bond, huh? Gotta keep up the tough-guy image."

Her smile was tinged with sorrow. "I suppose so. That tough image protected him for so long...." Her voice trailed off with a sadness that said she wished Ethan's life had been different—easier.

She raised her eyes to meet Gabe's and the connection he'd felt from the first time they'd locked gazes hit him once again. It was both unfamiliar and potent, and went straight to his gut. It made him want to do extraordinary things. If anyone had ever told him he'd pursue a woman like he was this one, he would have called them fifteen kinds of a fool.

With concentrated effort, he dropped his hand back to his side. "I'll check on you two later."

"Okay."

He started to walk away.

"Gabe."

He stopped and turned around. She was standing there wet and dirty, looking more vulnerable than he'd ever seen her.

"Thank you. I don't know what would have happened if you hadn't taken me up there. It could have been hours—"

"But it wasn't. You listened to your instincts and the boys are all safe—" He started to add *and sound*, but considering Jordan's condition, he felt that would draw fire from the levelheaded journalist. "You did good."

Chapter 3

THE NURSE WHO TOOK Ethan's temperature was a soft-looking grandma type with dark brown skin and a gentle touch. She looked at him with a sympathetic smile and pitying eyes.

Unsettled, he looked away. He was accustomed to strangers looking at him with wariness, suspicion. Even though he'd been with M for nearly two years, he was still getting used to kindness. Consideration continued to settle upon him with a sense of expectation, of measuring what would be demanded in return. Mistrust was a habit he could not seem to break.

"There now," the nurse said after the thermometer beeped. "You appear to be warming right up."

Kids down here were all about "ma'am" and "sir." Jordan would have given a clear, "Yes, ma'am." Ethan only managed a nod. Southern manners still felt like wearing scratchy wool without anything underneath.

The nurse wrote something down on a clipboard that

hung on the wall. "I'll see about getting you something to eat. Growing boy like you must be starved. You just close your eyes and rest now." She slipped outside the curtain.

Rest? Ethan didn't dare close his eyes. Every time he did, he saw the bloody crater in Mr. McP's skull—and the terror on Jordan's face.

There had been plenty of times he'd seen Jordan scared. It seemed Jordan lived most of his life scared—but never anything like last night. Jordan had been scared right out of his mind, scared enough that it had frightened Ethan— and Ethan couldn't remember the last time he'd been truly afraid.

The sharp edges of fear had a way of wearing off when you lived in a constant state of risk. For as long as Ethan could remember, uncertainty and chance had ruled his world. As he'd gotten older, things had become more dicey; it was more difficult to slip through life invisible and unnoticed. It seemed the more hazardous life got, the more danger it took for fear to slice into Ethan's heart. He decided that living the life he had had developed a sort of anti-fear force field in him. But that had been before . . . before M had come into his life.

Last night, he'd been as afraid as he could ever remember being. Maybe living with M—living with less risk, less danger—had worked in reverse, sucking away the power of his protective force field. Maybe he was turning into an ordinary kid.

There was only one problem with his anti-fear force-field buildup theory. Jordan. The kid didn't seem to be building any fear-deflecting powers. In fact, he seemed to be moving in the opposite direction. But even for Jordan, his reaction last night had been crazy—way too crazy even for seeing his stepdad like that.

That was another thing Ethan hadn't figured out—the stepdad. It was one of the reasons he'd wanted to go on this camping trip in the first place. Jordan was his friend, and Ethan always looked out for his friends. But to take care of Jordan, he needed to sort some stuff out about Jordan's family.

He and Jordan came from places as different as the earth and the moon. But they were alike in a lot of ways. Neither of them fit where they'd been planted. Jordan seemed as uncomfortable in his life as if he'd been dropped into it by an alien mother ship. Ethan had often wondered if it had been different before Jordan's mom married Mr. McP. Had Jordan been happy and comfortable at home? Or had he always skittered, ratlike, along the edges of his family as he did now? It wasn't something the two of them talked about, so Ethan needed to find out on his own.

Unfortunately, things had gone terribly wrong. Still, Jordan needed to be protected. And Ethan had to figure out a way to do it.

He glanced at the curtain that closed him off from the rest of the emergency room. Where *was* Jordan? Ethan had been straining to hear his voice, or the mention of his name. So far nothing. The ER hadn't seemed that large when they'd come in. Had they taken Jordan off some-place else?

M came back in. He was glad to see she'd changed out of her wet stuff and had on some dry nurse clothes.

"Can I see Jordan yet?" he asked.

"Not yet."

"Did the sheriff tell them? He said he'd tell them."

"He told them." She came closer and pushed his hair off his forehead. As always, he turned away; reacting as if she was admonishing him for his long hair. But somewhere along the way, he'd actually gotten so he looked forward to her doing it. In fact, he guessed that was one of the reasons he refused to wear his hair shorter.

"I know you're worried about Jordan, but he's where he needs to be right now. It might be a while before he can have visitors."

"I just need to see him for a second. I won't stay. I promise."

She sighed and looked really tired. "Ethan, I don't think you should expect too much. He might need a few days—"

"No!" He sat up straighter and threw off the blankets. "I need to see him now."

As he started to get out of bed, M put her hand on his shoulder. "All right, all right. We won't leave until you see him, okay?"

He eased back and looked her in the eye. "No bull?" Unlike lots of adults, M didn't say stuff just to get you to do what she wanted; if she said no bull, he could trust her to her word.

She smiled, looking like herself for the first time since they'd gotten here. "No bull. But I don't want you to be upset if he's the same as when we got here. It might take time."

"I know. I just need to see him."

The nice nurse reappeared with a tray of food. "We're between food-service shifts. I had to go down to the kitchen myself." She slid the table over his lap and set the tray on it. "Since the dietitian didn't have any part of it, I could pick out the good stuff." She gave him a wink.

"Thank you." Again, he had to shake off that feeling of being set up; remind himself that sometimes people did things just to be nice.

"You should eat up. I think your dismissal papers are almost ready."

M said, "That's great. Thank you."

The nurse nodded to M and then smiled at him again before she left. This time he made himself look her in the eye and smile back.

Ethan asked M, "Would you go ask how soon I can see Jordan?"

"Sure. I need to call someone to take us home, too. I won't be long."

He nodded and picked up his fork.

Most kids complained about "cafeteria food" and "hospital food," but Ethan had been hungry often enough that he knew better. That's why he felt so guilty when he couldn't eat it; that and the fact that the nurse had gone to so much trouble. He uncovered everything and rearranged it enough that he hoped it looked like he ate some of it. He really didn't want to hurt her feelings, but if he swallowed anything right now, he'd spew for sure.

GABE WAS ANXIOUS to get a firsthand read of the situation. He had no reason to believe McPherson's death was more than a tragic accident. Nevertheless, it was his job to investigate every death thoroughly. He'd delayed questioning the other boys for fear he'd run out of daylight before he could get McPherson off the mountain. He didn't want to have to assign someone to spend the night up there, plus he needed confirmation of death so he could inform Kate without further delay.

He tried to radio Carter while driving to the trailhead. He wasn't surprised when he didn't get a response. Once he got within range, which would most likely be partway up the trail itself, he'd try his small two-way.

While he'd been inside the hospital, the rain had cleared. Now the sun shone in the late afternoon sky. Good news; they would have at least thirty more minutes of daylight than if it had remained overcast. They were going to need every second of it.

Gabe pulled into the trailhead. Carter had brought one of the department's SUVs, which was parked next to McPherson's white full-size van. The coroner's wagon and a Search and Rescue truck from the fire department were there, too. Gabe parked next to Carter's vehicle and tried his two-way. He was pleasantly surprised when Carter's crackly response came through.

"Have the ME and FD made it on scene yet?" Gabe asked.

"Dr. Zinn came up with me. She's almost finished. Four FD rescue guys just got here. We're burning daylight. How long before you're on scene?" Carter asked.

"The body's at the base of Black Rock Falls?"

"Yes."

"I'm starting up now."

"You're cuttin' it close. The doc and I agree; McPherson fell. These damn rocks are slippery as hell. Doc estimates TOD was most likely last night. I took plenty of photos. You sure we can't just load him up and start down?"

"No. I'm moving as fast as I can."

Carter was the best-trained officer he had. And Gabe had confidence in his deputy's ability to investigate a scene. Still, they hadn't had a homicide in Forrest County

since Carter had come on staff—hell, there had only been
a handful in the eleven years Gabe had been with the
department. With various pieces of this puzzle still having blurry edges, Gabe wanted to have a look for himself
before the body was moved.

The muscles in Gabe's legs burned and his lungs were
huffing, but he made it to McPherson's campsite in just
over fifty minutes. The sight of the abandoned camp gave
him a rippling chill. The pup tents' flaps were open; the
sleeping bags inside sodden with rain. A skillet full of
water sat on a rock next to the ashes of a dead fire. An open
bag of marshmallows had a steady stream of ants entering
and leaving. A box of graham crackers had been trampled
under someone's careless foot, smashing the crackers
and splitting open the sealed packages, before the rain
turned it all into a gray-brown, spongy pulp.

Just as Ethan had said, Gabe could hear the distant
rush of the falls.

In another seven minutes he was standing next to Steve
McPherson's cold corpse.

The body was near the small, shallow pool at the base
of the falls, far enough away that the mist spray didn't
reach it. The boys had folded a jacket and placed it
under McPherson's head and put one over his chest and
another over his legs. It appeared that they had wrapped
a T-shirt around the head wound. The medical examiner
had peeled the makeshift bandage away and it now lay in
a bloody lump on the ground.

McPherson had been an experienced climber and
hiker, probably the best in the entire area. He'd not only
mastered the Appalachians, but had conquered most of
the peaks in the Pacific Northwest. Of course, accidents

happen to even the most experienced outdoorsmen. But the idea of him being off by himself without any of the boys didn't make sense. His entire purpose for taking kids up there was to teach them respect for the elements and the land, to give them wilderness survival skills. Why would he have gone off alone?

Gabe walked closer to Dr. Zinn, who was kneeling beside her large backpack, carefully loading her equipment. Her hiking boots and cargo pants were caked with mud. She was a woman whose active lifestyle allowed her to wear her fifty-five years well enough to pass for ten years younger. He'd gotten to know her long before she'd been appointed county ME; back when he'd been a new deputy he'd had to deliver the news that her then-fourteen-year-old son, Jimmy, had tried to jump Bear Creek with his dirt bike and had ended up in the ER. The boy's trouble had been compounded by the fact he'd been on private property without permission when he'd done it. It was the first call of that nature Gabe had had to make. It had been more difficult than he'd imagined.

Gabe's respect for Dottie Zinn had begun that day, when she'd made his job easier by staying calm, and showing uncommon regard for *his* uneasiness.

Young Jimmy had recovered. Dottie and Gabe had become friends.

Standing, she gave him a nod. "Gabe." Her gaze moved to the body. "Looks pretty straightforward; head trauma. Of course, the autopsy will confirm. I've bagged his hands, just in case."

"Can you estimate time of death?"

"Based solely on rigor and livor mortis, I'd say any-

where between six last evening and six this morning.
Pathologist will likely be able to call it closer."

He scanned the immediate area, looking for a possible
scenario for McPherson's fall.

The ground was a mix of dirt, gravel, and various-
sized boulders and rocks. Stony outcroppings flanked the
falls. There plant life clung tightly; saplings, mountain
laurel, and ferns sprouted from what appeared to be solid
rock. At the base of the falls, there was a jumble of stone
chunks that, with the passing of time, the rushing water
and vegetation had pried away from the body of the cliff.

The exposed layers of dark stone beside the falling
water were unstable in many places. Steve would have
known better than to have climbed there. Still, Gabe gestured toward the top of the falls and asked the question.
"Possible that he fell from up there?"

She shook her head. "Doubtful. His body is too far
from the drop. Even with this rain, we'd see some evidence that the kids had dragged him this far. Unless they
were strong enough to carry the dead weight." She raised
a brow in his direction.

With a half-shrug, he said, "With as rough as the footing is here, probably not."

"Most obvious trauma is to the left temporal region, but
there are other suspicious areas on the head." She pointed
to the gash in McPherson's skull. "My best guess is he lost
his footing and fell sideways—maybe even tumbled and
had more than one impact."

"I suppose the rain didn't help in locating the rock that
inflicted the wound?"

She shook her head. "Carter's gone over everything.

He photographed all of the rocks within ten feet of the body, as well as those near the falls."

Gabe walked slowly around the body, then worked his way out, looking for anything that could speak of what had happened here. Interspersed between stones was a jumbled assortment of footprints in the mud. They were concentrated near the body, lots of them positioned in a way that said people had been sitting on the rocks. The only discernible trail of prints led up the narrow path toward the camp. Of course, with the rain arriving this morning, only the tracks made today would have left deep depressions in the mud.

He saw nothing that would contradict the theory that this was an accident. "Carter, bag the jackets and the T-shirt. Then you can go back down with Dr. Zinn." He turned to the four rescuers shifting restlessly nearby. "All right, let's get him off this mountain."

While the SAR team secured McPherson's body to the stretcher, Gabe continued to look around. He started at the body and worked his way out in a spiral pattern. The woods thickened quickly as he moved away from the creek. About twenty feet from the body, he knelt down, inspecting the broken branches of a mountain laurel. The injury was fresh, the green wood still moist, and the foliage showed no signs of wilt. There could be any number of reasons for broken branches—an animal; J.D. had said Jordan was running around in a panic—it might have no significance at all.

He moved a little deeper into the woods, slipping on the wet, uneven ground more than once. Nothing out of the ordinary caught his attention. Then, just as he was about to loop around and return to the falls, he saw something small and light-colored on the ground near a two-foot-diameter boulder. He moved closer.

Cigarette filters, discolored from use and swollen from the rain. Impossible to tell how old they were. Brand marking said they were Marlboros—probably the most popular cigarette in town. He reached into his pocket and pulled out a ziplock baggie. He turned it inside out, placed his hand inside, and picked up the butts without contaminating them with his touch.

He remained kneeling, the slope of the land making him work at keeping his balance. He examined the ground around him carefully, then scanned the surrounding foliage and trees. Once he was satisfied that he wasn't missing anything, he straightened, stretching the knots out of his back. After spending the next several minutes working an increasing circumference from the spot of the cigarette butts and not finding anything noteworthy, he worked back toward the body in a zigzag pattern.

The light beneath the heavy canopy of trees was dimming rapidly. By the time Gabe reached the falls, the rescue team had already left with McPherson's body. For a moment, he stood alone and admired the beauty of this place. It was easy to be seduced by such splendor, forget that beauty sometimes disguises danger. Had Steve forgotten that most valuable of lessons? Or had it simply been an odd twist of fate, one of Mother Nature's little ironies?

He made one last pass around the area, then started back down the mountain himself.

ETHAN WAS BEGINNING TO THINK M was never coming back. How long could it take to call somebody to pick them up and find out where Jordan was?

His stomach tightened with nerves. What if Jordan had snapped out of it and started talking?

He was just throwing off the covers, determined to go find Jordan himself, when M reappeared. She had a paper bag in her hand and didn't look happy.

"What's wrong?" Ethan's mouth went dry.

"Jordan doesn't appear to have any real physical injuries, but . . . ," she said slowly, as if hesitant to speak the words, "he's still uncommunicative."

Ethan nearly pissed his pants with relief, but he tried to look unhappy, too.

M gave him her "sorry to disappoint you" look. "Maybe we should come back later. I'll bring you—"

"No!" He jumped off the bed and faced her. "No! You said no bull!" He punched a finger in the air between them. "You said I could see him."

Her eyes widened and she leaned back, away from him, as if he'd startled her.

He dropped his hands to his sides and added more quietly, "You promised."

"Take it easy," she said. "I did promise. And you *can* see him. I just thought it might be better for you to wait."

"No."

"All right. I picked up some sweats at the gift shop." She handed him the bag. "Get dressed. I'll go sign the papers to get you out. I'll be right back and we'll go see him."

He gave a brusque nod and grabbed the bag. His hands were shaking so much he could hardly get the ties of his hospital gown undone.

Once he was dressed, he stepped outside the curtain.

M put her arm around his shoulders. "This way."

Since his shoes were trashed, he was still wearing

those dorky socks with grippers on the bottom that the hospital had given him. He felt stupid running around in the hallways without shoes. As they passed the open doors, he tried not to peek inside to see the people lying in the hospital beds, but his curiosity overcame his manners. It looked like everyone in here was old...and dying. Was Jordan dying, too?

This place had the same weird overly clean smell that doctors' offices had. But here there was an unmistakable underlying odor of...*sickness* was the only way Ethan could think to describe it. He didn't like it.

M stopped in front of a closed door. "Jordan has a private room. Do you want me to go in with you?"

Ethan stared at the closed door and shook his head. He was torn between wanting to slam it open and hurry inside and running in the other direction.

He pressed his lips together, took a breath, then put his hand on the door and pushed it open. The room seemed dim after the bright lights of the hallway. It was nearly dark outside. The fluorescent light over the bed was on, but not real bright, more like a night-light. Jordan looked like old sour cream; white and green at the same time. His eyes were open, staring, just like they'd been when Ethan last saw him.

He was halfway across the room when he realized that Jordan's mom and dad were sitting in chairs shoved into the corner beside the door; a place where the light didn't quite reach. Todd McPherson was standing next to Jordan's mom, leaning against the wall.

"Oh, sorry...," he started to apologize.

"It's okay, Ethan," Jordan's mom said softly. "Go on. Maybe he'll talk to you."

Ethan nodded, then walked up to the side of the bed. He was worried that Jordan's parents would come up and stand there, too, but they stayed where they were. His back was to them, giving him just a little privacy.

He leaned over, so he'd be in Jordan's stationary line of sight. "Hey. It's me."

Jordan didn't move. He didn't even blink.

Ethan said, "Everything's going to be okay. You need to rest and get better."

Jordan remained motionless.

"You still look cold." Ethan leaned across and pulled the covers higher. When he did, he hovered close to Jordan's ear and whispered, "Whatever you do, don't say *anything*. I've taken care of it."

As he straightened, he sent a cautious glance over his shoulder. Nobody was looking at him; nobody heard.

Chapter 4

THE CUP OF COFFEE in Kate's hand had gone cold. How long ago had Todd brought it to her? The black darkness of night had turned Jordan's hospital room window into a mirror, a mirror in which her reflection showed a woman she barely recognized. Self-consciously, she smoothed her hair behind her ear. Hating what she saw in the glass, she looked down at her coffee where congealed swirls of cream had risen to the top. Her stomach rolled. She set the paper cup on the floor beneath her chair, back where it couldn't be knocked over.

"Can I get you a fresh one, Kate?" Todd pushed himself away from the wall. He'd been standing there, strong and silent, while they waited for Jordan to "wake up"— while they waited for news of Steve's condition.

"Oh, thank you, no. I'm too jittery inside already. How much longer do you think it can be before we hear...?" She couldn't bring herself to finish the question.

Steve's brawny build and rugged manliness had captured her attention the moment they met. He'd seemed larger than life, and she'd felt small and pale in his shadow. But, oh, how she'd wanted to be in that shadow. He'd made her feel safe.

There had been times during their two-year marriage when she'd paced the floor with worry. Back when he'd climbed Mt. Hood and the weather had abruptly changed, trapping his climbing team in a freak snowstorm. And the time he'd been a day late checking back into the lodge after hiking in Yosemite. For a man who lived the life Steve did, an overnight camping trip in what amounted to his own backyard shouldn't have caused even a moment's pause.

Todd knelt in front of her. "We'll hear soon. But he's going to be *fine*."

She straightened in her chair and looked into her stepson's eyes. "Do you really think so?" She wanted to believe. She had to believe. Todd had said Steve was going to be all right those other times, and he had. It was just like Mt. Hood. He was going to be okay.

"I do," Todd said, holding her gaze. "Dad knows what he's doing. And he's strong. He'll get through this."

She managed a smile of faith. "Maybe I will take that coffee."

Todd patted her hand and stood up. He seemed so much more than five years older than Jordan. So strong and confident—like his dad. It seemed he'd been a man from the time she'd first met him.

Bobby's voice broke into her thoughts. "I never liked the idea of Steve taking Jordan up there. A boy like Jordan had no place in the wilderness. Just look at him—"

He stood up and shoved his hands on his hips. "Steve shouldn't—"

"Hey!" Todd spun back around from the door and grabbed Bobby's arm.

Fear rippled through Kate. She and Bobby had had this disagreement a hundred times but Todd had never known of it. She didn't think she could take it if Todd and Bobby got into it right now. She held her breath, but could not make herself stand up and put herself between them.

Todd leaned close to Bobby's face. "My dad was just trying to do something nice for Jordan and that freaky friend of his! He doesn't have to spend his time—" Todd clamped down on his words. After a deep breath he continued, his voice sounding slightly more in control. "Dad's the one who's up on that mountain hurt." He released his grip on Bobby's arm and walked out of the room.

She watched Bobby's shoulders rise and fall. She knew him well enough to see he was barely controlling his anger. After a moment, she stood and touched his elbow. "Todd's upset...."

"I know."

"He's right, too. Steve is always trying to help Jordan fit in better, helping him with sports and things. He's—"

"Being a father?" Bobby's sharp gaze turned her way. "Is that what you're saying? Steve is being a better father to Jordan than I am? Don't you see, Kate? He's trying to make Jordan into something he's not. And in the process, he's making him feel like a failure. Steve needs to understand that playing baseball and climbing mountains and"—his face contorted with anger—"wrestling freakin' grizzlies is not the mark of a man."

He pulled his elbow out of her grasp and stalked out of the room.

Kate felt one more piece of solid ground crumble beneath her feet.

TODD HANDED KATE a fresh cup of coffee. "I'm sorry. I didn't mean to run him off." He nodded toward Bobby's empty chair.

"It's okay. Everyone's upset." She took a tentative sip of coffee. Todd had added cream, just like she liked it. "He'll be back." *For Jordan,* she thought, *not for me. I'm alone. So alone. Dear Lord, please let Steve be all right.* She didn't think she could stand being alone again.

Todd sat in the chair next to her. He leaned forward with his elbows on his thighs and looked deep into his own cup of coffee. "I'll apologize when he comes back."

She managed a nod and a weak smile. Todd was a good boy, a good example for Jordan. Todd had had his share of disappointment lately. The collegiate baseball scholarship he'd been counting on hadn't materialized. She'd been so proud of the way he'd kept his chin up and focused on his future. He was going to junior college and working; saving his money and planning on transferring to the University of Tennessee next year. If only Jordan could have that kind of resiliency and optimism.

Todd had lost his mother when he'd only been ten. He and his dad were so close; who could blame him for being short-tempered at the moment? He'd be absolutely devastated if something happened to Steve.

Fate couldn't be so cruel as to take his father from him, too. She clung to that thought. Steve would be okay and come back to her...to Todd. It seemed impossible to think otherwise.

After a few minutes, Todd got up and switched on the TV. "Maybe Jordan would like to watch *Sunday Night Football*." He leaned down and put his face in front of Jordan's. "It's me, buddy. I'm here. I won't leave. Remember how we like to watch football? Sorry, it's NFL, not UT." He pulled a chair right up to Jordan's bedside. "It's the Ravens and the Colts. Lots of bad blood there. Should be a real killer."

Kate smiled her appreciation. At least Todd was trying to pull Jordan back, not off sulking like Bobby. Jordan was what was important now, not some macho pissing match between Bobby and Steve. Todd, bless his heart, knew that.

For the next hour Kate half-listened to the TV. The penalty whistles seemed unnaturally shrill and the drone of the commentators ground at her nerves. She stared intently at Jordan, looking for the slightest response: the light of recognition in his eyes, the flicker of an eyelash, the quiver of a lip. So far nothing. How could he hold his eyes open for so long without blinking?

She heard a man's footfall behind her. Relief rushed through her. *Bobby*—

But it wasn't Bobby. It was Gabe Wyatt.

One look at his face confirmed what she'd been trying so hard to deny.

Her insides turned to liquid. She tried to push herself to her feet, but her hand slipped off the armrest. Her throat was suddenly too dry to make more than a choked whisper. "No..."

She heard Todd's chair scrape across the floor as he stood.

"I'm sorry." Gabe stepped closer.

She recoiled away from him, as if he was responsible for the news he carried. Bowing her head, she covered her ears, shutting out what he had to say.

"He's dead?" Todd asked, his voice sounding very far away.

Gabe's answer came as if filtered through a thick blanket. "He had a severe head wound. There wasn't anything anyone could do."

Suddenly, Todd's arms were around her, pulling her out of her chair, gathering her close. The smell of her favorite fabric softener filled her nose as she buried her face against his chest.

As he held her tight, Todd asked, "Was he conscious at all?"

"No. It appears he died last evening."

Todd's hands soothed her back. She felt him nod, his chin hitting the top of her head. "Where is he?"

"There will be an autopsy. You have plenty of time to make arrangements with the mortuary."

"I thought you said he had a head wound. We'd rather they not"—he lowered his voice, as if that might take the pain out of the words—"have him cut open."

Kate jerked her head upright. "No! No autopsy."

"I understand your feelings. Unfortunately, it's required by law for an unattended accidental death like this. I'm sorry." Gabe left the room.

Through her tears, Todd's face was blurred enough that she could almost imagine it was Steve standing there with her. "What am I going to do?" she whispered.

"Shhh." Todd squeezed her hand. "It'll be all right."

How could it be all right? She was alone.

* * *

GABE SAT IN HIS JEEP in the hospital parking lot, his hands on the steering wheel, staring at the dark sky. Minutes ticked by, but he made no move to start the car. The last vapors of the adrenaline he'd been running on slipped slowly and silently from his system. His legs began to cramp from this afternoon's rapid ascent to Black Rock Falls. His neck and shoulder muscles felt like they had been twisted like a wrung-out towel. But the worst discomfort came from the cold dull ache in the center of his chest.

He wasn't often called upon to deliver the devastating news of a death to a family; the low population and peaceful nature of Forrest County ensured that. But this was the second time in the space of a single week that he'd had to tell someone a loved one had died. Last Thursday it had fallen to him—since the football field sat just outside the city limits—to inform the parents of seventeen-year-old Zach Gilbert that their son had collapsed during football practice. The paramedics had had no luck restarting his heart. Kid had no prior history of health problems; looked healthy as an ox. It was a mystery that could only be answered by the autopsy report, which wouldn't be back before next week. The age of the victim and the lingering unknown had made that message particularly difficult to deliver.

And now Steve McPherson…Damn. He hoped his grandmother's rule of three wouldn't apply, or Gabe would be playing the messenger of death again soon. He tightened his grip on the steering wheel until his arms burned. He tried to close his eyes, but the devastated faces he saw behind his lids made him snap them back open. God knew he didn't want to lock gazes with one more woman who looked as if he'd just knifed her in the heart.

Poor Kate reminded him of a stray in a storm; so small and forlorn, eyes shining with loss. He wished he'd waited until he'd rounded up Bobby before he'd broken the news. It appeared that Todd was doing an admirable job of holding her together. But the boy had grief of his own to deal with.

At least in McPherson's instance there wouldn't be a boatload of extended family hounding Gabe with questions he couldn't answer. Unlike Forrest County's previous victims of abrupt and unexpected deaths, McPherson wasn't a native. He and Todd had moved from Michigan six years ago. Once, as they'd sat next to one another at a high school football game, McPherson had told Gabe that he'd come here because of the mountains and the wilderness. His wife had died and he and his son needed a place to heal, and to Steve McPherson, healing meant spending lots of time with nature.

Some things were just too ironic to contemplate.

Gabe exhaled deeply, then started the Jeep. At times like these, he wished he didn't live alone. How comforting it would be to return to a home full of life and light and love, instead of dark windows and desolate silence.

And for the first time, the person he imagined there waiting for him wasn't a nameless, faceless woman. It was Maddie Wade.

He thought of her and her little cedar-sided house up on Turnbull Road. It wasn't on his way, but after he'd basically abandoned her at the hospital, he owed it to her to make sure she was safely home. It was the least he could do.

It was nearly ten p.m. when he approached her house. He hadn't realized how desperately he wanted to see her until he felt the rush of relief when he saw the downstairs still blazed with lights. He pulled into the little unpaved driveway that ran alongside the house.

Even before he shut off the engine and opened the door, Maddie appeared on the front porch. She crossed her arms over an oversized, orange University of Tennessee sweatshirt whose hem hit her jeans at mid-thigh.

He got out, rested his left elbow on the top of the open driver's door, and looked at her over the top of the Jeep. As he did, he realized he was feeling every single heartbeat. For a long moment, neither of them said anything. She was backlit by the windows behind her; he couldn't read her expression.

Just as he was about to present his excuse for his unannounced appearance, she said, "I was hoping you'd come." It was a quiet, reserved statement; not laced with yearning or any other emotion. He couldn't read it any better than he could her expression. She turned and walked back toward the front door. "I've made coffee."

By the time he crossed the threshold, she had disappeared into the kitchen at the rear of the house. He took his time following, surveying the living room as he went. The furnishings fit Maddie's no-nonsense personality far better than they did this country house: spare and contemporary, leather, glass, and metal. An Xbox with two controllers sat beneath an expensive flat-panel television. A black-lacquered bookshelf filled one wall. Gabe delayed his curiosity to see what titles were housed there—from what he'd seen of her, probably lots of literary works, and maybe a few political exposés.

When he entered the kitchen, she had her back to him, pouring coffee. This room was much like the living room, personal items a sharp contrast to the architecture of the house. The Cuisinart espresso machine and sleek stainless-steel toaster stood out against the knotty pine and wrought iron of the cabinets. One wall housed a glass-paned triple door that would have a killer view in the daylight.

His gaze settled back on the woman. The deep walnut waves of her hair contrasted with the orange of her sweatshirt. "I see you've come over to the dark side," he said.

She shot him a look over her shoulder. As she turned her hair caught on her shoulder, creating a soft frame around her face. "Pardon me?"

"You've seen the light." He pointed at her shirt. "Abandoned Penn State football for UT."

"It's Ethan's. His first purchase after we moved here." Quirking her brow, she said, "*I'm* still a staunch Nittany Lions fan."

"Don't let anyone in this state hear you say that."

She chuckled. "I have been getting the impression that not embracing the big orange T is an offense punishable by law."

He sauntered closer, Western-style, hanging his thumbs on an imaginary gun belt. "Well, ma'am, as county sheriff, I'm in charge of enforcing the law around here. Lucky for you, you're wearing orange."

She turned and handed him a coffee mug—a Penn State coffee mug. "I guess I'd better make you drink out of this one, then."

He took the mug with a grin.

Sitting at the table, she motioned for him to do the same. "I forgot to ask if you take cream or sugar."

"Neither."

"That's what I like, a man who can stand up to my coffee without flinching."

He lifted his mug in a mock toast and took a sip. The coffee hit his tongue with the power of a sledgehammer. By the time it reached the back of his throat his body was already cutting it off at the pass. He only managed to swallow it with concentrated effort.

He closed one eye with a shiver and a grimace. "Good God, woman. How can you drink this?"

"I suppose it's an acquired taste."

"Only after you've completely annihilated your taste buds."

She smiled, somehow looking both sweet and condemning at the same time. "I'll try not to let your candy-ass taste in coffee stand against your masculinity, Sheriff."

He pushed the mug away. "Nice try. You can't even shame me into drinking that stuff."

She answered with a shrug as she took a drink from her own mug.

"How's Ethan?" he asked.

"Shaken. Exhausted."

"Did he talk any more about what happened up there?"

With a half-shake of her head, she said, "I gave him plenty of opportunities. But he said he was too tired to talk about it. He went to bed as soon as we got home." She set down her coffee. "I'm not sure how to help him." Her gaze locked on the mug she turned in absentminded circles. "I'm afraid I bit off much more than I can chew. What made me think I could raise a teenager? Ethan started out in this world behind the eight ball. He needs someone who knows what they're doing."

Her hair curled in an utterly feminine way that begged to be touched. He took a lock between his fingers. "From what I've seen, you're doing great."

She raised her gaze to meet his and those brown eyes became a clear window to her soul. Tucking her chin, she gave a breathy scoff. "Yeah, well, things always look better from a distance."

Then, before he could respond, that open window snapped shut. She straightened her back, the movement pulling free the curl wrapped around Gabe's finger. "What about Mr. McPherson? Did you get his body off the mountain?"

"Yes."

"And Kate knows?"

"I stopped at the hospital and told her and Todd before I came here. I didn't get far enough into the room to get a read on Jordan's condition though."

With a sad shake of her head, she said, "Ethan went to see him before we left—no change."

"Poor kid. The other two boys have been sent home. I plan to question them tomorrow."

"Question? Why?"

"You're a journalist. You know the drill; unattended death has to be investigated."

"Yes, but…the boys told you he fell. No one else was up there. What other explanation could there be?"

"The law says *every* death, not just those I personally question."

She gave him a sly look. "Extra vigilant with your father running for governor?"

He leaned his forearms on the table and leaned closer. "That sounds like a probing, journalistic question."

Lifting her chin, she said, "I do have a paper to run. Gotta keep abreast of the current political winds."

He held her gaze and tapped his index fingertip against

the tabletop. "Here's a quote you can print. 'I'm always vigilant when it comes to my job. My father's political career is moot.'"

"Oooooh, touchy."

Leaning back in his chair, he ran a hand through his hair. He'd been working hard to distance himself from his father's political campaign. He admired his dad and his commitment to serving their state. And he and his dad got along fine…as long as they didn't discuss politics. So while Marcus Wyatt was on the campaign trail, Gabe kept a very low profile.

"Not touchy," he said. "Tired."

"Yeah. Tomorrow morning is going to be a bitch. I haven't decided if I'm going to make Ethan go to school. He's so worried about Jordan."

"A boy like Ethan, having been on his own for so long and having to concentrate on his own survival…his concern for Jordan shows a lot about his character."

She pressed her lips together for a long moment. "Of course, you're right. I just don't want him to get so involved that he'll be hurt if Jordan doesn't fully recover."

"Looks to me like it's too late. First, he's Jordan's friend, and a good one at that. Second, he was there when it happened. If Jordan doesn't get over this, it's gonna hurt. Only thing you can do is be there, make sure he knows this is one loss he won't have to go through alone."

Wrapping her hands around her coffee mug, she heaved a sigh that spoke of both exhaustion and worry.

Gabe stood and stepped behind her. "I should go." He settled his hands on her shoulders. His fingers massaged the tightness he felt even through the bulk of her sweatshirt.

She rolled her neck and released a throaty moan. It was a sound that drew sensual thoughts that Gabe shouldn't be thinking at the moment. Stopping mid-massage, he gave her shoulders a pat with both hands.... Had she noticed the abruptness?

Leaning her head back, she looked up at him. Her brown eyes were sharp with recognition. Raising a challenging brow—which somehow lost its meaning when looking at it upside down—she asked, "Did I scare you?"

"No. Of course not. Why would you ask some—"

"Maybe it's that look of pure fear on your face." She spun around in her chair to look at him without contorting her neck. Her eyes glinted with wicked humor. "I have to admit, I'm a little surprised... after the dogged pursuit and all." She batted her lashes dramatically.

"Oh, but you misread. That wasn't fear. Not fear at all." He leaned closer, until their faces were inches apart. "Restraint. What you saw was gentlemanly restraint. Southern mommas teach their boys not to take advantage of an emotionally exhausted woman. Besides, I didn't feel it was the appropriate time for our first kiss. But since you called me on it . . ." He moved slowly closer and brushed his lips against hers, only allowing himself the briefest taste.

But when he pulled away, she came up out of her chair, her lips following his. Slipping her hands around the back of his neck, she kissed him, *really* kissed him...and his momma would have slapped him clear into next week for his ungentlemanly response.

Two steps forward backed her up against the glass door. Their bodies remained intimately close as they moved. He pressed his palms against the glass to keep his hands from traveling where they really wanted to go.

She'd once told him, "Good mothers don't have boyfriends. I can't put my feelings before Ethan's needs." It had taken him months to begin to lure her away from that conviction. *Don't blow it now.*

She was a passionate woman, invested to the gills in everything she did; he'd seen that in the first five minutes after they'd met. Now, with a single kiss, a fissure began in the wall behind which she'd locked all of her own needs. Her body hummed with dammed-up passion. He tasted starvation in her kiss.

His own body responded like a tuning fork, set to vibrating in harmony with hers. It took all of his willpower to put his hands on the tines and silence them. It had taken him too long to coax her closer; he could not let this go so far that she'd regret it.

He eased away from the kiss, keeping his palms plastered to the glass.

She looked up at him with eyes clouded by passion. Her lips were reddened from his kiss. He dipped his head and kissed her nose. "I'd better go or my credentials as a Southern gentleman will be revoked."

Her tongue traced her bottom lip. Her sensual haze began to clear. Unfortunately, watching her mouth only inflamed his own desires.

She looked up at him and although she grinned wryly, disappointment colored her expression. "Yes, well, we can't have that happen. I've already stirred things up enough in this God-fearing Southern town with my Yankee ways."

She started to slide sideways from between him and

the door. He held her in place with the pressure of his body and kissed her again.

With his lips still against hers, he said, "Oh, Maddie, you have no idea what your Yankee ways do to a country boy like me."

He felt her lips spread into a smile. "You ain't seen nothin' yet."

Chapter 5

WHAT WAS IT about that man's voice that made her lose all sense? Madison rolled over in bed, looking out the window at the pink light of dawn. Her heart hummed happily as she ran her finger along lips that had gone too long without a kiss. Trouble was, she'd been blissfully ignorant of the lack until last night. Gabe had reawakened desires she'd buried when she'd taken on the role of guardian, and then parent.

Her wild response to his gentle kiss had taken her by surprise. The simple sweet kiss he had offered should have been enough. But instead of keeping her butt in that chair, she'd given in to her aching need for comfort. In doing so, she'd leapfrogged over several steps in laying the foundation for a good, stable relationship, which was the only kind she could allow herself now that she was a mother.

No matter how much she liked Gabe, Ethan's well-being had to remain foremost in her mind. Last night she'd begun to hope that Ethan's best interests didn't preclude a relationship for her and Gabe. But she had to take it slowly; as much as she might want to, she could not embark on a wild ride with no guarantee where it would end. No more bunny-in-heat behavior.

Lucky for her, last night Gabe had come to his senses— and managed to coax her to hers without making her feel like a love-starved bubblehead.

Yes, with a considerate, selfless man like Gabriel Wyatt, there just might be some way to balance a relationship with her responsibilities to her son.

She pulled the covers up over her shoulder, delaying facing the realities of the day. Ethan would no doubt want to go to the hospital. She had to prepare, just as she prepared herself for an important journalistic interview. She wanted to be ready with her arguments and explanations, ready to go to battle for what was best for Ethan in the long run. As his mother, it was her job to make the hard decisions.

When she'd first taken on this role, she'd read every book on parenting and adolescent behavior she could get her hands on. One element that ran true in every one of them was the deep need a child, no matter what age, has for rules and boundaries. In the beginning Ethan had chafed under newly imposed restraints. After a while, beneath the bristling protests, she'd begun to sense his feeling of gratitude, his appreciation that someone cared enough to be concerned about where he was and what he was doing.

It was funny really; their no-bullshit pact didn't seem to come into play in this particular area of their relationship. When push came to shove, they squared off just like every other adolescent and parent. And afterward, just like most parents and half-grown children, they never came right out and said what they felt, but saved face by resorting to subtle conciliatory nuances.

Of course, having started this whole parenting thing halfway through the process, she had to be extraordinarily careful in choosing her battles. So, before she laid out judgment, she always thought it through, making certain she could justify her stand. That way there was no destructive waffling or backing down.

Today would be crucial. She had to consider the pros and cons of Ethan missing school, and of his visiting Jordan at the hospital. Even though Ethan had experienced more trauma than most boys his age, he was at such a vulnerable stage, agewise as well as socially. He was still adjusting as "the new kid." Considering that, wouldn't it be better for him to face school today, and not delay the inevitable questions of curious classmates?

As far as she could tell, Jordan Gray was his only close friend. And Jordan might well be in for a long recovery. Ethan had to be prepared for that possibility. Keeping to his normal routine might be the best way in which to do that.

On the other hand—

A soft knock sounded on her bedroom door. "M? Are you awake?"

Decision time. He was going to school. "Yes. Come on in."

Pushing open the door, he hung in the doorway. He was already dressed and his face looked as if he hadn't had a single minute of sleep. His hair looked like a rat's nest, as if he'd been tossing and turning, or repeatedly running his hands through it.

She had to choke back the sympathetic sound that

automatically formed in her throat and ignore the urge to draw him into a hug. Instead she said, "You're up early."

"Yeah. I was hoping to go by the hospital to see Jordan before school."

She was just a little ashamed of the relief she felt. She wasn't going to have to take the role of Dictator-of-What's-Good-for-You and force him to attend school today.

"What if he's the same?" she asked. "Maybe it would be better to give him the day and go see him after school. I can be done early at the office—"

"Come on, M! You know I'm not gonna freak if he's still...out of it." He locked gazes with her. "I won't be able to think in school unless I see him—just for a minute. And maybe it'll help him to see me, too."

She sighed, sat up, and pushed the hair out of her eyes. Sometimes her own teachings came back to bite her in the ass; thanks to her, the kid knew how to present an argument.

"Give me a minute to throw on some clothes. I'll come back and shower after I drop you off at school."

He nodded and backed away, pulling closed her bedroom door.

Twenty minutes later, they entered the hospital. Madison said, "Visiting hours don't start until one in the afternoon, so just keep walking like you're supposed to be here."

On a normal day, Ethan would have given her a load of crap, throwing her own lectures about picking and choosing which rules to follow right back in her face. Today wasn't a normal day.

They took the elevator to the third floor and walked past the nurses' station without pause. Not that it looked like any one of them had an interest in who was coming and going anyway; they were deep in conversation about a television drama that had aired last night.

The door to Jordan's room was closed.

"Let me check it out first," she said.

Ethan looked uneasy. She resisted the urge to smooth his hair away from his eyes.

Easing the door open, she slowly peeked inside. The drapes were open. Bright sunlight flooded the room and reflected in Jordan's unblinking stare. Disappointment sat like an indigestible meal in her stomach. If it hit her this hard, how was Ethan going to feel?

Before she could consider that question further, he walked past her and up to Jordan's bedside. To her surprise, Ethan took Jordan's hand. "Hey."

Jordan didn't show a flicker of response. She was struck then by his eerie resemblance to a wax figure. If anything, he looked worse than he had yesterday.

Madison tensed, waiting to see how Ethan handled the lack of improvement.

He only hesitated a second. "You're lucky, dude," he said in a tone remarkably close to regular guy talk. "You get to lay here in bed all day instead of going to listen to Mrs. Hillenberg go on and on and on about O. Henry's 'incredibly deep and multi-layered' short stories." He altered his voice to sound remarkably like the English teacher. Then he reverted to himself to add, "She never mentions the fact that the guy was a drunk and a convict."

Madison was impressed with the way he managed to make this one-sided conversation seem natural. And she was more than a little shocked with his expanded knowledge of O. Henry. It made her wonder if maybe

his outward derision of the author was just for adolescent
show—a defensive carryover from his previous life.

It hadn't taken long for her to see that he used postur-
ing and tough talk to camouflage his fascination with
books and language. She supposed in the cruel world of
his childhood, such interests would have been considered
weak. And to show weakness was to open the door to
being a victim.

After a short pause he said, "It's okay. You don't have
to talk until you're ready." Suddenly his face brightened,
as if he'd found the key to a mystery. "In fact, I want to be
the first one you talk to. So keep quiet until I get back to
torture you with all of the garbage Mrs. Hillenberg lays
on us today."

She wondered if his challenge had gotten through to
Jordan. Would it be motivation for the boy to reach out
when Ethan returned?

He took a step back from the bedside, keeping his gaze
on Jordan for a second longer. Then he turned his eyes
toward Madison. He was a master at disguising his inner
feelings, but she swore she saw relief there, running somewhere just beneath the worry and sadness.

THE BUZZ AT THE SMOKY RIDGE CAFÉ was all about Steve
McPherson's accident. Gabe didn't need to hear the comments to know that. It was written on every face in the
place as they looked at him when he walked in. Curiosity
filled the eyes of people who knew from experience he
wouldn't discuss anything associated with his job. That
fact didn't keep them from wanting to ask.

He took a seat at his usual breakfast table in the rear of
the dining room. Today he placed his back to the crowd,

just in case anyone's inquisitiveness overrode their good sense.

He didn't pick up a menu. Every weekday morning for the past two years Gabe had sat at this table and ate the same breakfast. All he had to do was show up and the rest was on autopilot. So he was a little surprised when the waitress, Little Peggy—who couldn't be called just Peggy because that was her eighty-five-year-old momma's name and she was still using it—stopped at his table without coffee or food.

"Just you this mornin', Sheriff?" Her eyes traveled to the empty chair across from him.

"It's just me every mornin', darlin'."

"Well...um, yeah...but I heard that yesterday you had some company. I just thought..." She let the suggestion hang there.

He should nip this now, before Maddie got wind of it. But he kinda liked the idea that people linked the two of them together as a couple.

He smiled and winked. "Just me today."

She tilted her graying head and winked back. "All righty then. I'll be right back with your coffee." She started away, then stopped and turned to him again. "Glad to hear that newspaper woman is finally mixing with the rest of us folks. Gotta be lonely, bless her heart."

Even with the "bless her heart," there was an undeniable undertone of censure in the statement. Gabe wondered how long it would be before everyone stopped thinking of Maddie as an outsider, an interloper in their community.

Probably just after hell froze over.

Was Maddie lonely? He couldn't imagine her ever admitting to being lonely. But he agreed with Little Peggy. Sometimes, in unguarded moments, Maddie's eyes revealed her desire for closeness. But those moments were always gone in a flash, long before he could capitalize on them.

So far anyway.

Just after his coffee arrived, so did Dottie Zinn.

She slid into the chair opposite him. "Morning, Gabe."

"Morning, Dot. Surprised to see you here. I thought you shied away from cholesterol in the morning."

The waitress arrived and set Gabe's standing order of bacon, sausage, eggs, grits, and biscuits in front of him.

Dottie gave a visible shiver. "Jesus, Gabe, you tryin' to cement up your arteries?" Then she smiled at the waitress and ordered black decaf coffee and oatmeal with skim milk.

"If I had to eat oatmeal every morning," he said, "I'd be *looking* for a way out."

"Big talk from a strapping, healthy thirty-five-year old."

He forked half of a sausage link into his mouth. "Thirty-three."

She grunted. "Rub it in."

The waitress delivered Dottie's coffee and a bowl of globular tan muck. Gabe mimicked Dottie's earlier shiver. "How can you eat that stuff?"

"I plan on living long enough to annoy my grandchildren. It's worth the sacrifice." As she poured the watery-looking milk onto her oatmeal, she said in a quiet tone, "Listen, I just sent Steve McPherson's body to the forensic pathologist in Knoxville. He said it had been a slow weekend, so we should have his preliminary results tonight."

"Slow weekend, huh? He and the undertakers are probably the only people who are disappointed."

"Hey, don't get sassy." She pointed her spoon at him. "Somebody's gotta do those jobs. Besides, he read me the report on Zach Gilbert that you'll be receiving later today."

Gabe's fork paused halfway to his mouth. "And?"

"Cause of death is officially heart failure. Kid's cholesterol was sky high, he had liver cysts—"

"And let me guess, toxicology screen tested positive for anabolic steroid use."

She nodded.

"Damn. I hate to have to tell a mother her kid's death was totally avoidable. What a friggin' waste."

"I'll contact the Gilberts. You've delivered more than your share of bad news this past week. Of course, that's only half the issue."

He set down his fork and exhaled. "I'll talk to the football coach today—make sure he's keeping close tabs on his players. Let's hope this is an isolated incident."

"Let's hope."

Gabe's grandma always said bad things came in threes; plane crashes, natural disasters, deaths. Gabe chose to lump in Jordan Gray's mental state with the two deaths and call this rash of crap done.

MADISON DECIDED TO WRITE THE ARTICLE on Steve McPherson's accidental death herself. She hoped Kate would see her personal interest as a nod to Jordan's friendship and appreciation for Steve's inclusion of Ethan.

According to back issues of the *Daily Herald,* McPherson had damn near been a saint when it came to donating his time to the youth of Buckeye. He coached basketball at the Boys & Girls Club, helped with peewee football, and had been a major force behind the formation of youth club baseball. He'd received a service award from the mayor just last year.

As she researched further with a few phone calls,

she discovered that Steve had never missed a single one of Todd's football or baseball games. Also, it appeared McPherson had focused more on his extracurricular activities than on a career. Although he held a degree in electrical engineering, he was completely content with his hourly-wage job in the Chevrolet dealership service department. The co-workers she interviewed all spoke very highly of him.

Madison wondered if perhaps she should offer to set up a scholarship fund in McPherson's name. She'd bet his co-workers would be willing to help. Maybe Todd could be the first recipient. Certainly no consolation for his father's death, but it could offer a boost toward his future. She really liked that idea.

She called the bank and made a mid-morning appointment to discuss it with the vice president. If she got it set up, she could include the donation information in this article.

AFTER LEAVING THE SMOKY RIDGE, Gabe decided to head out to the high school. As always when he was driving around town, he made an unnecessary swing past the *Buckeye Daily Herald*'s office.

The instant he turned the corner, he saw Maddie walking down the sidewalk on the right side of the street with her back to him. Her posture was ramrod straight, hair was pulled back into a sleek ponytail, and she wore a skirt suit that couldn't look more out of place on their homey downtown streets. To complete the Philly-business shell, she had an expensive-looking tote slung over her shoulder.

He couldn't help thinking how much he preferred her in that huge UT sweatshirt with her hair loose and naturally curled.

A smile played on his lips. *Maybe wearing nothing but that sweatshirt...*

He drove slowly. Once he got just behind her, he matched her speed.

She kept up her businesslike pace, eyes focused straight ahead.

Oh, well, hell. This was just too tempting to pass up.

He flipped on his siren—just one loud blip.

Every muscle in Maddie's body jerked tight. Her step faltered and her foot tipped off her three-inch heel.

She turned. The look of surprise on her face clouded with irritation the instant she saw him...laughing.

Stalking to the curb, she motioned for him to put his passenger window down. The look on her face reminded him of his third-grade teacher's after he and his best buddy liberated the classroom's pet gerbils from their cage. "Are you, like, what...twelve?"

Trying to suppress a chuckle, he said, "I'm sorry, sugar, but you were asking for that one." Little Peggy was right; it was time for Maddie to begin to fit in.

"What do you mean, asking for it?"

He could see her annoyance beginning to fade, so he went for it. "Be a good idea to stop walking around here like an alien from another planet. Get yourself some sensible shoes, maybe a pair of Dockers pants."

"I'm working! *These*"—she ran her hand down the length of her body, as if displaying a prize—"are my work clothes."

"All I'm sayin' is if you want to fit in around here, maybe it's time to knock the formality down a notch or two. Slow down. Stop and say howdy to folks you pass."

She straightened and fixed a mocking glare on him. "Who says I want to fit in?"

She turned and resumed her Yankee march up the street.

When he tooted his horn as he passed, she wrinkled her nose and gave him an I'd-delight-in-wringing-your-neck look—however, she did wave.

What a proud, stubborn woman. Why couldn't he leave her alone?

WHEN GABE SIGNED IN at the high school office, he wasn't surprised to discover that both Colin Arbuckle and J.D. were absent from school today. Spending a night on a mountain with a dead body would have taken an emotional toll. As a teenage boy, Gabe had always capitalized on each and every reason to miss school; this should qualify in spades.

Apparently not for Ethan Wade, however, who hadn't even been late in his arrival this morning.

Gabe hadn't planned on questioning the boys here anyway. Better to address them away from their peers. He'd call on Colin and J.D. as soon as he left here.

He found Coach Lawrence watching game tapes in his little office off the gymnasium locker rooms. The smell of this place hadn't changed in the fifteen years since Gabe had graduated—shower steam and dirty socks. If he closed his eyes, he'd be right back in freshman phys ed, fighting the combination lock that never worked right and dreading old Mr. Phelps's lazy man's approach to gym class...running endless laps.

Gabe rapped a knuckle on the door jamb.

Lawrence jerked his gaze away from the TV screen. "Sheriff." He stood. "What can I do for you?"

Stepping inside the cramped office, Gabe got right to the point. "Zach Gilbert tested positive for anabolic steroids. That's what killed him."

He waited, gauging Coach Lawrence's reaction. Had he known Zach was doping? Had he encouraged it? Lawrence had been brought in last year after the previous coach had gone three years without a winning season. High school football was damn near a religion in this town, and folks were impatient.

For a beat or two, Lawrence stood stock-still. Then he spun around and slammed the playbook in his hands against the side of a metal filing cabinet. Gabe flinched as the bang reverberated in the close space.

"Damn it!" the man swore between clenched teeth. He kept his profile to Gabe. His breath came in angry bursts from his barrel chest. "God-fucking-damn it."

"I take it this is news to you," Gabe finally said.

In the next instant, Gabe feared lightning bolts would actually shoot from the man's ice-blue eyes.

"What kind of man do you think I am? Holy Christ…"

"I just know the kind of pressure you're under here—"

"Hey! I want a championship as much as everyone else in this town, but I would never compromise the safety of a single player to get it." He shot Gabe another stabbing look. "There are thousands of high school coaching jobs. I don't need *this* one that badly."

Plenty of men had been tempted by less. But Lawrence's reaction seemed genuine. For the moment, Gabe believed him. "What about others? I can't imagine this is an isolated case. It just doesn't work that way."

Lawrence sank down in the chair he'd been sitting in when Gabe entered the room. "If I missed it in Gilbert, it's entirely possible that I've missed it in others." He gave his head a slow shake. "I made my policy clear at my very first summer practice. Zero tolerance." He ticked them off on his fingers. "No alcohol, no failing grades, no knocked-up girlfriends, no drugs—which I made clear included performance enhancers. An undisciplined athlete is an unreliable athlete."

Gabe nodded. "I'd appreciate it if you keep a close eye on your team. And let the other coaches know to do the same. I want to know if we have a serious issue in this community."

Lawrence stood again. "No problem. I'm gonna be all over this."

"Be in touch," Gabe said as he shook the man's hand.

On his way out of the building, Gabe paused by the double doors to the cafeteria and looked inside. The clothes and hairstyles had changed, but if he closed his eyes for a single second, as he had in the locker room, the rumble of dozens of adolescent conversations and the smell of sticky spaghetti and burnt garlic bread shot him right back to his high school days.

"Excuse me, do you need some help?"

Gabe turned to see a young woman with a blond ponytail and a photo ID badge that marked her as a teacher looking at him with concern.

Feeling like an idiot, he said, "Thanks, no. I was just on my way out."

She smiled and went on into the cafeteria.

It struck him then that he was older than many of the teachers. Man, when he thought back, all of his teachers had seemed friggin' *ancient*.

Nostalgia had a way of stacking the years into a visible mountain between you and your youth. He decided to put it away and not drag it out again any time in the near future.

Then another thought rolled down the steep slope of life's reminiscences. When his dad had been thirty-three, Gabe had been twelve years old. He tried to imagine himself with a twelve-year-old child.

He might never be a father at the rate he was going.

Knock it off, Wyatt.

As he started away from the cafeteria door, he noticed Ethan sitting at the end of a long table all alone. In a sea of youthful movement, he was an island of stillness. He painted such a picture of misery that Gabe stopped and studied him for a moment. The boy had pushed his untouched food tray away from him. His elbows were planted on the table and he rested his forehead on the heels of his hands. It was the defeated droop of his shoulders that struck Gabe the hardest.

He almost walked through the door, but stopped short. True, he wanted to talk to Ethan further about what had happened on the mountain, but this wasn't the time or place. The kid had enough trouble without Gabe pulling him out in front of the entire student body.

Besides, if he waited until Ethan was home, Gabe would have an excuse to see Maddie.

He left the school thinking he shouldn't be so looking forward to questioning a kid about a death.

THE PRESSURE IN ETHAN'S HEAD threatened to make it explode. With every heartbeat, he felt his eyes bulge. He pressed the heels of his hands against them to keep them in their sockets. He could almost see the top of his head blown open by the force of his own pulse; his blood and brains on the cafeteria wall.

Blood and brains...blood and brains...like Mr. McP.

The thought kept circling in his head, building more pressure.

He tried to stop thinking. He'd been trying for two days. But there was no relief, no sleep, no peace.

All Ethan had wanted to do was protect Jordan.

It had been that way from the start. The first time Ethan had laid eyes on Jordan, the kid reminded him of a whipped dog, so unaccustomed to anyone reaching out to him except to bully and punish that he instinctively shied away. Ethan knew that feeling all too well.

But while Ethan's life had made him strong, Jordan's seemed to have knocked all the toughness right out of him.

They'd met the first week after he'd moved to Buckeye:

Ethan approached the skateboard half-pipe at the public park. He didn't have a skateboard, but looking at the cool skate park, he thought maybe he'd ask for one for his birthday next week. M had been bugging him about what he wanted. Since she couldn't give him what he really wanted—to not have his fifteenth birthday before he started his freshman year in high school— maybe a skateboard would be fun.

The park wasn't real busy, just a couple of guys with their boards inside the fence. Ethan leaned his elbows on the top of the chain link and watched. They were both younger than him and they were pretty good working the half-pipe; one of them was getting some pretty serious air.

Then Ethan spotted a skinny kid sitting on a bench just outside the gate. He held his skateboard across his bouncing knees. His fingers drummed on the board. He kept his gaze lowered, looking at everything except the kids inside the fence.

Ethan recognized the posture, that desire to be invisible, right away. He'd been the same way his first weeks on the street.

He walked around the fenced area and sat on the bench next to the kid. He couldn't tell how old he was; he looked twelve or thirteen, but as pale and scrawny as he was, Ethan guessed he was probably older than he appeared.

"Hey," Ethan said. "You going in?"

The kid's gaze came up for a fraction of a second, then returned to the skateboard in his lap. He shrugged. "Maybe later."

Ethan pointed to the skateboard; it was new, the wheels barely even roughened. "Pretty sweet."

"Thanks." The word was almost too low to hear over the rumble of the other skaters' wheels.

"Hey, dweeb, thought we told you to go home," one of the guys inside the fence called.

Ethan watched as the kid on the bench retreated like a frightened turtle, drawing his head lower into his shoulders.

The other skater kicked up his board and carried it over to the fence. "Yeah. You're too scared to do anything. Why are you hanging around here?"

Ethan looked up. "How 'bout you guys leave him alone? He's not bothering you."

"Wrong. He's bugging the shit out of us. Little nerd can't even ride that thing."

"Looks to me like he just got it," Ethan said.

"Yeah, well, he's too chicken to use it."

Ethan looked at the kid sitting next to him, who was totally focused on the skateboard wheel he was fingering.

Ethan asked quietly, "Did they throw you out?"

One bony shoulder rose. Then he looked sideways at Ethan without raising his head. "My brother Todd gave me the skateboard," he whispered. "I *have* to learn to ride it."

"Hey, dude," one of the kids called from just inside the fence, "you don't want to hang with that pussy." He pointed to the scared kid.

Ethan was off the bench and had the kid by the shirt-front in a heartbeat. He lifted Skater Boy's shoes off the ground, pulling him up until they were nose to nose over the fence. "Leave him alone, or I'm going to shove your head up your buddy's ass." His teeth were clenched as he ground out the words.

Skater Boy's eyes widened and he raised his hands, palms up. "Dude, relax."

The other skateboarder hung back, out of Ethan's reach. "Yeah, dude. What's wrong with you?"

"Pricks like you, that's what's wrong with me. Leave him alone. Next time, I'll feed you your own balls." He let the kid down.

The instant the kid's feet hit the ground, he jerked away, taking a step back. "You're a crazy fucker."

"Crazier than anything you've ever met. Remember it."

Instead of coming out the gate, the two skaters went to the side fence and climbed over, shooting nasty looks at Ethan as they did.

Once they were over, Ethan made a move like he was going after them.

They broke into a run and didn't look back.

He grinned down at the kid on the bench. "I'm Ethan."

The kid looked up, gratitude in his eyes. "Jordan."

"Come on, Jordan, let's get you riding that thing."

Jordan had been the most cautious, least coordinated kid Ethan had ever seen. But by the end of that afternoon they'd gotten him so he could coast along on the thing without falling and busting his ass.

They'd parted friends that day.

Over the summer, they'd hung out a lot, enough that Ethan could tell something was wrong with Jordan as they'd driven up the mountain on Friday. He'd been silent the entire drive—which wasn't entirely unusual, as he tended to be quiet around his stepdad. But there was a weird nervousness about Jordan: jittery hands, bouncy knees, and a scared-rabbit look in eyes that would not meet Ethan's.

Why hadn't he asked Jordan about it? Why hadn't he *made* him talk?

Ethan knew why. Because he really hadn't wanted to know, not that day. He'd been excited about this wilderness trip—he hadn't wanted it ruined by seeing the very thing he was looking for.

Could things have been different? If he'd confronted Jordan, would Mr. McP still be alive?

The cafeteria bell rang, a screwdriver jabbing in Ethan's ears. He didn't cover them to muffle the sound because he deserved the pain.

Chapter 6

J.D. HENRY'S MOTHER WAS A NERVOUS, underfed redhead who gave Gabe the impression that she ran solely on the "ines"—caffeine and nicotine. He had never seen her without a cigarette in her hand. Except in the hospital yesterday, which was a strictly non-smoking facility. Every time he'd laid eyes on her in the ER, the jittery woman was pacing around with a cup of black coffee in her hands.

When he knocked on the door of the Henry duplex, she opened it and peered at him through a ribbon of smoke that curled from the cigarette pinched between the first two fingers of her left hand.

"Mrs. Henry, I'd like to speak to J.D. for a few minutes, if I may."

For a moment, she simply stared at him. He thought perhaps she didn't recognize him. "I'm Sheriff Wyatt."

"I ain't blind. I seen the uniform. I ain't stupid neither; you talked to me yesterday."

Nervous *and* bitchy. Gabe felt a stab of sympathy for

J.D. And, he thought, just maybe J.D.'s older brother had been driven to the crime he was sitting in jail for. "May I speak to J.D.?"

"Sorry, he's at school." She started to close the door.

"Mrs. Henry, I just left the school. He wasn't there."

Gabe heard J.D.'s voice from inside the house. "It's okay, Mom."

She spun around and said, "He don't have a warrant. You don't need to talk to him."

Gabe didn't need a warrant; he was simply taking a statement. "Mrs. Henry, your son hasn't done anything wrong. I just need to ask a few questions about Steve McPherson's accident. It's just a formality to get the paperwork completed."

She drew on her cigarette and blew the smoke out of her nose, shooting Gabe a mistrustful look.

J.D. wedged himself between his mother and the door jamb, forcing her to open the door wide enough for Gabe to enter.

She looked mad enough to spit nails. "Go on ahead then, James Dean, if you ain't got no more sense than that. Have them lock you away like they did Jeffery." She stomped up the stairs.

J.D.'s brother had been sent to jail last year for assault after he'd beaten up his girlfriend, breaking her nose and her arm. Gabe hadn't had anything to do with that arrest, since it was in the city police's jurisdiction.

Mrs. Henry slammed a door upstairs.

"Sorry," J.D. said. "She gets worked up about Jeffery. She's convinced it was Shelly's fault."

Shelly, the girlfriend Jeffery outweighed by fifty pounds.

Gabe thought it was more likely leftover rage from living with his own mother.

"And you? What do you think?" Gabe asked out of curiosity.

J.D. glanced up the stairs. "I dunno." He shrugged. "Sometimes Jeff can have a temper."

"Can we sit down? I just want to go over what happened with Mr. McPherson's accident for my report."

J.D. led him into a living room that smelled like a bar after a Saturday night. Gabe sat on the edge of the recliner and J.D. sprawled on one end of the sofa.

"Okay," Gabe said, "can you tell me what was going on before Mr. McPherson left camp that last time?"

"Jordan and Ethan had gone off to get more firewood. Me and Colin were supposed to get the stuff ready to cook supper."

"About what time was that?"

"I wasn't paying much attention. I guess around four or four-thirty."

"Go on."

"Mr. McP was checking the tents, 'cause it was getting windy. He said we had to have a small fire because of the wind, too. Once he got done with the tents, the guys were supposed to be back with the wood and he was gonna show us how to build a fire that would stay small. But then when Ethan and Jordan didn't come back, he tried to call them on the walkie-talkie he'd sent with Jordan.

"Jordan didn't answer. So Mr. McP—he was pretty mad—went off to find them. Me and Colin were supposed to stay in camp."

Gabe hadn't found a walkie on McPherson. "Did he take the walkie, or leave it with you two?"

"He took it. We were supposed to have Jordan call him if they showed up back at camp." He picked at a hangnail. "But they didn't show up. Later, we heard Ethan yelling for help."

"How much later?"

"I'm not sure. It was starting to get dark."

"Where was Ethan when you heard him calling you?"

"Somewhere between camp and the falls. I couldn't see him or anything. When we yelled back, he didn't wait for us."

"And when you got there?"

"Jordan was going nuts. Ethan had his shirt off; it was all bloody and pressed against Mr. McP's head. Colin started yelling, 'What happened?' and Jordan was walking around pulling at his hair saying, 'It was an accident. It was an accident.' Over and over. He wouldn't stop, until Ethan finally yelled for him to shut up."

"Do you know if Mr. McPherson was still breathing?"

He shook his head. "Ethan said he wasn't . . . said he was dead, but neither me or Colin got close enough to tell."

"Why?"

J.D. shrugged. "Didn't really want to, I guess. Colin got one look at the blood on Ethan's shirt and was puking in the creek. Ethan seemed to know what he was doing."

"What about going for help?"

J.D. shook his head. "No way. It was getting dark. And up there, I mean it gets *really* dark. None of us thought we could find the way. We decided to stay there and wait for daylight."

"Did Ethan tell you how he found Mr. McPherson?"

"He said he and Jordan were getting wood and heard a yelp. They found him on the ground by the creek."

When Gabe stood, he had a couple of new questions in his mind. Where was the walkie that McPherson was supposed to have had? And why had Jordan been yelling, "It was an accident"?

"I appreciate you talking to me," Gabe said pointedly.

J.D. looked slightly embarrassed. "Sorry about my mom."

"No need to apologize."

Next Gabe went to the Arbuckle house and got pretty much the same thing, minus the combative attitude of the mother. Colin Arbuckle's mother had been a clucking hen, worrying over her son's recent trauma and the long-term effects it might have at such an impressionable age. Gabe left wondering if there were any middle-of-the-road mothers anymore.

The more he contemplated the questions he'd left the Henry house with, the simpler the answers seemed to be. The walkie could very easily have bounced into the creek, especially if it had been in McPherson's hand when he fell. And, although he couldn't completely explain Jordan's hysterical comment, he also couldn't take it too seriously. From everything Gabe had gathered, the kid hadn't said anything that made sense from the moment he'd seen McPherson's body.

Once he confirmed all of this with Ethan and received the autopsy report, the case could be officially closed.

MADISON'S CELL PHONE RANG just as she was leaving the office at five o'clock. She'd intended to get away earlier, to be home for Ethan. But one problem after another had cropped up and the afternoon was gone. She answered her phone as she simultaneously juggled her laptop tote, her purse, and the keys to lock the front door of the editorial office of the *Buckeye Daily Herald*.

"M, can you pick me up at the hospital on your way home?"

"How'd you get to the hospital?" It was four miles from the high school to the hospital.

"Walked."

A pinprick of guilt needled her conscience. "I told you I would take you as soon as I got home from work."

"I know."

She nearly asked how Jordan was, but realized if there had been any improvement, that would have been the first thing out of Ethan's mouth. "I'll be there in five minutes."

When she pulled her Saab up to the main hospital entrance, she spotted Ethan sitting with his back propped against the base of the flagpole. Exhaustion was written in every movement as he got up, picked up his backpack, and ambled over to the car.

He got in and she said, "Hi. How about some dinner on the way home?"

He ignored the question. Keeping his gaze out the windshield, he said flatly, "They're moving Jordan to a stress center in Knoxville tomorrow."

"Oh?" Not that she was surprised. She supposed she should have prepared Ethan for this possibility.

"His mom said the doctor said he needs psychological help." He balled his fists in his lap. "They think he's crazy...but he's not." He finally turned to look at her. "He's just scared. That's all...just scared."

"Scared is a psychological and emotional state, Ethan. He's going where they can help him."

"But it's so far from here."

"Let's hope he won't have to be there long. And we'll go visit him."

He didn't look reassured.

She reached over and brushed his hair away from his forehead. "You're doing all you can. You're showing him you're there for him."

He responded with a half-grunt.

She wished she could offer him more encouragement, but empty promises and hollow words would break their no-bullshit pact. And this was one of those important things; Ethan needed to know he could rely on her for the bare-assed truth. Unfortunately, the bare-assed truth was that it might take a very long time for Jordan to recover, if he ever did fully recover. That was something she decided she could ease Ethan into. He didn't have to face the worst-case scenario today.

During the fifteen-minute drive home, out of the corner of her eye she saw Ethan's head bob. She looked over and saw he'd fallen asleep with his head leaning against the window. Guess they'd skip dinner out and scrounge up something at home. Poor kid, more tired than hungry... that was a first.

Through diligent research she'd been able to prepare for lots of things about being a parent. But nothing in this world had prepared her for the piercing pain in her chest, the aching lump in her throat, the heavy sickness in her belly that came when she saw her son hurting and unhappy. Nothing had prepared her for the raging impotence over not being able to do anything to alleviate that pain or to lift that shroud of despair.

Her mother's words echoed in her mind: *One day you'll understand... when you have children of your own.*

Jesus, it seemed like her mother could have done more to prepare her than quote platitudes.

An unwilling smile curved Madison's mouth. *Like I would have listened.*

With a deep breath, she realized how much anguish she'd dealt, both inadvertently and willingly, her own mother. (Deep down, she figured her dad deserved every heartache he'd received. Although she doubted he cared enough to notice the arrows she intentionally flung his way.) She supposed she was getting her due. But why did Ethan have to suffer for it?

In an effort to lift her spirits—she needed to be in better mental shape when Ethan awakened—she focused on her surroundings. She loved driving the narrow road to their house. It was mostly uphill, which was why she had such a great view from her kitchen window, and why it seemed so much farther out of town than it was.

She slowed as she approached the railroad overpass. It had been built so long ago that only a single vehicle could fit through at a time. It was situated in the middle of an S curve, which made it really difficult to see if there was oncoming traffic, not that Turnbull Road was heavily traveled. Still, caution was prudent.

One of the first times she'd driven this road she'd nearly had a head-on with a pickup that had a deer carcass strapped to its hood. She'd come around the corner too fast and there it was, a deer, stretched on its side, heading right for her windshield.

The old guy driving the truck had laid on the horn, then followed up by flipping her off as he passed her. Sitting stock-still in the road, she'd looked in her rearview. The only thing that jumped out at her was a huge "Jesus is Lord" sticker on the back bumper—not a rare thing in these parts. Consequently, she'd never figured out who the old codger was. Too bad, because it hadn't been deer season. She could have paid him back for his kind gesture with a call to the Department of Natural Resources.

She threaded the eye of the needle beneath the railroad, tense as ever. Obviously today the peaceful scenery wasn't doing the trick to unwind her.

Maybe deep breathing…

When she rounded that last curve, she got the emotional boost she'd been looking for—from a most unexpected source. Gabe's SUV was parked in front of her house. He got out, smiled, and waved as she pulled into the drive. She shivered with a spark of sheer happiness.

Ethan didn't stir when she shut off the engine. She got out of the car, closing the door softly.

Gabe walked up the driveway in that unhurried Southern gait of his. All of her nerve endings readily snapped to attention.

He gave her a crooked grin as he said, "Evenin', Maddie."

The warm roughness of his voice slid over each and every one of those eager nerve endings, soothing and exciting them simultaneously.

"Evenin', Sheriff." Her imitation of a Southern drawl was both pathetic and comical.

He was kind and didn't laugh, but he did give her a smile that had probably scored him more points with women than he ever imagined. "Left the sheriff back at the office." He pulled out a large brown paper bag from where it was tucked behind his back. "Gabe the Gourmet brought dinner."

"Mmmm, from the grease spots on that bag, I'd say I'm gonna like what's in there."

"Baby-backs, bar-b-que beans, slaw, and home fries."

"Hope you brought plenty. Ethan can eat two racks all by himself."

"Well, so can I." He cocked his head. "Maybe you'll have to eat peanut butter."

"Ha!" She snatched the bag out of his hand. "We'll see about that." She went around to the passenger door and tapped on the window.

Ethan lifted his head and blinked, as if he was reacquainting himself with his bearings.

She opened the door and waved the bag under his nose. "Gabe brought ribs, the universal language of all American males."

Ethan's nostrils flared as he took in the smoky aroma. "I'm starved."

Looking at Gabe, she said, "Uh-oh. Looks like maybe we'll both be eating peanut butter."

Once inside, they sat down around the kitchen table with the food and a large stack of napkins. Ethan and Gabe started talking UT football. Although Ethan's eyes didn't shine with their usual light, his spirits seemed to be lifting.

As they talked, the guys piled up mountains of stripped bones at a rate that would rival those competitive eating contest guys on ESPN.

Hope rose in her chest. This could be a turning point for Ethan. Life would never be exactly the same after what he'd been through on that mountain, but perhaps it was sliding back toward normal—or at least normal-ish.

She smiled, feeling warm and at peace as she watched

the two guys talk. Licking her fingers, she continued to eat
Gabe the Gourmet's unhealthful, artery-clogging, fat food.
She decided she'd wait until later to feel guilty about it.

GABE WATCHED RELIEF GROW IN MADDIE'S EYES as Ethan
ate like the teenager he was and got swept up in the subject
of football, which had just switched from the fall schedule
for UT to the prospects for the local high school team, the
Buckeye Rebels.

"Have you considered playing?" Gabe asked. The kid
certainly had the build.

Ethan shrugged. "It's way too late for me to start. I
mean, most of those guys have been playing since they
were in grade school. I wouldn't have a chance."

Madison said, "If you think you'd like to, maybe we
could find a football camp next summer."

"Nah. I don't want to play for losers...everybody says
without Zach Gilbert, the Rebels are royally screwed."

Gabe saw that for the self-defensive move it was. Ethan
was already in a tenuous social position; new kid, best
friend hospitalized for what the rumor mill was calling a
nervous breakdown.

"I understand it was steroid use," Maddie said sadly.
"At *seventeen*."

Before Gabe's surprise formed a question on his lips,
Ethan said, "No shit?" He paused with a rib halfway to
his lips. "That's just stupid."

"It is. And a horrible, tragic waste," Maddie agreed.
She shifted her attention to Gabe. "We push and push
these kids, and for what? A winning *high school* season?
Where are our priorities as parents and coaches?"

Gabe didn't know which took him more off guard, her

jumping in with both feet on a subject that could be upsetting for Ethan, or the fact that she already knew about the autopsy findings.

She seemed to read his surprise. "It's my job to stay on top of the news." She sounded just a tad defensive. "Part of that is communication with the ME's office—especially in a case like this. It *is* public record, after all."

Gabe lifted a palm in her direction. "I'm not criticizing. Just surprised at the speed of your acquisition of the fact."

"News has a short shelf life—that's why they call it news. I have to obtain information quickly."

"Yeah," Ethan piped up. "M won an award in Philly because she's the best there is."

Maddie harrumphed. "Hardly."

"I have no doubt about that." Gabe locked his gaze to hers. "I could tell first time I saw her at a city council meeting."

For a moment, her gaze flirted with Gabe's, probing, suggesting possibilities that he had been hoping for for weeks. His pulse actually kicked up a notch. After a pause in conversation that was bordering on obvious—even to a teenager—she disentangled her gaze.

Apparently not quickly enough; Ethan made a sound of disgust, then said, "Hello?...Impressionable teen in the room."

Maddie rolled her eyes. "Yes, well," she said, the first syllable just shaky enough to tell Gabe she was as affected as he, "this whole steroid situation needs to be exposed. I did a little research today; it's a serious and growing problem in high school athletics." Her eyes glittered with enthusiasm; her attention now solely focused on what she was saying.

Gabe recognized that kind of enthusiasm; the kind that was borne of a passionate soul. He longed to probe that passion, get under that beautiful skin and see what dwelt deep in her heart; to have her eyes light up like that with his touch.

His thoughts must have been written on his face, because she blinked, looking away from him, color rising in her cheeks. She moistened her lips and went on, "I plan to focus front-page space of the *Herald* on it. Maybe we can prevent another athlete from inadvertently killing himself."

He gave a nod. "I think that's a very good idea."

Maddie asked Ethan, "Do you know anything about kids at school doping?"

Ethan's eyes widened. "Seriously, M! If I did, do you really think I'd rat somebody out? They already don't like me 'cause I'm from up north."

To Gabe's surprise, Maddie laughed. "Okay, don't get your boxers in a bunch. I was just checking... you know I access all of my sources...."

"Yeah, well, this source is a dead end." Ethan's untroubled tone said this was a gentle battle, one these two had danced around before. Ethan wiped his sticky fingers on his third napkin. "Do we have dessert?"

After they nearly polished off a bag of Oreos, Ethan went to his room to watch TV. Gabe took the opportunity to say something he'd been hesitant to bring up in front of him.

"I saw your piece in tonight's paper on Steve McPherson. Very nice."

Maddie smiled a smile that said his opinion mattered. "Thanks. He'd earned it. He was a good guy." She started to clear the table. "I feel really badly for Kate—she doesn't seem to have the kind of fight in her that it takes to push through all of this. And Todd...poor kid. Is his mother around here?"

Gabe dumped the rib bones from their plates into the paper bag. "No, she died before Steve and Todd moved here. I think when Todd was around ten."

She made a sound of sympathy. "Cancer?"

"Not sure. Steve didn't ever seem to want to talk about it."

Madison picked up the Oreo bag. "How on earth did we leave just one?" She pulled a single cookie out, then dropped the empty bag in the trash. She took a step closer to him. "Open up."

"*I* get the last cookie?" He raised a brow.

"You're the guest." She moved the cookie closer to his lips.

"You're the lady."

Inching closer, she said, "The lady has to watch her figure." She rubbed the Oreo lightly against his bottom lip.

He put his hands on her waist. "I'll be glad to watch it for you."

Those possibilities bloomed in her eyes again. "How gentlemanly of you. How about we split it?" She slid the cookie between his teeth.

He held it there, half out of his mouth, and leaned closer to her lips. His words were muffled around the cookie when he said, "Come ge' 'our haah."

With a little grin that could only be called wicked, she took the other side of the cookie between her teeth. Then she surprised him by snapping it downward, breaking it off, leaving him with far less than his fair share.

He watched three-quarters of *his* Oreo disappear behind those lovely lips.

Laughing, she tried to twist away from him, but he tightened his grasp on her waist and pulled her against him. "Cheater."

Her hands settled on his upper arms. She made a show of chewing and swallowing. Challenge sparkled in her whiskey eyes. "What you going to do about it?"

"Get it back." He ducked his head, his lips finding hers.

Her hands slid over his shoulders, pulling him closer. He tasted Oreo and her hunger as he slipped his tongue between her lips. The sweet flavor of her passionate soul nudged away his good sense. Instead of backing off, taking his hands and shoving them in his pockets, he slipped them inside the back of the low waistband of her slacks and cupped her backside. The electric shock of intimate skin contact shot from his fingertips to the pit of his stomach.

One of her hands rested on the back of his head. None-too-gentle pressure urged his mouth toward her neck as her head dropped back.

His fingertips dug into her hips, anchoring their lower bodies together as he traced kisses along her ear and down her neck, sucking at the soft flesh, teasing, tempting. His blood was lava pounding through his veins, the pulse of it drowning out everything except the taste and feel of her.

He'd wanted this woman since he'd laid eyes on her. Over the past weeks, his desire had grown into a need. And with this hint of intimacy, it was suddenly much more, a wildfire that once set loose would be impossible to extinguish. And it was close to breaking free.

The low moan in her throat told him she wasn't any more inclined to put a halt to this than he was.

That one small, sultry sound put an effective end to all thoughts of smothering this fire. It was going to have to burn until it had consumed everything that fueled it.

But not today. Not now with her son upstairs.

It was wrong.

Still she clung to him.

Maybe the kid was asleep....

Suddenly, her hands pressed gently against his chest. "You'd better get that."

He looked at her. "Get what?"

"Your cell."

As the sound of his heartbeat receded in his ears, he heard a distant electronic melody.

Pulling back, he looked at the phone clipped to his belt. "Oh." He blew out a quick breath that puffed his cheeks. He hoped it cleared the huskiness that had to be in his voice.

He opened the line. "Sheriff Wyatt."

"Gabe, it's Dottie."

"Hi, Dot." With his mind miles away from his job, it took him a few moments to register the possible reasons for her call. None of them were good.

"Remember back when you were in training and they told you to treat every unattended death like a homicide?"

"Yeah." He took a couple of steps away from Maddie.

"I hope you did it on the McPherson case. It looks like we have something other than an accidental fall—unless he bounced."

"More than one blow?"

"Several. And the positions of some are completely inconsistent with a fall."

"Shit."

"That pretty much sums it up. The pathologist is faxing the report to your office right now."

"I'll take a look at it tonight."

"Figured you would." She hung up.

Maddie was staring at him, questions burning in her eyes.

"I need to leave."

"Okay."

He started toward the back door. Then he stopped. She'd have the news in the morning anyway. "I'm talking to Maddie, here, not the editor of the *Herald*."

She nodded. "All right."

"McPherson's autopsy says it's very unlikely the man fell."

Maddie echoed his words, "More than one blow..."

He moved back to her. "I'd appreciate it if we kept this quiet for a few hours."

Her back stiffened. "I would never use something said in confidence in my work."

He gave her a sideways glance.

"Okay, not when I have a personal relationship involved."

He managed a smile. "Good."

As he kissed her forehead, movement caught his eye.

There standing in the doorway to the kitchen was Ethan, as sickly white as when he'd come down from that mountain.

"You okay, kid?" Gabe asked, wondering how much Ethan had heard.

Maddie turned. "Oh." She moved to feel Ethan's forehead.

Ethan pulled away and headed back toward the stairs. "Fine."

Maddie didn't argue, so Gabe certainly wasn't going to. But he didn't buy Ethan's denial—not in the least.

Chapter 7

THE TELEPHONE AWAKENED Madison with a start. She sucked in a breath and knocked away the lingering fingers of the nightmare that had been tormenting her most of the night. The clock said four-ten.

She picked up the phone and mumbled, "Hello?"

"It's Gabe."

She shifted to a half-sitting position. "What's wrong?"

"I have Ethan. He was caught sneaking into Jordan's hospital room. I'm bringing him and your car home."

She jumped out of bed and looked out the window at the empty driveway.

Her waking reality was worse than her nightmare.

MADISON WAS PACING AT THE KITCHEN DOOR. Dawn had come, but it was still shadowy enough beneath the trees for the headlights to be visible when her car pulled into the drive.

She ripped open the door and waited on the back step.

Her arms were crossed tightly over her chest to hide her trembling hands.

Ethan got out of the car and passed her with his jaw set, careful not to make eye contact.

"You wait in the kitchen," she said, then pulled the door closed. The night air was cool, but she didn't really think that was the reason for her shivering.

Gabe stopped at the bottom step. "I have a deputy picking me up."

The grip of disappointment she felt was startling. At that moment it struck her that she'd been counting on him to help her get through this. Suddenly she realized how dependent she'd become on Gabe's interpretation and guidance with the adolescent male psyche. She hadn't had adequate time to plot her course, examining the pros and cons of each action and argument. What if she acted on impulse and screwed up?

"Did he have any excuses?"

Resting his right foot on the lowest step, Gabe rubbed the back of his neck. "No. He didn't present any argument at all, just took what I dished out."

"Which was?" *Please, give me a guidepost here.*

"I used the only weapon I thought would get through to him...you."

She furrowed her brow. "What?"

"I told him how much a stunt like this hurts you." He paused, glancing toward the new set of headlights that pulled in the drive. "Listen, the security guard said he got the impression that Ethan was planning on taking Jordan out of the hospital...he brought extra clothes." Gabe handed her a plastic grocery sack.

"Why would he do something like that?"

"Maybe you'll have better luck getting that answer out of him than I did." He backed a step away. "I'll talk to you later."

"Thank you, Gabe." She bit down on her tongue to keep from asking him to come inside and help her deal with this.

As if sensing her unspoken need, he came back to her. For a moment he looked into her eyes, then he put his hands on her shoulders. It took all of her willpower not to throw herself into his arms, bury her insecurities in his strength.

"Trust yourself, Maddie." He held her gaze. "You can do this. I'm sure he'll respond to you."

The fact that her need had been so evident made her draw back. She hated weakness, in herself most of all. This was a road she'd embarked upon alone. It wasn't fair to burden Gabe with the difficulties she now faced.

She nodded and turned, not looking back as she opened the kitchen door.

Shaking the tension out of her shoulders, she took a breath and stepped inside the kitchen.

Ethan was slumped in a kitchen chair. The sun was just coming up. A single ray slipped through the trees, illuminating the contrast of his bright blue irises against bloodshot red.

"I think it's time for you to tell me what's going on in that head of yours. You *steal* my car? And where did you think you were going? Why would you try to take Jordan away from the help he needs?"

Ethan sat stone-faced, his fingers busy shredding a paper napkin he'd plucked from the holder.

Madison lurched forward and slammed her palm against the table. "Talk to me!"

Ethan's flinch was barely perceptible. He kept his gaze on the napkin and continued tearing.

Closing her eyes and reining in her temper, she pulled out a chair and sat across from him. "Where were you taking Jordan?"

Ethan's chest rose and fell with deep breath.

"You may not believe it now, but the stress center is the best thing for him. Don't you want him to get better?"

His startled gaze snapped up. There, running deep beneath the surface, was something that sent a cold shaft of fear through her chest—guilt.

"Why would you ask that?" His voice quivered just enough to seal the deal.

Frost encased her heart. God, she didn't want to ask, but she had to. "Is there something you need to tell me about what happened up there?"

For a long moment, he chewed his lower lip, keeping his gaze averted. He swiped up the thin ribbons of napkin and balled them in his fist. His knuckles blanched white. Finally he said, "No."

"Ethan," she said softly, "look at me." Reluctantly, his eyes met hers. "I'm not an idiot. It's easy enough to connect the dots between you overhearing the results of Mr. McPherson's autopsy and you trying to run off with Jordan."

"Who says I was trying to run off with him? I just wanted to see him before they moved him."

"Ethan." She used the same don't-bullshit-me tone her mother had used on her. "You had spare clothes in a bag."

He looked up from beneath his brows, his mouth pulled

into a frown. "Can I go now? I need to take a shower before school."

She knew from experience that once Ethan shut down, that was it. She'd have to take another run at him later. "Go. We'll discuss your punishment tonight."

The chair rattled across the pine plank floor as he pushed it back with his knees as he stood.

Before he got through the door to the living room, she said, "You do know how lucky you were tonight, don't you?"

"Some luck." He hurried on.

Madison sat for a few minutes, just staring out the window at the brightening day. For a moment she felt completely rudderless. She saw something deep in her soul she'd never faced; she, Independence Incorporated, wanted someone—no, not just someone, she realized—she wanted *Gabe* to take her hand and weather this storm at her side. She needed help. There was too much at stake for one person to be solely responsible.

The reality of that horrified her. Ethan was savvy and resourceful enough that, had he gotten out of town with Jordan, it would have been very difficult to find them. Her entire insides felt as if someone had filled her with broken glass and shaken her. She decided she'd be sleeping with her car keys under her pillow for a while.

GABE LOOKED AT the autopsy report again. Not that he was going to see anything different, but he didn't like where the most logical trail was likely to lead.

In addition to Steve McPherson's most obvious wound—which now proved to be the result of at least three separate blows, all from angles extremely unlikely to have been caused by a slip and fall—he also had four fractured ribs, three on the left and one on the right, classic defensive wounds on his hands and forearms (bruising most likely caused by fending off blows), a broken nose, and six fractured teeth. If they'd found him in a back alley instead of at the base of a rocky waterfall, their first conclusion would have been that he'd been beaten to death.

The pathologist suggested the most likely instrument used in the cranial blows would have been a fist-sized rock, or something similarly shaped. Gabe pulled the photos of the scene—the *crime* scene—and spread them on the desk. No shortage of possible weapons in the immediate area. In fact, a person would be hard-pressed to put his hand down anywhere within fifteen feet of the body and not have it land on a rock of the appropriate size.

After careful review, he was no more enlightened than he had been when he'd opened the folder containing the photos.

The only scrap of evidence he'd brought down from that mountain had been the cigarette butts. He held the baggie up in front of his face. Filtered. Marlboro. Could there be enough DNA after being exposed to the elements? Would it tell him anything if there was? Those butts could have been left by anyone over the past weeks.

He set a box on his desk to load all of the evidence so it could be sent to the forensics lab. The cigarette butts. The paper bag with the T-shirt that had been wrapped around McPherson's head, and the jacket that had been under it. The two bags with the jackets that had been used to cover McPherson's body. His clothes were already there, as they'd traveled with the body.

He'd have to go back up on the mountain and do another search. Maybe he'd discover something of value.

Scrubbing his hand over his face, he wished Ethan had not tried to pull such a stupid stunt this morning. Damn kid. This wasn't the time for him to be doing stupid things.

Gabe ached for Maddie; she'd looked so, so... *betrayed* was the only word for it, when he'd taken Ethan home.

Gabe paused with a marker in his hand, the case reference number half-finished on the box. For a moment, he studied the phone on his desk. How was Maddie doing? No. He shouldn't call. He'd done what he could. And he'd told her to call him if she needed anything.

Besides, this had now become a homicide investigation. And currently the only suspects were the four teenage boys—one of whom was Maddie's son. Until this was cleared up, he had to take a step back. It was his job. It was his duty. And it totally pissed him off.

As he picked up the last bag containing one of the jackets, he paused. Then he slipped on a pair of latex gloves and unrolled the top of the bag. He lifted the jacket out by its collar, holding it over the bag in case anything fell off of it. He looked it over for signs that the wearer had beaten McPherson. Nothing, at least nothing visible to the naked eye.

He replaced that jacket, changed his gloves, and opened the bag with the other one. It was Ethan's Philadelphia Eagles jacket. Gabe had seen him wearing it. There were a couple of small blood smears on the sleeve, no droplets. He felt the pockets. The one on the right side had something in it.

With two fingers, he spread the pocket opening and looked in. Shit. An open pack of Marlboro filtered cigarettes.

* * *

IT HAD BEEN A HELL OF A DAY, and it was only one-thirty in the afternoon. Of course, Madison thought, it had begun at four-ten this morning. She still hadn't decided on the proper punishment for Ethan's misconduct. She'd left him with the instructions to phone in hourly once he was home from school. Thanks to caller ID she would be certain he was home. She'd drawn on their no-bullshit pact in a way she'd never imagined.

It was time to draw on one of her old talents, compartmentalization. She would take care of problems at home when she was in a position to do something about it. Now it was time to work.

She finished her last proof of the story she'd written for the front page. It was good. Gathering her facts for it had made her itch for the old days. Back when investigating stories and ferreting out sources had had risk, when she had constantly ridden the edge between what was ethical and what was necessary to get the job done.

Since Zach Gilbert's funeral was this afternoon, Madison had been able to locate his girlfriend, Julia Patterson, at home. The girl was angry enough over her needless loss, and young enough to have very little rein on her emotions, that she had given Madison an earful. She didn't name names, or direct Madison toward the source, but she had confirmed Madison's suspicion that doping was a much more widespread problem than one lone football player.

Madison hoped this article would open the eyes of the parents and coaches enough that Zach's death could be the beginning of the end. She'd keep digging, looking for more specific information, keeping this from slipping into the background and hiding behind the fog of everyday life.

It felt good. Damn good. She hadn't realized how much she missed this part of her old job. She'd been a tenacious shit-stirrer in her day. Nice to feel that rush again.

As soon as she sent the story off to press, that rush disappeared as fast as bacon on Ethan's breakfast plate. Now that her crusade was off the ground, she was left to face her own, more personal problems. If only they could be fixed by a sharp-witted exposé.

Ethan was hiding something. She had to get him to open up to her. It might not fix the problem. In fact it could very likely kick off a whole new set. But she had to know the truth—so they could prepare.

KATE MCPHERSON ANSWERED THE DOOR in her bathrobe, even though it was two in the afternoon. There was a crumpled tissue in her right hand. She wore no makeup, and her pale hair was in a sloppy ponytail. Her red-rimmed eyelids were so puffy, Gabe might not have recognized her if she hadn't been in her own house.

"Kate," he said, "I know this is a bad time, but I'd like to ask you a few questions."

With a sniff and a nod, she opened the door wide enough for him to enter. The room was dark, the draperies blocking out the clear sunny day. She motioned for him to take a seat on the sofa. He stubbed his toe on a cast-iron cat-shaped doorstop that he hadn't seen as his eyes adjusted from the bright outdoors.

"Oh," she squeaked. "Careful."

He made it the rest of the way and sat down without further incident.

"Steve gave me that doorstop for my birthday. I love

cats...but Jordan's allergic so I can't have a real one. Steve started me a collection."

Gabe rested his elbows on his knees, leaning forward, as if to make his questions less painful by making them more intimate. "Dr. Zinn informed you of the autopsy results?" It was a question he already knew the answer to, but it seemed the best place to start.

"Yes. I still don't believe it. There has to be some sort of mistake."

With a sympathetic shake of his head, Gabe said, "I wish I could say it was a mistake. But the report was conclusive. Steve's injuries weren't the result of a fall."

"You said he was by Black Rock Falls. He could have fallen from the top. He could—"

"I'm sorry, Kate. That's just not the case."

"But everybody loved Steve."

After an appropriately respectful pause, he asked, "Did Steve smoke?"

She swatted away the idea with a tissue-clutching hand. The movement was lethargic, as if despair had leached away all of her strength. "Heavens no. Never. None of us in this house smoke...Jordan's allergies. I used to have to watch Bobby like a hawk to keep him from smoking around Jordan."

"Does Bobby still smoke?"

"Oh, yeah, no gettin' that man to quit." Underneath the exasperation rode a tone of true fondness, as if she were talking about a beloved, but slightly misbehaving child.

"Had Steve mentioned any incidents lately, someone angry with him at work, a disagreement with a friend... anything like that?"

"No, like I said, everybody loved St-steve." His name came out half-hiccup, half-sob.

Gabe waited for her to regain control of herself, then asked, "How about Steve and Bobby? What was it like between them?"

"Fine." Her answer came quickly, sharply enough to set Gabe's intuition buzzing. "They got on fine."

He let the silence play out, a technique he'd found more useful than beating a person with questions they didn't want to answer.

Kate touched her nose with the tissue again. "I mean, sometimes they disagreed about what was best for Jordan.... Steve didn't want to take Bobby's place, he made that clear, but he was tryin' real hard to help Jordan fit in better...sports and things, you know."

Gabe nodded and waited.

"It wasn't like they fought over it or anything; don't get the wrong idea. Bobby wouldn't hurt anybody—you know him, he wouldn't hurt Steve."

"I'm not looking to accuse anyone," Gabe assured her. "I'm just working to get a sense of what was going on around Steve over recent months."

"It doesn't make sense," she said, her voice quavering. "He was just up there helping those boys...." Her eyes widened and she sucked in a breath. "You don't think...one of them . . . ?"

"No, no." He raised his palms to halt her train of thought. Last thing he needed was for rumors to start flying, or a grieving family to start a groundswell of public opinion. "I don't think *anything* yet. I'm just gathering information."

She settled back in her chair. "You know we moved Jor-

dan today—to that great place over to Knoxville. Well"—
she rubbed her palms on her robe—"I didn't...I just
couldn't. Todd and Bobby took him." She sighed. "I just
don't know what I'd do without Todd right now."

"It's good you have someone here with you. I'm sure
it's good for Jordan, too."

She nodded.

"What can you tell me about Steve's relationship with
Jordan?"

Her gaze snapped up. "What do you mean? They got
on great. He took a real interest in Jordan, that's why he
took all those boys camping, it was for Jordan. He doesn't
fit in very well.... We're hoping he'll come out of his shell,
be more like Todd."

That statement shot straight through the bull's-eye of
Gabe's intuition. "So Steve encouraged Jordan?"

"With Jordan it takes a little more than 'encouraging.' I swear that boy just has to be pushed sometimes, or
he'd spend all of his time in his room. Last summer Todd
got him a skateboard and taught him to ride it. They had
such a great time together. I think Jordan's really making strides"—she caught herself in mid-sentence—"or at
least, he was."

"It sounds like both Steve and Todd were doing their
best." He paused, knowing the minefield he was tiptoeing
through. "And Jordan, he was comfortable with all of this
encouragement and attention?"

"Well, you know teenage boys; they're almost as
moody as girls sometimes. There's been times Jordan
would go through mopey weeks, just like all boys. All in
all, Jordan and Steve got on real fine for Steve bein' his
stepdad."

A qualifier. Interesting.

He stood. "Well, that's all I have for now. Thank you."

She walked him to the door. "Dr. Zinn said y'all are holding Steve's . . ." The words trailed off, as if she couldn't bring herself to refer to his dead body. "When can we have him back?"

"Dr. Zinn will be in touch."

"How can we plan a . . . a funeral?" Her lower lip trembled.

He paused with his hand on the doorknob. "I know this is hard. But you want us to catch whoever did this, don't you?"

She nodded and wiped her eyes. With a look bearing more strength than he'd ever seen in her, she said, "You find him. Find him and make him pay."

"I'll do my best."

Gabe's next stop was Gray Insurance, where Bobby worked with his father and brother.

They leased the second floor over a storefront that had been the five-and-dime back in the sixties. Now the downstairs housed an independent bookstore. Luckily for the owners of the store, which was truly a mom-and-pop operation, all of the big chains were still too far away to siphon off all of the business.

The warped, narrow stairs that led from the street-level door squeaked and groaned—more reliable than a door-bell, Gabe thought.

The door to Gray Insurance was open. Gabe entered with a soft knuckle rap on the frame, not that he needed it. All three faces in the little office were focused on the door in anticipation, thanks, no doubt, to the incredible moaning stairs.

The office was a single large room with four desks, he assumed one for each Gray and one near the door for the receptionist/secretary and her copy/fax machine. Hanging on the wall over her head was the mounted head of an eight-point buck. This was mountain country—a taxidermist's dreamland.

The receptionist grinned up at Gabe, her false teeth perfect and white beneath her perfectly coiffed gray hair. "May I help you?"

Bobby was already heading in his direction. "I imagine the sheriff is here to talk to me." As he and Gabe shook hands, he said, "Am I right?"

"If you have a minute and don't mind."

"No problem." He waved an arm in the direction of his desk, which had a plum view of the Fashion Nook across the street. "Step into my office," he quipped.

Gabe took one of the two seats in front of Bobby's desk, not missing the glare he was receiving from the other Gray present. Bobby's brother, Brooks, didn't make the slightest effort to conceal his disdain. He walked to the front of his own desk, leaned back, crossed his ankles and arms, and looked at Gabe as Al Gore might a belching smokestack. Gabe had a feeling if the elder Gray had been in the office, he'd be parked right next to his son, sending matching hate signals.

Bobby waved a hand toward his brother. "Don't you have work to do?"

Brooks didn't move.

"My apologies for my brother's manners. Sometimes he forgets that I'm grown now and don't need him to protect me."

Gabe ignored the apology and the brother. He didn't

bother to pretend that news didn't travel faster than flies to roadkill in this town either. "I assume you've heard that it appears Steve McPherson's death was no accident."

"Kate told me this morning. She's so torn up that she won't even leave the house." He ran a hand over his jaw. "I don't know what to do to help her. And Jordan...Jesus, what a mess."

Gabe nodded in understanding. "I'm going to have to ask you about your whereabouts on Saturday."

Brooks shot off the desk as if somebody had branded him. "We were hunting, up on the ridge. First day of bow season. We always spend the first Saturday hunting"—he nodded toward the empty desk that Gabe assumed belonged to the elder Gray—"the three of us."

Gabe shifted his gaze from Brooks's angry face to Bobby.

Bobby said, "It's true."

"Have any luck?"

Bobby's brow furrowed.

"Deer. Did you get any deer?" Gabe's gaze scanned Bobby's desk. There was a pack of Marlboros sitting beside a lighter and an ashtray filled with a dozen filtered butts.

Leaning back in his swivel chair, Bobby crossed his arms over his chest and narrowed his eyes. "No. No luck."

"And you were with your brother and father all day?"

Brooks piped up. "Hell yes. And just 'cause we didn't bag a deer, don't mean any one of us killed McPherson—"

"Brooks!" Bobby leaned forward, raising a hand to halt his brother's comments. "I didn't kill Steve. You sure it wasn't an accident? The man liked to do dangerous stuff."

Gabe stood. "I'll let y'all get back to work."

He got in his truck and made a few notes. Bobby and McPherson disagreed about Jordan's upbringing. Bobby's alibi: a defensive brother. Bobby's brand of cigarettes: Marlboro.

It wasn't much, but it was the first thing that pointed away from the boys... from Ethan and Jordan, to be more specific. And it gave Gabe just a little hope.

Chapter 8

A T NOON ON THURSDAY, Gabe stopped just before he pulled open the glass door to the deli.

Maddie stood with her back to him, placing her order at the counter. They hadn't spoken since he'd delivered Ethan home from his midnight misadventure at the hospital. And things hadn't gotten any less complicated since then.

He stood there for a long moment with his hand on the door.

He should go; come back later.

He went in.

At the sound of the little bell on the door, she turned. The way her face instantly brightened when she saw him made his chest tighten.

"Oh, hi," she said. There was an unusual awkwardness in the way she said it.

"Speak of the devil," Mrs. Conway called from behind the counter. "I was just trying to sell this young lady a piece of my homemade Oreo cheesecake—told her you can vouch for it; it's one of your favorites."

Was Maddie blushing?

Gabe held her gaze while he answered Mrs. Conway. "Why yes, I can. Oreo has recently become my favorite flavor in everything."

Mrs. Conway said, "I figured she'd listen to you, since y'all are dating." She rushed on before he could respond. "These girls today all want to be shaped like pogo sticks. But a man wants some curves on his woman, right?"

He loved the way Maddie's eyes pleaded with his for intervention.

Finally she turned back to Mrs. Conway. "Actually, the sheriff and I aren't dating. We're just friends."

"Sure y'are." Mrs. Conway winked.

Gabe chuckled. "So, Ms. Wade, what say you on the Oreo cheesecake?"

She scowled at him. "No." Then she smiled at Mrs. Conway. "Thank you." She snatched up her order receipt and walked over to sit at a small table situated by the front window.

Gabe placed his own order and then joined her.

"Thanks for the help," she said dryly.

"Hey, I like the idea of us dating. You're the one who has the problem with it."

"We haven't had a date yet."

"We had breakfast."

"Breakfast is not a date. People don't go out for breakfast on their first date."

"It depends on how long that first date lasts. Besides, in this town, the only reason two people of the opposite sex eat breakfast together is because they climbed out of the same bed."

"You're enjoying this! I have a reputation and a son to think of. You promised me we would go slow; you wouldn't push."

"*I'm* not. I can't control what the rest of the town thinks." Even though, for Maddie's sake, he probably should—especially now. But it felt so good to leave the load of his job behind and just simply enjoy the woman.

Mrs. Conway brought over their orders and placed them on the table. Included was a large slice of Oreo cheesecake on a plate with two forks.

Maddie rolled her eyes at him, pushed her sandwich aside, and picked up a fork. "As long as it's here . . ."

Gabe would never in his life be able to look at a bag of Oreos and not think of her sweet mouth. The cookie of his childhood had just taken on some very adult associations.

As they ate, her banter disappeared and she fell unusually quiet.

Finally, she said, "I want to thank you again for interceding on Ethan's behalf the other night."

He just nodded. This was a road he didn't particularly want to travel right now. He was enjoying his break from being Sheriff Wyatt.

"I mean—"

"Maddie. Let's just have lunch and leave everything else until another time."

Her relief was visible. "Deal. Just two friends having lunch. No parent talk. No sheriff talk."

"We're entitled," he agreed.

And they were. Maddie was under plenty of stress dealing with Ethan. And Gabe had been living and breathing this investigation every waking hour. He didn't want to delve into *why* Ethan had gone after Jordan. He didn't want to probe about those cigarettes he'd found in Ethan's jacket. He didn't want to have to dance around, avoiding giving away too much about the case while digging for details about her son.

They both deserved a brief reprieve from reality.

So why did it feel as if he was neglecting his duty?

ETHAN STOOD AT HIS LOCKER at the end of the day on Thursday. Colin Arbuckle's locker was directly across the hall. Ethan kept his back to the group of freshman boys that had gathered around Colin's big, blabbering mouth.

"Like I said," Colin boasted, "I know what went down on that mountain—"

Ethan slammed his locker door hard enough that all of the guys huddled around Colin looked startled when they turned around and saw Ethan right behind them. Most of them got busy looking other places.

Ethan inched closer, his hands twitching. This school made a big deal out of any violent contact. *Zero tolerance. Zero tolerance.* He kept the mental chant going. He couldn't forget. This wasn't Philly.

Colin didn't take the hint and shut up. "I could have told the sheriff it wasn't no accident—but my mom was right there, cryin' and stuff. But I knew it the second I looked at Mr. McP, saw it right off. And I know who—"

Ethan slammed his hand against the locker right beside Colin's head. It had taken everything in him not to actually slam the guy's head. He was in enough trouble with M as it was. "Yeah, yeah, you saw all right"—Ethan leaned closer to Colin's face—"while you were *puking in the creek.*"

Was it possible that Colin actually did see...? No, no way. He'd have spilled his guts by now.

It had only taken about five minutes for Ethan to figure out that Colin Arbuckle liked to be the center of the universe. He always put on a show. Now it was clear the guy would say anything to get attention.

And his diarrhea of the mouth wasn't just here and now. Ethan had overheard a bunch of kids talking in the cafeteria at lunch. Colin had started mouthing off as soon as word got out that Mr. McP had been murdered.

A couple of the kids slipped away, moving down the hall. Others stood stock-still, waiting for a fight.

Colin said, "Hey, man, chill. I was just talkin'."

Ethan clenched his jaw. The look of disappointment on M's face when the sheriff had brought him home Tuesday morning filled his mind. He gave a disgusted shake of his head and stalked away.

"Stupid bastard," he muttered. Who knew what he'd say next.

Dear Editor:

Since you came so recently from a crime-ridden, drug-laden gangland, we can see how you might misinterpret a single, tragic incident as a widespread problem. We all know the Internet is probably to blame for Zach Gilbert's unfortunate death. With the click of a button, our kids are so easily victims of drug dealers and pornographers—people *outside* of our community.

You can take your high-and-mighty attitude, your
fancy foreign car, your big city views, and your lies
about our kids, and go back to where there is plenty
of crime and drug use. We don't want you polluting
our town with your suspicions and ugly thinking.

We here in Buckeye take the word of Jesus Christ Our
Lord and Savior to heart. We take care of our own and
have since long before you swept in here with your
city ideas and your city assumptions. We *do not* need
someone like you to turn us against one another and
our own kids.

A Concerned Citizen

Madison flipped the single sheet onto her desk and
picked up the envelope. No return address. Buckeye post-
mark (hence the rapid delivery). Printed on plain paper by
a computer printer. This was one of five letters about yesterday's article. This one was the most well written. One
had ranted in nearly unintelligible form. But they were all
similar in sentiment. All without identification. All either
unsigned, or signed with a righteous moniker.

It really pissed her off when people wanted to take a
bold public stand hiding behind an anonymous name...
and Jesus.

Even though newspaper policy was not to print anonymous letters to the editor, Madison was going to print
all of them. The authors had unknowingly lightened her
workload; she didn't have to verify the identity of any of
the senders.

She wondered briefly if she should have had reporter
Judy Jenkins put her byline on the article. Maybe it

wouldn't have seemed like a frontal assault on the community if it had come from one of their own.

This problem was entirely new to Madison, speaking to an audience who actually knew her. She hadn't realized how delicate her relationship with her readers could be. Too bad she hadn't considered this before she published the article. This message was too important to let it get shot down just because nobody liked the messenger.

Judy had locked the front doors on her way out at five, after turning off the lights out in the front office. The building was empty. Madison was in her element: cocooned alone in her own little office, the only sound the hum of the fluorescent lights, the fan on her computer, and the rain drumming on the roof—with the print deadline clock ticking.

Undaunted by her unpopular status, she was doing her second front-page installment on the dangers of anabolic steroids. She was delaying sending it to press because she was waiting for a call from Zach Gilbert's girlfriend, Julia.

Madison had received the e-mail at four o'clock this afternoon:

From: editorial@RebelNews.com
To: M.Wade@BuckeyeHerald.com
Subject: (none)

ms wade,

you told me to contact you if i have any information
i'm using the school newspaper's computer will call
before 8 tonight

When Madison had first read it, she'd wanted to get up and dance a little jig around her desk. Julia Patterson, bless her heart, was coming through. And it couldn't have come at a better time. Madison needed ammunition to counter the rash of crap she was going to publish in tomorrow's "Letters to the Editor" column—which of course would be on page three, while her solidly researched article, complete with startling statistics concerning small towns and rural communities, would be on the front page under the banner.

Madison looked at the time on her computer. Eight-ten. *Come on Julia, don't get cold feet.*

Her cell phone rang. She snatched it up off the desk.

"Ethan Wade reporting as ordered."

"No need to be a smart-ass. You're ten minutes late."

"I fell asleep watching TV."

She responded with an appropriately skeptical grunt.

"Seriously, how long are you gonna make me do this?"

"Maybe forever. I like hearing your voice."

"I feel like I'm on a leash."

"Good."

He groaned and hung up the phone.

Madison tossed her cell back on the desk. Grounding a kid who'd lived the life Ethan had seemed a little like closing the barn door after the cow was already out in the storm, but she had to do something. If she could only get him to open up and tell her what was going on.

With an exasperated sigh, she dragged her focus back to her work. Instead of finishing her article, she caught herself staring at her phone, urging it to ring. It was obvious that Julia was nervous about someone discovering she was talking about Zach's doping. She'd used the school computer and the newspaper's e-mail account; her name wasn't anywhere on that e-mail. In their conversation on the day of Zach's funeral, Madison had assured Julia that if she shared information, she would remain protected, anonymous...and much more deserving of it than those asses who wrote those letters.

At eight-thirty, Madison gave up waiting and finished typing her article. She'd wanted to be able to print that she was close to confirming the source of the steroids. But that would have to wait. After she did get the information, there would still be fact-checking and confirmation. But with a lead from Julia, she'd be that much closer to discovering where those drugs came from—be it Internet, mail order, or Joe Blow who lived on Main Street.

At eight-forty-five Madison picked up her jacket and favorite Kenneth Cole tote—Ethan had saved his dog-walking earnings and given it to her last Christmas—and then turned off her office lights. The streetlights would be shining through the large plate-glass windows on the front of the building, so she didn't have to worry about breaking her neck on the way out.

After locking the door to her office—a habit even living in this sleepy town couldn't break after years of protecting sources and guarding information—she turned to head toward the front of the building. She shrugged into her jacket as she juggled her tote. The tap of her heels on the hardwood floor echoed off the empty desks and silent electronic equipment.

As she straightened the collar of her jacket, she looked up and froze in mid-step. There, silhouetted by the streetlight, stood a tall figure against the glass door. He was broad shouldered and it appeared he had on a sweatshirt with the hood up. He remained so motionless that for a moment Madison thought perhaps it was a trick of light and shadow, a product of her eyes adjusting from the bright light of her office. But that thought was simply an attempt by her mind to overcome fear. The man was real—and he wasn't leaving.

Keeping her gaze on the figure, she took a slow step backward, gradually reaching inside her tote for her cell phone. She couldn't explain why she moved with the slow caution of a person faced with a snake coiled to strike. Stealthy movements weren't likely to alter the outcome of whatever was in play here.

She forced herself to breathe as she groped in the deep tote for her phone, thankful for the fifteen feet and a locked door between her and whoever it was out there. Finally her fumbling fingers located the phone. She employed the same slow, steady movement in pulling it out and flipping it open, not daring to take her eyes away from the front door. She half-expected the man to come crashing through, even though logic told her that if that had been his plan, he'd have done it already.

Logic didn't slow her racing heart or put spit back in her dry mouth. Her fingers were trembling so badly she had to look at her phone in order to dial 911. As she pressed SEND, she looked back up at the door.

The man was gone.

She sidled closer to the windows, but didn't see him on the nearby sidewalk.

"911. What's your emergency?"

She was at a loss. What was she going to say, *Someone was looking in the window of a downtown storefront*? The guy probably hadn't even seen her inside; nobody was ever here this time of night. Then she realized that maybe he wasn't even facing this way. With the light directly behind him, he could as easily have been facing the street; maybe he'd ducked into the recessed door opening to get out of the rain.

"I'm sorry. No emergency. I just got a little spooked."

"Where are you? Do you want an officer dispatched?"

"No. No, everything's fine." Her car was only halfway down the block. There wasn't even an alley for someone to hide in between here and there. And Killroy's Bar on the corner was still open; no doubt people were coming and going. "Thank you." She disconnected.

She'd walked truly dangerous city streets in the dark more times than she could count—investigating things that only transpired on shadowy streets in the dead of night. She was ashamed of her ridiculous overreaction to this shadow outside her front door—in *Buckeye,* for crying out loud.

Grabbing an umbrella from the bucket they kept by the door for short runs to the bank and such, she unlocked the front door and slipped out. She took a moment to survey the street, confirming it was empty, before she turned her back and put her key in the lock.

Feeling more like herself and back in control, she opened the umbrella and stepped out onto the sidewalk. She hurried toward her car, telling herself she was rushing only because of the rain.

When she stepped off the curb beside her car, she found herself in ankle-deep water.

"Crap." She shook off her shoe and moved to the driver's door. As she reached for the door handle, she noticed her front tire was completely flat. "Uuggh!"

A hand landed on her shoulder. "Hey."

With a screech, she swung the open umbrella around.

It bounced ineffectively off her attacker and landed on the wet pavement, spinning like a top. She had her foot drawn back when the voice penetrated her adrenaline-fueled reaction.

"Hold on, Maddie! It's me." Gabe had her by the shoulders, trying to keep her out of striking distance.

"What the hell is wrong with you!" she shouted. "You should know better than to sneak up on a woman like that." Her face burned from the burst of fear, and then anger. The cold rain drenching her now was a welcome relief.

Gabe bent over and picked up her umbrella, which had stopped spinning and sat upside down collecting rainwater. He shook it out before he held it over her head. "Sorry. I forgot you're not used to our small town ways."

That remark shot through her like a fiery arrow. "Seriously! You don't do that *ever*. Didn't they teach you anything in police school? God!" She swiped the rain from her face.

After his last comment, there was no way she was admitting to being on edge because she'd been creeped out by an innocent pedestrian trying to shield himself from the downpour in the newspaper office's entry.

She took a couple of deep breaths to dissipate the adrenaline rush.

"I *am* sorry," he said sheepishly. "Won't happen again."

"If it does, you'd better guard your nuts."

He stood there laughing with the rain running off the end of his nose. She was torn between throttling him and kissing him.

"I just came out of Killroy's"—he lifted his chin over his left shoulder to indicate the bar cattycorner across the street—"and I saw you leave the office."

She took pity on him, even though her heart was still racing from the start he'd given her, and stepped closer, lifting the umbrella over his head.

"Out drinking on a Thursday night?" she asked.

"Eating. I'm a horrible cook and Killroy's has great chili."

"Hmmm, maybe I'll pick some up to go. I'm sure Ethan's starved—even though he ate dinner at six-thirty. That is"—she looked down at her flat tire—"after I put on the spare."

His gaze followed hers. He made a *tsk*ing sound. "Bad night for a flat. Want me to hold the umbrella over you while you change it?"

"How chivalrous."

"I know how you Yankee city girls are...independent and all. Don't want to piss you off."

"Independent, not stupid. I'll have you know, I've never turned up my nose at the idea of letting a man change a tire or carry heavy objects for me."

"I see, then. You want your cake and eat it, too."

"And why wouldn't I?"

With a crooked smile, he said, "Indeed." After a pause that Madison couldn't quite read, he said, "How about I drive you home instead. It's supposed to stop raining around midnight. I can pick you up in the morning, then change the tire in dry daylight."

She sure as hell didn't want to kneel in that puddle and change the tire. It didn't seem fair to ask him to either. "Okay."

"You want to pick up that chili?"

"Not really. I'm too tired to eat—and Ethan can snack on a whole ham or something."

He chuckled. "My truck's around the corner." He put his arm around her as they huddled side by side under the umbrella and walked to his Jeep.

She tried not to like the feel of him pressed against her side or the gentle weight of his hand on her shoulder. She reminded herself that this was a small town and there was an ongoing criminal investigation that involved her son.

He opened the door for her to slide into the passenger seat. Then he leaned in, across her, and reached behind the console between the bucket seats. His chest was intriguingly close to her face. His body gave off comforting warmth and the clean smell of Dial soap rose from the opening in his jacket. She caught herself drawing in a very deep breath.

When he pulled back, he handed her a towel. "Here, you can dry off a little."

She took it and dabbed her face. As she did, she wondered if the rain had turned her mascara into raccoon eyes.

Gabe closed her door, then went around and got in the other side. He collapsed the umbrella and put it behind her seat.

She handed him the towel. "Looks like you could use this, too."

She liked the careless way he ran the towel over his hair and face; an utterly masculine move.

"I appreciate the lift," she said.

He started the truck. "My pleasure."

There was just something about the way he said that phrase to her that made her all warm inside.

Her mother's voice rushed forward from her memory, "Ah, your daddy, he's such a sweet talker." There had been an almost dreamlike quality in the way her mother had always said that phrase—and it usually came up after her father had disappointed them once again. Madison had always wondered if perhaps her father had hypnotized her mother, using his love and his voice to get her to forgive anything he did.

Now she could see how easily it could happen. Her own good sense told her she should put as much space between them as possible—especially until she uncovered exactly what was going on with Ethan.

They drove out of town in silence, the steady thump of the windshield wipers and the patter of raindrops the only sound. Their lunchtime vacation from reality was over. Now silence was the best way to avoid all of the unpleasant subjects that stood between them.

Just as they turned onto the road that led to her house, he broke the hush that had grown increasingly awkward.

"How is Ethan getting along?"

Was that a loaded question? "Fine."

His gaze cut her way at her abrupt answer. He prompted, "Have any revealing conversations after the other night?"

"Is this Gabe the friend asking, or Sheriff Wyatt?"

"There's a difference?"

She shot him a sharp look. "You know there is. Sheriff Wyatt is concerned with things like Ethan driving without a license and violating visiting hours at the hospital." She pointedly avoided mentioning the murder investigation and the fact that just prior to Ethan's escapade he'd overheard the autopsy results.

"And Gabe the friend?"

"Is worried about Ethan's welfare and state of mind."

"I am." He glanced over at her. "I truly am. As well as his momma's."

"And Sheriff Wyatt?"

"Is chalking the entire incident up to extenuating circumstances."

"Which are?" The words were out before she could stop them. Why did she always have to dig for the red-hot center of everything?

He cast her an incredulous glance, which looked even more dubious in the dim glow of the dash lights. "You're kidding, right?"

"Extenuating, as in he suffered a trauma and is upset by his friend's condition? Or extenuating, as in we're almost dating?" Might as well get this over with.

He shook his head. "You're one blunt woman."

"Makes things easier that way."

"Not always." He blew out an exasperated breath. "I cut him a break because of the emotional stress he's under." He took his eyes from the road long enough to make her squirm. "I'd have done it for any one of those boys who were on that mountain."

She didn't know if she was relieved or disappointed. But she said, "Good."

After a moment, he said, "About Saturday night...I know Ethan needs you right now."

"Gabe, seriously, you forget who you're talking to." She paused, then handed him the out he was too gentlemanly to ask for. "I know that unless you've got another good lead, you're going to have to look long and hard at these boys, question them again.... It's going to be uncomfortable enough as it is. We haven't even gone out and people in this town are already talking. Let's just leave this whole dating thing alone for the time being."

He turned into her driveway, put the truck in park, then rested his hand on the top of her seatback.

She tried to ignore the closeness of his hand to the back of her neck—a total dating gesture. Before he could offer an argument, she reached back for her umbrella, forcing him to put his hand back on his side of the bucket seats. She picked up her tote and opened the door.

"Thanks for the ride."

"I'll be back to get you in the morning. Seven-thirty okay?"

"Probably not a good idea...considering. I'll call Judy to pick me up."

"Then give me your car keys and I'll get your tire changed first thing."

"I'll take care of it."

"Maddie, don't take this to extremes. We can still—"

She reached across and put her index finger against his lips. "Don't. Just leave it there." The last thing she needed was for him to sweet-talk her out of her better judgment.

She closed the door and hurried to the front porch before she changed her mind.

Chapter 9

MADISON SAT ON THE SOFA, waiting for the eleven o'clock news to come on. Ethan moved like a cat behind her, going from the kitchen to his room upstairs. He'd been avoiding her since she'd gotten home. She'd been too preoccupied with worry that Julia Patterson was backing out of delivering specifics and her own mixed feelings over Gabe Wyatt to address it. But now that Ethan was headed to bed, it was her last chance.

"Is your shirt pressed for the funeral tomorrow?" She found the oblique line of attack to be much more successful when approaching touchy subjects. Honest as they'd promised to be with one another, Ethan was still a teenager.

He stopped, his hand lingering on the banister. He didn't turn around when he said, "I don't want to go."

She nearly said, *Neither do I,* but caught the words just before they tumbled out of her mouth.

"Come back down here for a minute." This wasn't a

conversation she wanted to have shouting halfway up the stairs.

After a pause where she imagined he was rolling his eyes, he turned around and slowly clomped down the steps. "What?"

"Sit down."

He walked around the sofa and sat at the opposite end. Then he focused all of his concentration on cracking his knuckles. It was a nervous habit that had all but disappeared over the past year.

"Why don't you want to go?" she asked.

"It's not like I knew Mr. McP that well."

"But you're friends with his stepson. It'd be a show of respect for that friendship to attend the funeral."

"It's not like Jordan will be there. I'd rather go to Knoxville and see him." The emotion in his voice escalated as he spoke. "Everybody's making such a big deal over Mr. McP. Nobody's thinking about Jordan!"

"You and I are thinking about Jordan. And so are his mother and Todd. It's just that this is the last time anyone will be able to do anything for Mr. McPherson. The temporary focus on him doesn't mean they love Jordan any less."

She tried to put herself in Ethan's shoes. Jordan was the first real friend he'd had in a long time. "I know it's hard," she said. "And we'll go see him on Sunday. You know that's the only day he's allowed visitors right now.

"But remember," she added, "Mr. McPherson was very nice to include you. You should attend his service."

Ethan's eyes were cold when he looked at her. "I don't think Mr. McP *was* nice. You never should have written the article saying he was all that."

A chill rippled down her spine. "What do you mean?"

"I mean I don't think he was nice to Jordan."

Madison's lungs froze, locking her breath inside. "In what way?"

"He kept trying to make Jordan be like him—sports, mountain climbing, all that crap. But Jordan wasn't ever going to be like him. Pushing him to do stuff he didn't like just made Jordan feel worse."

"Jordan told you this?" At least her initial fear proved invalid. She supposed investigating child predators had colored her thinking.

Ethan gave a cynical snort. "He didn't have to. If you'd only seen the way he was at home…" He put his elbows on his knees and scrubbed his hands over his face. He sounded really, really tired when he said, "That's one of the reasons I wanted to go on that trip, to see if I could figure out what was going on with them. I mean, yeah, I wanted to go camping and all, but it was a chance to watch Jordan and Mr. McP together."

"Was there anything in particular that made you think there was something going on?"

He lifted a shoulder. "Just a bunch of little stuff." He turned, resting his bent knee on the sofa between them. "Like Jordan always seemed half-scared when he was around his house—like he was really afraid to mess up. And one time he had this ugly bruise on the back of his neck. He tried to tell me he'd fallen on his skateboard and hit a curb."

"And you don't think he did?"

"Seriously? How do you hit your neck and make a bruise go halfway around? Besides, he *hated* that skateboard. He only rode it at all because Todd had given it to him and he didn't want to hurt Todd's feelings. He *never* rode it after that first week."

"Maybe he was practicing in secret so he could show everyone he could do it." Admittedly lame, but she wanted Ethan to think this through.

Ethan vehemently shook his head. "No. He would have told me. I taught him how to stay on it in the first place. And it wasn't just that. He told me he broke his arm a year ago when he fell out of a tree he was climbing."

"And?"

He looked at her like she was dim-witted. "M, can you imagine Jordan *ever* climbing a tree? He doesn't even like to be outside! He *hates* dirt under his fingernails. I think that's just the story they cooked up for the emergency room."

She really couldn't imagine Jordan climbing a tree— well, maybe if he was being chased by a particularly dangerous dog, certainly not just for fun.

"Ethan"—she held his gaze—"what you're insinuating is a very serious accusation. You can't go around saying things like this without proof."

"M, Jordan was scared—not just regular I-don't-like-to-ride-roller-coasters scared. He was scared of something at home."

Madison inched closer to Ethan. She put a hand over his. Her stomach was one tight knot as things eased into focus. "Were you there when Mr. McPherson was killed?"

He jumped off the couch. "Hell, no!" He paced around in a tight circle. "You're not understanding what I'm saying!"

"Then sit back down and tell me."

He continued to move back and forth across the room,

folding down the fingers of one hand with the other, cracking his knuckles again. "You have to promise me that you won't tell anyone what I'm going to tell you."

"Ethan—"

"Promise!" He stopped dead and stared hard at her.

"I—I can't. If you tell me something that will help solve this murder, I can't lie to the authorities about it. We have to do what's right."

He pressed his lips together. "Then I can't tell you."

She got up and went to him. Placing her hands on his shoulders, she forced the words out. "If you're in any way involved in this, I have to know now. Nothing stays buried. No matter how deep. Sooner or later it works its way to the surface. It'll be best if we're proactive about this. We have to prepare."

"I didn't have anything to do with his death." Ethan's steady gaze spoke of a troubled spirit, but a clear conscience.

"Then *tell me what happened*!" She hoped her forceful tone would have the desired effect.

"I can't. Not if you won't promise." He turned and hurried up the stairs with hard thudding footfalls.

The slamming of his bedroom door felt like a physical blow to her chest, the concussion reaching the very center of her heart.

THE NEXT MORNING, Ethan didn't offer more protests about attending the funeral. He came down for breakfast wearing black slacks and his dark blue dress shirt. He had his black tie in his hand. The last time he'd worn these clothes had been to the final hearing to approve the adoption.

"I don't have to wear the tie to school, do I?"

He looked so old in these clothes, more young man than boy. She realized how little time they would have together before he went away to college. She was suddenly glad his homelessness had put him a year behind in school.

"No. I'll bring it when I pick you up." She set his breakfast on the table. "You're going to have to ride the bus this morning. I had a flat last night and Judy's picking me up for work."

He groaned as he stuffed bacon in his mouth.

"It's just one day. I don't know what the big deal is—you ride it home every day anyhow."

He didn't explain; just kept eating.

"I called the service station," she said. "My car should be ready in plenty of time for the funeral. I'll pick you up at the main entrance at eleven. I already called school and told them you'd be leaving early."

She heard the groaning engine of the school bus coming up the road. "Better hurry."

He chugged his milk and grabbed his backpack off the floor by the kitchen door. "Bye."

Madison walked to the front of the house and watched him get on the bus. She noticed he took a seat alone near the back.

Crossing her arms, she closed her eyes and prayed whatever he was keeping from her wasn't going to bring his whole life crashing down around his ears.

AT TEN-FIFTY Madison hadn't heard from Mr. Whetzel, who was repairing her tire. Just as she was ready to pick up the phone and hurry him along, he moseyed into her office.

"Oh," she said, "I'm so glad you're here. I was getting worried."

Mr. Whetzel was eighty if he was a day, and probably hadn't had an urgent thought or hurried movement in his life. He smiled slowly, revealing teeth that proved his age. "Now Miz Wade, I told you I'd have your tire back in time. It's all set to go."

She was glad she'd already given him her credit card number, or she'd never get out of here in time to make the funeral. She gathered her purse and pushed back from her desk. "Thank you so much for rushing." She barely kept the chuckle inside. "What was wrong with it? Nail?"

"Well, now," he said with excruciating slowness. He leaned against the door frame, boxing her inside the office. "That's a very interesting thing." He took off his ball cap and rubbed a hand over his bald head. "Very interesting."

She stood, fighting the urge to reach in to pull the words out.

Finally he went on, "There weren't nothin' wrong with that tire, 'cept all the air was gone out of it."

"Really?"

"Yes'um. I checked it real careful." He drawled out the words. "No reason a'tall for it to go flat as a pancake. Can only think maybe some mischief maker done let the air out."

"Hmm." Some mischief maker who'd stood looking in the front window of the paper afterward, perhaps? "Well, thank you so much."

"Welcome." He didn't move from the doorway.

"Just put the charge on my credit card." She made a slight move forward, thinking he'd get the hint.

"Oh, no charge. Didn't do nothin' but pump it back full of air...well, other 'n checking for a leak. That didn't take no time."

"That's very generous of you. I really appreciate it."

"Way I figure it, this world is too full of people sayin' gimme. What we need is more helpin' hands."

She smiled. "You're so right." She took another step forward. "I'm sorry to rush, but I have to pick my son up at school before the funeral."

He stepped into the hall. "Now there was a man who believed in helpin' other folks. Terrible thing, what happened up there on that mountain. Terrible."

"Yes." She hurried past him. "Thank you again." She was going to have to hurry, or they'd miss the funeral altogether.

Madison and Ethan arrived at the church just before eleven-thirty. The parking lot was already filled, so they parked on the street a block away. They signed the register in the vestibule of the Mountain View Baptist Church, then entered the sanctuary. It was filled to capacity. The people in the last pew on the right slid closer together so Madison and Ethan could squeeze in. Ethan sat on the aisle.

This was Madison's first visit to the church, which was the largest and oldest in Buckeye. It seemed too bright for a funeral. Several tall, narrow, Gothic-arched stained-glass windows lined both sides of the sanctuary, spilling cheerful colors on the white plaster walls and dark walnut pews. Behind the carved walnut pulpit was a wall of shining brass pipes for the antique organ that sat directly in the center of the dais. The organist looked dwarfed in front of the massive double keyboard. Music thundered from the mouths of those pipes with bass notes so deep, Madison felt them in her chest.

She glanced at Ethan. He slipped his finger inside

his collar and tugged. His gaze was fixed on the flower-draped casket sitting at the head of the aisle.

A thought occurred to her that should have long before now. She leaned close and whispered to Ethan, "Is this your first funeral?"

His eyes were downcast when he nodded.

She gave his hand a brief squeeze, releasing it quickly, before she embarrassed him.

The service began. The minister read scripture, and then dwelt on Steve McPherson's love for his family, and his good works in the community. The only nod to the fact that Steve had been murdered was a buried statement about life cut tragically short by a violent hand.

A young woman Madison didn't recognize climbed the steps, took the microphone, and sang what the reverend referred to as Steve's favorite hymn, "Amazing Grace." Her young voice was clear and beautiful and would have made a person cry even if they weren't at a funeral.

When Madison glanced at Ethan, his head was bowed, his eyes closed.

Then the pastor introduced Todd, who wanted to say a few words about his father.

The room had been quiet, but now was completely hushed as Todd stepped up to the pulpit.

"You all know that Da-ad"—his voice cracked and he cleared his throat—"loved the outdoors. And he loved taking me and my brother camping."

A choked sob came from the front pew. Madison assumed it was Kate. This had to be tearing her heart out. The idea that funerals were for the comfort of the family suddenly seemed ludicrous.

Todd continued, his voice showing only a slight tremor. "And I just hope that everyone remembers that about him. Many of you know he got into more scrapes than most people, getting stuck on Mt. Hood, and that time we thought we'd have to send out a search party in Yosemite. And although I never imagined it would be quite like this, I always knew Dad would leave this world"—he paused, taking a shuddering breath—"from a place of beauty made by God's own hand.

"All I ask is every time you see something beautiful in nature, that you think of Steve McPherson and how he loved his family and the outdoors."

He stepped away from the microphone.

The minister stood up from the chair at the side of the dais and shook Todd's hand and clapped him on the back, bringing him into a half-embrace. For a moment Todd lingered with his head bowed on the minister's shoulder. Then he descended the steps and took his seat.

Kate's sobs were joined by other more discreet sniffles throughout the packed church.

The minister returned to the pulpit and said a concluding prayer. After the closing "Amen," the organist began a subdued and somber tune. Then the mourners, one pew at a time starting at the front, moved forward to pass the casket for their final good-bye. The family remained seated, accepting condolences from people as they filed by.

She felt Ethan stiffen next to her.

Sliding her arm across the back of the pew, she put her hand on the center of his back. She could feel the faint moisture of nervous perspiration through his shirt. "It'll be all right."

Once the mourners passed the casket, they moved back

up the central aisle, heading outside to await the removal
of the body for the procession to the cemetery.

The first time Madison saw someone scowl at her as
they passed, she thought it was her imagination. Grief
and disapproval could look very much alike. But she soon
reassessed her dismissal. Two or three other people cast
looks of condemnation her way as they inched toward
the rear exit. She could hardly believe they were bringing
their issues with her articles to this funeral.

Fighter that she was, she squared her shoulders and
stared right back.

That's when she noticed it. They weren't glaring at her.
They were glaring at Ethan.

From the corner of her eye, she saw him fold in upon
himself, as if he hoped to become small enough that no
one would see him.

Then Colin Arbuckle and his family passed. Colin
stopped and stepped close. He laid a hand on Ethan's
shoulder. A silent gesture of solidarity, a salute to shared
hardship. Of all the people here, only Colin knew how
Ethan was feeling.

Madison was more than a little embarrassed when
Ethan didn't look up or acknowledge Colin.

She smiled her thanks to the young man. He inclined
his head and moved on.

Time finally came for their row to proceed to the front.
After giving Ethan an encouraging pat on the back, she
stood and followed the rest of the people in their row.
She was all the way to the front when she turned to take
Ethan's arm.

He wasn't there.

She said distracted condolences to Kate and Todd and

Steve's elderly mother, then paused appropriately at the casket. The line moved slowly toward the exit. Once out the door, Madison paused on the top step scanning the crowd for Ethan.

She breathed a sigh of relief when she saw him standing on the corner near where they'd parked the car. He had his hands shoved in his pockets and his back to her.

When she started down the steps, she passed Julia Patterson. She touched the girl's elbow. "Hello, Julia."

Julia's expression was much more startled than friendly. "Ms. Wade . . ."

"Is everything all right?" The girl was pale and her eyes shifted quickly over the people around them.

She nodded and started away. Clearly everything was not all right. The poor kid just buried her boyfriend last week. Her eyes were red-rimmed and she looked like she hadn't been sleeping. Her movements reminded Madison of a skittish wild animal.

Madison stopped her with a hand on her arm. "Julia?"

"I have to go."

"I'm sorry I didn't hear from you last night." Madison kept her voice low.

"I made a mistake," she said without making eye contact. Then she pulled her arm away and hurried off.

With a sigh of disappointment, Madison headed toward the Saab. This wasn't the first time someone who was about to blow the whistle had gotten cold feet. She'd give the girl a day or two, then contact her and try to coax the information from her.

As she reached the outer edge of the mourners, she saw Gabe. He was dressed in a dark suit, white shirt, and blue tie, wearing sunglasses against the glare. He was turned away from the church. And even though she couldn't see his eyes, she could tell he was watching Ethan.

She walked up to him, resolved to put on a congenial, yet not too friendly public face. Business as usual. "I didn't see you in the church."

He shifted his gaze away from her son and looked down at her. "I got here late. Stood in the back."

"Oh." She debated for a moment before she said, "Um, this isn't the time or place, but I have something I need to discuss with you."

Over the sunglasses, he raised a brow. "Now you've got me curious."

"Don't get excited. You're probably not going to like it. Can I come by your office later this afternoon?"

"I'm taking the afternoon off. Why don't you meet me for a drink at Killroy's after you put the paper down for a nap."

With a shake of her head, she said, "You mean put the paper to bed."

"What's its bedtime?" he asked with a grin.

"I'll meet you there at five-thirty." She started toward Ethan. "And stop grinning. I said you aren't going to like it."

Chapter 10

GABE HAD TOLD MADDIE he was taking the afternoon off. That was only half true. He'd promised his father he would spend a few hours schmoozing members of the local Chambers of Commerce in Forrest County on behalf of the Marcus Wyatt gubernatorial campaign. It was something he didn't feel particularly comfortable about. He just hoped no one asked too many political questions.

It wasn't that he and his father didn't share the same fundamental ideals. But there was a major fork in their roads when it came to the means by which those ideals were to be achieved, and that made for a rough ride. All in all, he supported his father's bid for office. Unfortunately, the lead Marcus had been enjoying in the polls was shrinking; thus Gabe's capitulation on his staying-out-of-the-fray stance.

In a rural county like theirs, the constituents would undoubtedly receive him more warmly in khaki slacks and oxford shirt than his funeral suit. He changed and then left the house his mother fondly referred to as a "quaint cottage."

Her terminology was far too kind. In reality this house—which he'd purchased last year—was a fixer-upper just short of needing demolition. He looked upon it as an act of mercy, adopting a house too dilapidated and forlorn to attract the attention of a family. The roof sagged and the gutters sprouted a botanical garden all their own. It seemed each time he was ready to tackle one job on his list, another demanded immediate attention—and cash. So far he'd personally installed new plumbing, new electrical wiring, and a new furnace. Those gutters were next on his list…as long as something else didn't blow up, catch on fire, or spring a leak in the meantime.

He waved at his neighbor, Mrs. Caskie, as he walked to the garage. She was a retired elementary school teacher whose husband had passed away about the same time Gabe purchased the house. Consequently, he'd in essence adopted two houses. Luckily, Mrs. Caskie's didn't require as many emergency medical treatments as his own, which seemed to be on continual life support.

"Lovely afternoon," she called, looking up from her roses with her pruners in one gloved hand.

"Yes, ma'am."

As he swung open the double doors on his 1930s-era garage, she stood and looked with interest. "You getting Old Blue out? Haven't seen him in a long while now."

"Don't want him to start sprouting vegetation like my gutters." In truth, he couldn't drive his department vehicle, purchased by tax dollars, on a political campaign.

She chuckled and returned to her roses.

The garage smelled like cobwebs and used motor oil. He carefully rolled the cover off his 1965 Ford pickup and then backed it out of the garage.

While in storage, the transmission leaked like a shirt carrying rainwater. He shut it off, got out, and checked the dipstick. It was its usual quart-and-a-half low.

Once he topped off the transmission fluid, he backed out of the drive, giving Mrs. Caskie one last wave.

He passed Mountain View Baptist on his way out of Buckeye. It made him think of the way Ethan had bolted rather than follow Madison past the casket. The kid had practically tripped over himself getting out of there.

He wondered briefly if Maddie had felt about Ethan the same way Gabe had felt about his house. Had she taken mercy on a boy unlikely to attract the attention of a family in search of a child? Had she seen past the rough exterior and seen strength and character?

The connection was suddenly undeniable. Maddie, a woman not prone to sentimentality, had been drawn to the need in Ethan, just as Gabe had been drawn to rescue a tumbledown house.

But would the rest of the world ever see Ethan as anything other than a throwaway? Would they see the strength, the character? Or, Gabe forced himself to ask, was there something else dwelling deep inside Ethan Wade? Something even Maddie hadn't seen?

Gabe gave over to chewing on his suspicions in the McPherson murder.

He'd gone back up to Black Rock Falls on Monday; spent the better part of the day up there. And he'd found exactly what he'd expected—nothing.

Maybe something would come from the lab reports.

He didn't like his current list of potential suspects: (1) Jordan Gray. (2) Ethan Wade. (3) Colin Arbuckle. (4) J.D. Henry. (5) Suspect or suspects unknown. Of those, he'd give his right arm for the murderer to be behind door number five. He'd been digging all week and he'd only added one name to that list: Bobby Gray—with an additional shot-in-the-dark possibility of his brother, Brooks.

Neither Gray brother seemed likely, but none of the other suspects did either... except for one. His stomach had nearly eaten itself up this week as he'd thought about it.

There was nothing about Ethan Wade to suggest he had a killer inside him. But then, Gabe admitted to himself, he really didn't know much about the kid.

Maddie was smart and a woman of the world; not easily duped into believing the boy was something that he wasn't.

Not that that argument would provide a viable defense.

And Gabe was beginning to worry that Ethan might need one.

Gabe had already begun to beat back rumors.

What would he do if the fear in his gut turned out to be reality?

THE DOWNTOWN BUILDING that housed Killroy's was much the same as all the others on the block: Italianate-style brick with ironwork columns and panels flanking the front windows and recessed entryway. The one differentiating factor was the colored leaded glass in those front windows that prevented those on the streets from clearly viewing the interior.

When Madison opened the door, she expected to find a place where Southern-style barbeque influenced both the décor and the aroma. Instead she stepped into an Irish pub. The dark wood bar was complete with brass foot rails and tall spigots for beer on tap. Leaded glass lamps featuring shamrocks and harps hung over the booths. Gaelic music played in the background. Hardly the rodeo chili impression Gabe had given her.

The place was fairly crowded. She looked around, but didn't see Gabe.

For a few moments she hung by the door, hoping he'd arrive. But when the place started to fill up, she went ahead and took the last high-backed booth. It would afford more privacy than the bar and she didn't think she and Gabe needed to add more fuel to the gossip wildfire.

Seriously, she should have insisted on his office; even if it meant waiting until morning.

At least they wouldn't be seen walking in together. Once seated, she ordered a beer…a Guinness on tap, something she'd assumed she'd have to forgo in a town like Buckeye.

She'd sipped more than half of it by the time Gabe showed up. He slid into the booth across from her.

"Sorry," he said. "I got held up."

"Thought you were taking the afternoon off." She looked at him over the rim of her glass as she sipped.

"I was doing a little campaigning for my dad."

"Really?" She'd gotten the impression he didn't want anything to do with his dad's political campaign. "How's that going? It looked like he was slipping a bit when I last checked the polls." She couldn't help but add, "Which, if I were guessing, would be because of his plan for eliminating prison overcrowding."

He gave her an acknowledging grin. "That'd be my guess, too."

Narrowing her eyes, she leaned forward across the table. "Seems like with a son in law enforcement, he'd have an excellent source to help design a *good* plan."

He raised his palms in the air. "Hey, I've talked politics about all I can stomach for one day. Would you mind giving it a rest?" His words were delivered good-naturedly, but she could see in his eyes he meant it.

"My, my, with an attitude like that, how did you ever get yourself elected sheriff?"

Shifting uncomfortably, he said, "If you must know, I ran unopposed."

She let loose a bark of laughter. "Seriously? How did you manage that?"

"Sheriff Elliot had a heart attack two years into his term; had to retire. I was appointed to complete his term—guess people just liked me after that." He offered a schoolboy smile.

"I see."

The server appeared and Gabe ordered a beer. "You want food?" he asked Madison.

She was seriously starved, since she'd skipped lunch in order to attend the funeral. Ethan had been so depressed after the service that she'd taken pity on him and delivered him home with a foot-long Subway sandwich instead of taking him back to school.

"Um, I'm having dinner with Ethan, but an appetizer would soak up some of this alcohol before my drive home."

"Nachos?"

The hopeful glisten in his eye made her agree.

He told the server, "Extra jalapeños."

Madison cut in, "On the side."

As the server left them alone, Gabe lifted a challenging brow. "After that, no more nasty comments about my candy-ass taste in coffee. Who eats nachos without jalapeños?"

"Hey, I can take the heat. It's just jalapeños make me drink too much beer. I have work to do when I get home."

They spent the next minutes carefully avoiding any of the thorny subjects that hung between them, talking like strangers or old friends...saying a lot of nothing.

Gabe was enjoying it enough that he pretended there wasn't a reason that she'd asked to meet with him—a reason she'd warned him he wouldn't like.

Once the food was delivered, Gabe decided he'd better get his questions out there before she delivered whatever nasty news she had in her pocket. "So tell me about Ethan. I mean, what his life was like before . . ."

"Before me?"

"Yeah."

"He's an incredibly resilient and resourceful kid. He survived alone on the streets for over a year before I met him."

"How old was he?"

"When I met him?" At his nod, she continued. "Twelve."

"How'd he slip through child protective services?"

She smiled. "I told you he was resourceful. In that neighborhood, the population of street kids is in constant flux, impossible to tell who actually has a home to go to and who doesn't."

"No problems with the authorities then?"

With a dismissive shrug, she said, "Not really. Like I said, it was a rough neighborhood, lots of stuff going on."

"What about his parents?"

She picked at a nacho chip and nibbled the edge. "Same story as thousands of kids. Born into a rough world. His mother died of a drug overdose, but Ethan was already on the streets by then. He said it was easier than going home every day and opening that apartment door to the unknown…violence, drugs, men…you've heard the tale."

"His dad?"

"Never really in the picture."

"Was there an issue getting his consent for the adoption?"

With a brusque shake of her head, she said, "That wasn't a problem." She brushed the salt from the chips off her hands. "Listen, the reason I asked you to meet me—"

"Ah, yes, the one I'm not going to like."

Pointing a finger at him, she said, "That very one." She lowered her voice. "Ethan said something to me that I think you should know."

He set down the beer he'd been just about to drink and leaned his forearms on the table.

"He said that Jordan was afraid of Steve, afraid at home."

"Meaning?"

She slumped back in the booth. "I'm not sure. He clammed up before I got specifics. He did say that Steve was always making Jordan do things he didn't want to do."

Gabe's mouth went dry.

She read his face. "Not *those* kinds of things. Ethan said Steve pushed Jordan into sports and that type of thing. He said Jordan always acted terrified to disappoint."

"Lots of kids feel that way."

"This seemed out of the ordinary. Ethan was very worried about Jordan, even before the camping trip. He said there were bruises...and a broken arm."

He rubbed his thumb across his lips. "Are you saying that Steve was physically abusive to Jordan?"

"It feels that way to me. And look at the shape Jordan is in right now. It certainly lends credence."

"Is that why Ethan tore out of the church rather than pass the casket?" That was preferable to the other reason Gabe thought might have prompted it: guilt.

"Ethan is very protective of those he cares about. Jordan is his friend. He said he just couldn't walk up there, knowing what he knows."

"But does he really know anything? What you're telling me is conjecture and circumstance."

"I know." She tapped her index finger on the table between them. "I just thought you should know so you can ask the right questions of the right people. Jordan might be a victim in more ways than one. You know as well as I do that the number of blows the autopsy indicated Steve took indicates a whole lot of rage."

"You think he killed his own stepfather? The kid's hardly a mass of muscle."

"All I'm saying is that it's worth looking into the possibility. Ethan is—" She cut herself off. "It could have been self-defense."

He sat back and crossed his arms over his chest.

"I told you that you weren't going to like it."

"I don't. I don't like anything about this entire situation."

Chapter 11

"HEY, DUDE," COLIN's voice came through J.D.'s phone.

"Hey." J.D. rolled over in bed, pulling the blanket higher. "What's up?"

"It's Friday night. Get your shit together 'cause we're goin' out."

"I can't, man, I'm sick."

"Is that why you weren't at the funeral?"

"Yeah." J.D. was sorry he'd gone to bed last night wishing for some way to get out of going to the funeral today—it sure wasn't worth having the pukin' flu. Not that his mom gave a shit whether he went or not. But it'd look bad if he wasn't there, especially now that they said it was murder...considering his brother's record and all.

His mom had totally freaked when she'd heard Mr. McP had been murdered, saying they'd be coming after him just 'cause he lived on the wrong side of town. Just look at what they'd done to Jeffery, she'd said. J.D. didn't

think they'd arrest him, but it wasn't worth doing anything to risk it. He sure hoped missing the funeral didn't
screw him.

"Get unsick," Colin said. "You so don't want to miss
this. I got beer."

"You're shittin' me. How'd you get beer?"

"Never mind how. I got it and we're gonna drink it."

"You got it at home? Your dad's gonna kick your ass."

"It's not here with me," Colin hedged. "I'm meetin'
somebody at seven-thirty."

"Who?"

"You'll see. He asked me to ask you. He's bringing
enough for both of us. Come on. Meet me out by the
lumberyard."

"I'm wicked sick, man...been pukin' and shiverin' all
day. No way can I ride my bike clear out there—or suck
down a beer."

"Take somethin'."

"What magic pill you got in mind?" The thought of
beer made him want to barf again. Last time they'd gotten
their hands on some alcohol, J.D. had been sick for two
days.

"I don't know. Pepto or somethin'."

"Ugh. Gotta go." He hung up and raced to the bathroom, making it to the toilet just in time.

MADISON GOT HOME SHORTLY after seven. The kitchen
was dark and silent. She dropped her tote on the kitchen
table and walked into the living room looking for Ethan.
He was supposed to have the table set and a salad made.
She'd been both dreading and anxiously anticipating
their evening together. After his disappearing act at the

funeral and his silent behavior afterward, she was getting to the bottom of this tonight. She just had to pick the right moment and the right angle of attack.

She went into the living room, ready to use teasing as opposed to letting loose her frustration that he hadn't taken care of his tasks. Tonight she was picking her battles with particular care.

But Ethan wasn't in the living room. It was dark, too.

She turned on a lamp. "Ethan?" She started up the stairs.

The upstairs consisted of four dormers, one for each of the three bedrooms and one for the bath. All of the doors opened off a small central hall at the top of the stairs. Madison kept a night-light burning all the time in the hall, for fear she'd take a misstep and tumble down the steps on her way to the bathroom one night.

Ethan's door was closed. A yellow Post-it was stuck at eye level.

M

2 sick 2 eat C U in the morning.

She pulled off the note and crumpled it in her hand. Was this a ruse? Did he know the showdown was coming?

Knocking softly on the door, she tried the knob. It was locked.

"Ethan, you all right?"

An unintelligible muffled response came through the door.

"Ethan?"

She heard his feet thud on the floor, then shuffle toward

the door. The lock clicked, and the door opened a crack. "Stay back. I might be contagious."

She nudged the door open a little farther. "What's wrong?"

"Barfed twice this afternoon." He was wearing a T-shirt and boxers. The front of his hair was standing straight up. "I was finally getting to sleep when you knocked."

"Oh." She reached out, but he took another step back.

"Seriously," he said, "you don't want this."

"Can I get you anything?"

"I just want to sleep."

"Okay. Yell if you want anything."

He closed the door. She heard the lock click and his feet shuffle back toward his bed.

She almost told him to unlock the door in case he got sick enough that he needed help. But she'd always tried to give him space when he needed it. He never liked being fussed over when he was ill. She went back downstairs, figuring she could open the flimsy door with a butter knife in the unlikely event that she'd need to.

AT THREE A.M. Gabe finally gave up on sleep and got out of bed. He'd been tossing and turning since midnight. Visions of frightened teenage boys and bloodied camp chaperones kept flashing in his head. Every time he got those out of his mind, Kate McPherson's tortured expression and pathetic sobs replaced them.

He hated unanswered questions. They slid beneath his skin and irritated like splinters. Even worse, these particular questions would have to sit festering until Monday. There wasn't a damn thing he could do to get closer to the answers before then.

The loudest and most persistent question in his restless mind was whether or not Steve McPherson had been knocking his stepson around. Between Ethan's comments, Kate's careful answers about the relationship between her husband and her son, Jordan's current mental condition, and the obvious fact that Steve's death had all of the markings of a very personal attack, it was looking like a real possibility.

Could that pale, frightened boy have struck out with such brutal force? Gabe had heard of situations where people had exceeded their own apparent physical limitations in a violent act. Rage was a wild and powerful thing.

He needed to ask the crime lab if they could narrow down the size of the attacker by the injuries. What were the chances that the forensics folk would say, "Yes, without a doubt, the murderer couldn't have been over five-four and a hundred-and-ten pounds."

Right. If only it worked like it did on television, his job would be a snap.

Since no action could be taken until Monday, he formulated a plan of attack. He needed to question Kate again; that would be a tricky one. She wasn't likely to say she'd stood by while her husband relentlessly bullied her son.

And Todd—Gabe wanted to see if Todd could throw any light on his stepbrother's frame of mind. Of course, he couldn't see Todd admitting anything damning about his own father either. Still, he might shed a ray of light onto Jordan's psyche.

At this point any sliver of vision Gabe could gain might help assemble a clear picture. He knew Judge Preston was all about individuals' privacy; he wouldn't issue a subpoena for Jordan's medical records without a very strong case.

That thought spurred another idea. If there had been even the slightest suspicion of abuse by the medical teams who treated Jordan for his broken arm, they would have filed a report. As the McPherson family lived in town, the city police would have been involved. He'd check with Chief Davis of the city police and county child protective services first thing Monday morning.

Monday. Monday. Monday. Until then he just had to sit on his hands and wait.

God, as much as he hated for it to be true, an abused Jordan striking out at his abuser would make his life (both personal and professional) a hell of a lot easier.

If he could get this case off his back, he could return to wooing Maddie. The better he got to know her, the closer he longed to get. And that just wasn't going to be happening until he could say with certainty that Ethan wasn't a suspect in this case—not without a huge public outcry. Even Carter, his own deputy, had started dropping hints that Gabe might not be as objective as he should be.

He went into the kitchen, opened the refrigerator, and pulled out a beer—a real beer, not that coffee-colored crap Maddie had been drinking tonight. As long as he couldn't sleep, he might as well accomplish something. He gathered his tools and went to start on the most destructive job he had on his list, ripping the tile off the walls in the bathroom.

BY NOON ON SATURDAY, Gabe had worked himself to exhaustion. He was covered in dust and sweat. The floor of the bathroom was a jagged debris field of broken salmon-colored tile. He'd left the floor tile and the tile in the tub surround, since he hadn't actually planned this little demolition project and had no new tile to replace it. It was a hell of a mess, but he could live with mess, had since he'd moved in.

He went to the garage to get a box and the grain shovel that had come with the place. For the next hour, he scooped and carried until he once again recognized the gray, yellow, and salmon mosaic-tile floor.

Just as he stepped into the steaming shower, his cell phone rang. He considered ignoring it. All he wanted was to be clean and crawl into bed for the sleep that had evaded him last night.

With an exasperated sigh, he swatted aside the shower curtain and snatched the phone from the back of the toilet. "Sheriff Wyatt."

"Sorry to bother you, boss," Deputy Carter said, "but I thought you'd want to know. We've got a missing person. We're working on setting up a coordinated effort with Chief Davis for a search right now."

Fatigue forgotten, Gabe asked, "Who is it?"

"A kid, Colin Arbuckle. Parents said he was supposed to be at a friend's house overnight—J.D. Henry's. When they called this morning, Henry's mom said she hadn't seen him."

"Did someone question J.D.?"

"Yeah, that's how they found Colin's bike. J.D. was home with the flu yesterday. Said that he talked to Colin around dinnertime. J.D. suggested we start looking at the lumberyard. The bike was there, but no Colin."

"I'll be at the lumberyard in ten minutes."

"Roger that."

Gabe quickly soaped and rinsed, assuring himself that kids lied to their parents all the time. Colin was probably somewhere sleeping it off.

It was a thought that he clung to like a lifeline.

Chapter 12

THE LUMBERYARD WAS ON THE EDGE OF TOWN, city police jurisdiction. Unfortunately the city force consisted of only six officers—not nearly enough for a search for a missing person. When Gabe pulled up, there were already several of his own deputies and a dozen volunteer firemen milling around, getting ready to search the rough woodlands that stretched for miles behind the lumberyard.

Colin's parents stood nearby. Mrs. Arbuckle was staring at the bicycle lying beside the lumberyard fence, crying softly. Mr. Arbuckle had his arm around her looking grim and anxious. When one of the firefighters passed him, Mr. Arbuckle grabbed the man's arm. "Why are we waiting around? Why aren't we doing something?"

Gabe heard the beginning of the explanation of the need for organization to ensure an effective search before he got out of earshot.

He approached city police chief Davis with a nod. "Carter here yet?"

Davis shook his head.

"What can I do?" Gabe asked.

"Parents said they've checked with all of his friends. No one saw him last night. So we only have the bike and time last seen, which was when he left home just before seven last evening."

"Any sign of a struggle?"

"No. I've called for search dogs, but it'll be a while before they get here."

"Did J.D. Henry say why he thought Colin might have been here?"

"Nope. Just said Colin had asked him to meet him here."

"No reason why?"

"Well, I'm pretty sure there was a reason...but the Henry kid wasn't giving up anything. You know where that leaves us."

Gabe nodded and listed the most likely possibilities. "Drugs, alcohol, or vandalism."

"No sign of anyone messing with the storage yard or the office building, so my guess is one of the first two."

"Unless . . ."

Davis narrowed his eyes behind his glasses. "What are you thinking?"

"It's not likely, and I don't want to panic the family, but we could be looking at a kidnapping."

Davis followed his thought. "I'll have one of my officers check out the kid's computer. See if he'd been chatting with anyone who might have had an ulterior motive."

Just then, Carter's cruiser pulled up beside them and the passenger window went down.

Gabe walked over and rested his hands on the door, leaning in.

"Call off the search. I found him," Carter said.

From the grim look on his face Gabe didn't have to ask. Colin Arbuckle was dead.

GABE, DAVIS, AND CARTER stood on the narrow bridge looking down at the boy's body.

Carter said, "I just had a hunch and decided to drive past here before I went to the lumberyard. We used to hang out here in high school." He didn't elaborate on what he and his buddies *did* while out here.

He pointed toward the embankment near the bridge abutment. "I noticed the beer cans first. The sun glinted off one, caught my eye. Then I saw this knit cap here." The dark green cap was on the pavement near the bridge railing, not nearly dirty enough to have been lying there long. "Poor kid must have been drunk and fallen from here."

Colin was lying half on a large rock, his legs and feet in the rushing creek thirty feet below. His head was at an unnatural angle to the rest of his body.

Davis said, "We're in your backyard now, Wyatt. You need my people for anything?"

Gabe massaged his forehead with a thumb and forefinger. They'd managed to slip away from the search site without drawing Arbuckle's parents' attention. "If you'd take care of the family, I'd appreciate it. And send the rescue team on down to recover the body." Then he turned to Carter. "Before you run the chief back to the lumberyard, give me the crime tape, camera, and evidence bags from your trunk."

Once the handoff of equipment was made, Carter and Davis left Gabe alone to begin the preliminary work.

By the time Carter had made the short trip to the lumberyard and back, Gabe was standing in water up to his knees, finishing with the final photographs. He'd been in the creek just long enough for the deep ache to start in his ankles and calves from the cold and for the water to wick up to mid-thigh on his jeans.

He looked up as he started to rewind the film and saw the rescue truck pull up behind Carter.

He met Carter halfway up the embankment and asked him to bag the beer cans. Then Gabe went back to the small area on the bridge that he'd marked off with yellow police line tape, the spot where it appeared Colin had gone over the rail.

For a moment he stood there looking down as the rescue squad, all wearing hip waders, lifted the boy's body off the rock and placed it on the litter. There were a couple of missteps on the rocky creek bottom that threatened to dump the body into the creek before they made it to the bank. When they started to put the boy in the black vinyl bag, Gabe turned away.

Although he'd photographed this area already, he studied the concrete rail and the pavement. Not far from the hat was a metal button, like those on jeans and denim jackets. He bagged it. The he turned another plastic bag inside out and picked up the cap. He'd been avoiding doing it until this last minute, hoping his suspicion was wrong.

It wasn't.

The side of the cap that was facedown bore a Philadelphia Eagles logo.

* * *

GABE HAD SERIOUS DOUBTS that Colin Arbuckle had been out there drinking all by himself. His best hope of getting information was J.D. Henry. He headed straight to the Henry duplex without bothering to change his wet jeans.

Mrs. Henry was her usual charming self when she answered the door.

"What do you want?" She'd barely gotten the words out before she took a long drag on her cigarette. "They find that boy?" she asked after she blew smoke out through her nose.

"I'd like to speak to J.D.," Gabe said quietly.

She opened the door. "Since the kid ain't got no sense, I reckon there's no reason for me to keep you out. He already talked to the police once today." Turning her head toward the stairs, she yelled, "James Dean!"

J.D. came dragging down the stairs. His eyes were hooded and his face pale. Clearly his claim of illness yesterday was true. He croaked one word, "Colin?"

"Let's sit down, son."

Once Gabe revealed to J.D. that Colin was dead, he watched for the boy's reaction. Stunned shock paled J.D.'s complexion further.

It took all of about twenty seconds to get him to admit that Colin had mentioned someone was meeting him with beer.

"Who?"

"I don't know. I swear." He swallowed dryly. "Colin was all hotshot, like he gets. He acted like it was this big secret deal and said I'd find out when I got there."

"Did whoever it was know Colin was bringing you?"

"Yeah, I was invited. Colin said." A sudden look of

horror crossed J.D.'s face. "You think somebody just ran off after Colin fell—left him there?"

"Looks that way." Gabe made one more stab at him. "Did Colin say anything that would give you any kind of idea who he was meeting? Someone old enough to buy beer? A high school kid? Someone you already knew?"

J.D. shook his head. He looked like he was about to break down and cry.

Leaning forward, using a tone of confidentiality, Gabe asked, "Is this something y'all have done before...the beer?" Was J.D. protecting their supplier?

"No." Then J.D. looked at the floor and added quietly, "Once Colin snuck a bottle of whiskey out of his house. That's all, I swear."

Standing, Gabe said, "Okay, J.D. If any ideas pop into your head about who Colin might have been meeting, it's important that you tell me. I'll do my best to keep your name out of things as long as you're honest with me."

The boy's hand came up to rub the tears from his eyes. His chin quivered. "I don't know who it was. Swear to God. Why is all this crap happening?"

Gabe was wondering the same thing. Since he didn't have an answer, he let it lie. "You'll let me know if you get any ideas about it, right? You don't have to be sure. Any idea is a help."

J.D. gave a jerky nod.

Gabe let himself out the front door.

FOR A FEW SECONDS Gabe sat in Maddie's driveway, parked behind her Saab, steeling himself for what had to be done. His sour stomach churned in time with his throbbing head, the two combined like the rhythmic agitation of a washing machine. His itchy eyeballs even ached.

No sleep. A third dead body in his jurisdiction. Maddie's imminent pain. His personal life headed for the rocks. No wonder his body was rebelling.

He wanted there to be a logical explanation for that cap being on the bridge. He wanted the circumstances around McPherson's death to point miles away from Ethan. Hell, he wanted to wind the clock back a couple of weeks and start over—for all the good wanting did.

Worried that Maddie would look out and see him sitting here like a stalker, he got out and went to the front door.

A look of surprised questioning crossed her face when she answered. "Hi." She was wearing glasses. He'd never seen her in glasses. She looked hot—in an academic sort of way. He hated the reason he was here even more.

"Can I come in?"

"Sure." She stepped back and looked down at his dirty shoes and wet jeans. "What happened to you?"

No sense in beating around the bush. "Colin Arbuckle is dead."

Her eyes widened and her hand went to her chest. "When? How?"

"Last night. Fell off a bridge."

"Oh, how awful." Her hand lingered at the base of her throat. "How on earth did he fall off a bridge?"

"Good question."

She didn't react to his abrupt answer. Instead, she asked, "Do you want some coffee? You must be cold."

He wanted to say yes. He wanted to pretend they could sit down and she could help him sift through this bizarre rash of mysterious deaths. But this wasn't Gabe visiting Maddie. This wasn't even the sheriff discussing events with the editor of the newspaper. This was the sheriff here to question Maddie's son in a death investigation; best to treat it that way.

"No thanks. Is Ethan here?"

Wariness bloomed in her eyes. "Yes. He's in bed sick." She added pointedly, "Has been since yesterday afternoon."

"Would you get him? I only have a few quick questions."

She hesitated, only a beat but it was there. "All right. Have a seat."

A couple of minutes later, Ethan came down the stairs with Maddie following like a shadow.

He came and stood in the middle of the living room. Maddie sat on the fireplace hearth, far from where Gabe sat on the sofa. He felt her gaze on his skin like the faint pull of static electricity.

"M said something happened to Colin," Ethan said, shifting his weight from one bare foot to the other.

Gabe nodded. "He's dead." He kept his gaze on Ethan, gauging his reaction and assessing his state of health. The kid definitely looked tired...but *sick* and tired? He wasn't as drained of color as J.D. had been.

Ethan's brow creased and the corners of his mouth pulled down. After a moment, he asked, "What happened?"

"Maddie didn't tell you?" Gabe's gaze cut briefly to Maddie. Her distrusting stare didn't waver.

"No," Ethan said. "Just that something happened to him."

"He fell off a bridge and broke his neck."

Ethan's mouth fell open for a second, then he closed it. "How'd he manage that?"

"He was supposed to meet someone at the lumberyard last night, someone who was bringing beer. Do you know anything about that?"

"How would I? I barely know Colin. We don't hang out."

"You hear anything around school about who might be able to get their hands on beer?"

"I'm not exactly on the in, if you know what I mean."

Gabe reached in his jacket pocket and pulled out the ziplock bag that contained the knit cap. "Do you recognize this?"

Ethan took a step closer, but didn't reach for the bag. "It's a hat."

"Ethan." Maddie spoke for the first time in several minutes. Her voice trembled.

"It looks like my hat. I had it up on the mountain, but it wasn't in my stuff when I picked it up. I figured it got lost."

Gabe locked gazes with Ethan. "It was on the bridge where Colin fell."

Ethan didn't flinch, his gaze didn't shy away. "I suppose it could have gotten thrown in with Colin's stuff."

Maddie stood up and put a hand on Ethan's shoulder. "That's enough. Ethan's sick and doesn't need any more stress." To Ethan, she said, "Go back to bed. I'll see the sheriff out."

"M!" Ethan protested. "He thinks I—"

"Go!" She pointed toward the stairs.

Once Gabe heard a door close upstairs, he said, "You didn't tell him Colin was dead? Why?"

She raised her chin ever so slightly. "Because I wanted you to see his reaction when he heard it."

"Maddie, listen, I know this is hard—"

"Did you even ask Colin's parents if he was wearing that hat last night?" She jabbed a finger toward the bag in his hand. "Or did you see the logo and immediately jump to the *wrong* conclusion? I know that hat went up the mountain; I packed it. And I haven't seen it since."

"Did you unpack his stuff?"

"No. I didn't." She crossed her arms. "Ethan was in bed with the flu last night. He didn't go anywhere."

"Can you say that with certainty?" He had to keep his head on the job, but each word nearly dragged his heart right up and out his throat.

"Yes," she said, her eyes flashing with resentment. He could see her pulling up the drawbridge. He was no longer welcome in the castle.

"How?" he asked.

"Good God! I saw him in bed at seven. He locked the door. I was up until midnight. When I got up at six, he was still in there asleep."

"So he could have left the house between midnight and six."

"How? He was sick. He certainly didn't walk all the way out to the lumberyard and back."

"He wouldn't have had to walk."

"What?"

"He took your car without your knowledge before."

She drew a sharp breath and recoiled. "You can't be serious. Why are you leaping to all of these ridiculous conclusions?"

"I'm just asking questions. It's my job."

"He didn't take my car."

"You're certain? You check the mileage every time you get in and out?"

"No, smart-ass, I don't check the mileage. But I've been keeping the keys with me at night. He didn't take my car." Anger crackled around her like a blue-white electric charge. She took a step closer. "If Colin was out there drinking, he was most likely drunk enough to take a tumble off a bridge. I think you need to be looking for the person he was meeting...the person with the beer."

"I am."

"Get out."

"Maddie, I—"

"You're as bad as everyone else in this town! See a kid with a past like Ethan and you assume the worst." She turned her back to him. "I said leave."

Didn't she know what this was doing to him? She had to know he didn't want Ethan involved in this any more than she did.

He wanted to step close behind her and pull her against his chest. He wanted to assure her that he'd get to the truth and then everything could go back to the way it was.

But he had to shelve what he wanted and do his job.

He turned around and walked out the front door. The click of it closing behind him sounded everlasting and final.

FOR SEVERAL MINUTES after she'd heard the door close behind Gabe, Madison stood with her eyes closed, trying to put out the fire of her rage.

Tears stung in her eyes, but she would not let them fall—because they were for all the wrong reasons.

Once she banished the trembling of betrayal and her

shame over her selfishness, she headed up to Ethan's room. She didn't knock.

"All right, Ethan. I've known you're hiding something from me. After what just happened downstairs, I think you'd better let me in on it."

He was lying on the bed with his back to her. He rolled over and off the bed in one jerky movement. "You think I did something last night! You believe *him* over me!" He thumped his fist against his chest.

As much as she felt like yelling and screaming right along with him, she paused long enough to calm her voice. "No. I don't believe you were out last night. And I will never believe anyone else over you, as long as I feel I can trust you're living up to our agreement. We promised not to lie to one another, even if we knew it was going to hurt one of us. And lately, I can't say I feel you're doing your part. I don't think you've lied to me outright, but the lies of omission have to stop."

She waited, watching his shoulders rise and fall with angry bursts of breath. His jaw tensed, locking away anything he might have been thinking about saying.

"Ethan, this can look very bad. If only you hadn't taken my car that night—"

"I didn't take it last night!"

She raised a hand. "I know. But think about how this looks to someone who doesn't know you. You did get caught with my car the other night. Your hat was on that bridge. Because you're from the city, people here believe you know how to get your hands on things kids aren't supposed to have. Right now we're not fighting a battle of what is; we're fighting against the perception of what could be."

"Colin had to have had my hat. I swear it wasn't with my stuff when I got it back."

She took him by the shoulders and backed him up until the foot of the bed hit the back of his knees and he sat. "You don't have to convince me. I believe you. But I think there's more to what went down on that mountain than you're telling me."

He looked away.

"Ethan! You have to tell me—no matter what it is. You're only making it more difficult for yourself and everyone else. Let me help you."

She sat next to him and tried to kick open that closed door. "It has something to do with Jordan."

She waited. She would wait as long as it took.

Ethan cracked his knuckles and stared at the floor.

For a long while the only sound was his ragged breathing and that maddening pop of his joints.

Minutes dragged on. Madison forced herself to keep her pleading words inside.

Finally, Ethan got up and walked to the window. He kept his back to her when he said, "He didn't mean to do it."

Chapter 13

KATE SAT IN THE BLIND-DARKENED ROOM, thinking about how Saturdays used to be. She and Steve had been working so hard to get Jordan to come out of his shell, to fit in better with his peers. Up until she'd gotten together with Steve, she'd been so upset about her and Bobby's divorce that she hadn't seen how much her son had retreated from other kids.

Steve had seen it right away, thank goodness.

No matter how busy he'd been, Steve had always made time to do something with Jordan on Saturdays. He'd never let her go along, always saying they were going to do manly things, going off to do some serious male bonding. He'd wanted the time to be special, just the two of them.

Sometimes they had gone up the mountain. Sometimes, when Steve had been coaching, he'd taken Jordan along and tried to make him feel included, teach him the fundamentals. Afterward he'd usually taken Jordan to the sporting goods store, or to get wings at the sports bar on the edge of town.

She wrapped her fingers around the lapels of her chenille robe and pulled it tighter, curling her legs beneath her on the chair.

She tried to push away the dark thoughts that came when she thought about Steve dying like he did. But they were always there and wouldn't let her alone. How could someone have been so brutal to such a good man? And who? Everybody in town loved Steve. Everybody in town...

Stop it! Todd had told her she had to stop thinking such things.

She turned her thoughts toward tomorrow when she and Todd would go see Jordan. She'd see her baby.

She was ashamed of the relief she'd felt when she'd discovered that Jordan would only be allowed visitors on Sunday during his first weeks at the stress center. That had frightened her a little, not that she couldn't see him, but that they were talking in terms of weeks and months, not days.

She was a terrible person, to be so relieved not to have the burden of sitting with him every day. But how could she have stood it, sitting there all alone day after day looking at the zombie that had been her little boy?

She did call every day for an update, although she always put it off until the very last minute. It was time to make that call—not that she'd hear anything different. There hadn't been any improvement since he'd been admitted.

For a long moment, she stared at the cordless phone sitting on the arm of her chair. Maybe she wouldn't call today. Then she could pretend the news was good. Then she could look forward to seeing him tomorrow.

Just then the phone rang, startling her so much she jumped.

She'd been letting the answering machine pick up all week. All the calls were the same. People offering to bring food that she couldn't bear to look at, let alone eat. Hearing people talk about what a great guy Steve was and asking her how she was doing made her want to scream. How did they think she was? Her life had just imploded.

On the fourth ring, the machine picked up. When she heard the first words of the message, she snatched up the phone and clicked it on.

"Yes, hello, I'm here."

"Oh, good. Mrs. McPherson?"

"Yes."

"This is Carol Bishop at Pleasant Hill Stress Center. I thought you could use a little good news."

Kate's heart rocketed into the stratosphere. "Jordan's talking! I just knew he'd get better. Can I speak to him?"

"I'm afraid our forward progress is a bit more modest than that. Jordan isn't speaking yet, but he did make eye contact with the therapist today. And he shook his head when he was asked if he wanted orange juice this afternoon."

Although the giddiness in her chest evaporated like bubbles rising from the surface of a soda, Kate grabbed on to the positive. "Oh, Jordan hates orange juice. This is good news. He's coming back to himself, isn't he?"

"It's certainly a step in the right direction."

"Maybe when he sees us tomorrow, he'll be even better."

"We're hoping so, Mrs. McPherson. We're certainly hoping so."

"Um, will you call his father and let him know? I'd rather not make the call myself."

"Of course."

As soon as she disconnected the call, she jumped out of the chair and headed to the shower. She wanted to be ready when Todd got home from work. They were going out to celebrate!

FOR A MOMENT, Madison stopped breathing. She stared at Ethan's back and wished she could make this nightmare end. Even though he was finally going to tell her what had happened, she had the feeling that instead of waking up to the light, they were both going to be sucked deeper into darkness.

"Jordan," she finally said. "You mean Jordan…he didn't mean to kill his stepfather."

Ethan's head bowed. He ran both hands through his hair, tugging mercilessly, as though if he pulled hard enough the memory could be removed from his brain.

"Tell me," she urged, her voice no more than a choked whisper. "Tell me everything."

Ethan's knees buckled. He spun as he went down and leaned his back against the wall below the window. The bright afternoon sun shone in, mocking the dark desperation she saw on his face.

She slid off the bed and sat on the floor facing him. "Tell me."

Keeping his gaze on the floor, he began, "Mr. McP sent me and Jordan to find firewood. He stayed in camp with Colin and J.D. Jordan was complaining that Mr. McP just wanted to get rid of the two of us—that he only brought us along to make Jordan's mom happy.

"When we came to the waterfall, it was so cool. I mean, it wasn't like anything I'd ever seen. Jordan sat down and started throwing rocks into the creek while I looked around. When I stood at the bottom of the falls and looked up, I got curious about what it'd look like from the top. It looked like an easy climb, so I said we should go up there."

Ethan's face drew into a frown. "If only I hadn't..." He took a shuddering breath and continued. "Jordan said, no way. It was too dangerous. I tried to talk him into it, but he just got in a pissy mood and told me that if I wanted to climb it to go ahead and break my neck.

"So I went. At first it wasn't too bad. But the stone was crumbly in places. A couple of times, I had to grab on to some plants to keep from falling. I almost turned back, but I didn't want him to think he was right." He paused and looked up at her from beneath his furrowed brow. "Now I wish I hadn't been so stupid. I should have just given up.

"But I didn't." He rubbed both hands over his face. "It took a long time, but I made it to the top. When I got there, Jordan was standing at the bottom looking up at me. I was almost afraid he was going to try to climb up—I mean, if I had trouble, he was sure to fall. So I called down to him and told him not to try, that there were too many loose rocks and I was going to walk around and find another way back. It was too dangerous to climb back down."

Tears pooled at the corners of his eyes, but Madison didn't think he noticed as the first one broke free and slid down his cheek. "I wish I'd just gone back down the way

I'd come up. I probably could have made it. Even if I'd fallen, it would have been better...."

She wanted to interrupt. She wanted to assure him that no matter what had happened, she was glad he hadn't risked his own safety. But he looked as if he'd completely forgotten she was in the room. So she held her tongue and left him to his telling...

"It took me a while; I had to walk all the way around. I was almost back to the creek when I heard this weird noise. At first I thought it was an animal. I thought maybe something was hurt, or trying to hurt Jordan. I started running. As I got closer, I could hear Jordan crying.

"Man, I was so scared. But I kept running.

"When I got there, Mr. McP was on the ground...oh, God, he was so bloody...and Jordan was yelling that it was an accident, over and over again. His hands were bloody and there was blood on his face and his lip was swelling."

Ethan squeezed his eyes closed, as if he could block out the image.

Then, to her surprise, he crawled across the floor and laid his head in her lap. "I know he didn't mean to do it, M. I know he didn't. Maybe Mr. McP was trying to hurt him; maybe that's why Jordan was so afraid. I shouldn't have left him alone. If I hadn't—"

"Shhh." She felt his hot tears on her leg, spreading as her jeans absorbed them. "Shhh. It wasn't your fault, Ethan."

"But I wanted to keep him safe. I promised him I'd keep him safe."

"It wasn't your job to keep him safe. It was his parents' job. None of this was your fault."

She stroked his hair as he quietly cried. Each one of his tears was like acid eating up her insides. How had he carried all of this around without breaking? It was horrible enough spending the night alone with the body and taking care of Jordan on the mountain. But what he'd been through since...

And he hadn't trusted her enough to tell her.

She'd thought she was doing right by him. She'd thought they were solid. How wrong she'd been.

There wasn't anything she could say in this moment to make it up to him, no way to excuse her failure as a parent.

Finally, as the light was dying in the sky, he sat up.

"Why did you go to his hospital room in the middle of the night?"

"I thought it was going to be okay. I thought everyone thought it was an accident. But then, when I heard Sheriff Wyatt tell you about the autopsy, I got really scared. All I could think about was getting him away from here. If they took him to the stress center, I wouldn't be able to help him."

Ethan looked at her, pleading in his eyes. "You have to understand. It wasn't his fault. He never would have done anything like that unless he was trying to protect himself. But who'll believe him? Nobody believes a kid."

"Oh, Ethan, I wish you'd told me all of this in the first place."

"I couldn't. At first all I had to do was keep Jordan from telling anyone, and it would have been okay. Then it started to get so complicated...."

"What about Colin? Did he play a part in this? Is that

one of the complications?" She could barely muster the breath to say the words.

Ethan shrugged, the defeated movement of his shoulders visible in the fading light. "I don't know how he could have. He wasn't there until after."

"And you really have no idea who was getting the beer?"

He shook his head, the reflection of the night-light in the hallway a tiny pinpoint of light in his eyes.

"We need to tell Gabe."

"What good will it do? Jordan is already more messed up than if he was in prison."

"Listen to me. This will not go away by ignoring it. Murder investigations don't ever go away. We're not doing Jordan any favors by covering it up."

She put her hand on his arm. "There were extenuating circumstances. If Jordan acted in self-defense he won't be prosecuted. And just maybe, once the doctors know what happened, they'll be able to help him more."

"What if they don't believe it wasn't on purpose?"

"From what you've told me, I think it's perfectly logical. Why wouldn't they believe it?"

The look on his face froze her heart. "Because I'm the one telling it."

Chapter 14

AFTER SHE SENT ETHAN TO TAKE A SHOWER, Madison had second thoughts about calling Gabe. What if Ethan was right? What if no one believed him without someone to back him up?

Tomorrow was Sunday, visiting day for Jordan. She decided to wait to have Ethan talk to Gabe. She and Ethan would go see Jordan tomorrow, see if he was improving enough to substantiate how everything happened. If he was, great, things should sort themselves out quickly. If it looked like he was making progress, then they'd wait a few more days and hope that progress continued. If not... she tried not to think about the rough road ahead if Jordan remained totally uncommunicative.

Perhaps Ethan's visit would be helpful to Jordan's state of mind. Maybe it would be the springboard for recovery. She held hope.

In any case, they'd waited this long to tell his story, a few more days couldn't make things much worse. It was worth the risk to keep this train from heading down the wrong track; they needed Jordan's corroboration.

GABE SAT AT HIS DESK, staring at the bag containing the green knit cap. He'd just returned to his office from the conference room where he'd taken statements from Mr. and Mrs. Arbuckle separately. Neither one of them could remember if Colin had been wearing a hat when he'd left home last night. In fact, neither one of them could remember what he'd been wearing at all.

They'd each become righteously indignant when Gabe mentioned the beer cans, insisting Colin would never, ever do such a thing. He was a good Christian boy. Mr. Arbuckle had added the indisputable fact that just because the cans were in the vicinity didn't mean his son had been drinking. Anyone could have left them there.

Gabe had nodded and put the subject away. Once they got the fingerprint analysis and blood alcohol level back, the truth, whatever it was, would be undeniable.

This would be one hell of a coincidence if it was as simple as an inexperienced drinker consuming too much and falling over the bridge rail; especially when that drinker was one of the four people on the mountain when Steve McPherson died.

Gabe didn't believe in coincidences.

Could Colin have been drinking to drown his guilt? Had he had something to do with McPherson's murder?

Picking up the bag holding the metal button, Gabe held it up to the light. Diesel brand. Pretty pricey for most kids around here. And Colin hadn't had on a denim jacket, or jeans for that matter. He'd been wearing athletic pants and two sweatshirts layered over a white T-shirt.

Maybe the button wasn't connected. He'd still send it off for fingerprint testing along with the beer cans. Of course, that report would take a day or so.

And until then, he had nothing at all to directly tie Ethan to this scene. He prayed it stayed that way.

SUNDAY MORNING ARRIVED after a long, sleepless night. Madison and Ethan went silently about their morning routines surrounded by a volatile and unstable atmosphere. Madison kept her words to a minimum, unable to shake the impression that opening the subject that occupied her mind would spark an everlasting chain reaction that would blow apart the rest of their lives.

And truly, there was nothing new to say... not until after they'd been to see Jordan.

During the drive to Knoxville, Ethan remained quiet; the kind of quiet that gave off a conspicuous and contagious tension. It had crept across the car and invaded Madison's every muscle until her neck and shoulders ached with it. She flexed her fingers to relax their too-tight grip on the steering wheel.

At twelve-thirty, they pulled into the parking lot of Pleasant Hill Stress Center and passed Kate and Todd pulling out. Kate had such a cheerful expression on her face that Madison had to believe Jordan was improving. Hope warmed her chest. She waved, but they must not have seen her; her Saab didn't stick out nearly as much in Knoxville as it did in Buckeye.

Once inside the main entrance of the facility, they had to sign a visitors log and then wait to be escorted to Jordan's room. As they sat in the lobby, which was designed with a gently burbling water fountain and soothing colors,

Ethan became fidgety. He sat bouncing his heels, setting his knees into a jittery dance. All of that frenetic motion grated against Madison's frayed nerves. She reached over and briefly laid a hand on his knee.

His legs stilled. "Sorry," he whispered. It was the first time he'd spoken in hours.

A young woman appeared and asked, "You're here to see Jordan Gray?"

"Yes," Madison said as she and Ethan simultaneously shot to their feet. This felt more like a court appearance than a hospital visit.

"I'm Vanessa. I'll take you to his room."

Madison fell in step beside the woman, while Ethan trailed behind.

They followed a carpeted hallway until they reached a desk beside a door with wire-reinforced glass in the upper half.

Vanessa said, "I'll have to ask you to leave your purse and jacket here."

Madison handed over her purse to the security attendant behind the desk, then took off her jacket and gave it over as well. Ethan wasn't wearing a jacket.

The security officer stood up behind the desk and held out a small plastic basket. He nodded to Ethan's cargo pants. "Please put any pocketknives, nail clippers, pens, pencils, over-the-counter or prescription drugs that you have in your pockets in here."

"I don't have any."

The security officer's gaze moved to Madison, as if to confirm Ethan was telling the truth. It pissed her off, but she nodded. What made her incapable of lying if Ethan wasn't trustworthy?

"All right," the officer said to Vanessa.

She then punched a security code into a panel beside the door. It buzzed and she pulled it open.

As they started down the hall, this one tiled, not carpeted, Vanessa said, "Jordan's mother and brother just left a few minutes ago to get lunch. They'll be back shortly, in case you want to visit with them, too."

Madison didn't comment. She wasn't sure if she wanted to see Kate right now, not with the bombshell they were about to drop.

Vanessa stopped outside a partially closed door. "It's been a good day for Jordan. The more you talk to him the better. Just push the call button next to his bed if you need anything."

Madison thanked the woman. After she walked away, Madison gave Ethan a bolstering look. He paused only a second, then gave her a resolute nod and pushed the door open.

ETHAN DIDN'T KNOW what he expected after the lady said Jordan was having a "good day," but it wasn't what he saw when he walked into the room. He felt just a little sick to his stomach.

Jordan was dressed and sitting in a chair; that part was normal enough. But he still looked out of it, zoned to another planet.

The TV was on. Tuned to football. Now that really pissed Ethan off.

He reached for the remote and changed it to the Discovery Channel.

"There," he said. "That's better."

Maddie said, "I agree. I just love this channel. Don't you, Jordan?"

Man, M sounded just like she was talking to a normal person. He looked at Jordan—who was at least blinking his eyes.

As much as he'd wanted to get here, Ethan suddenly wanted just as much to take off. He didn't want to talk to a cardboard Jordan. He wanted his friend back.

He took a deep breath and sat down in a chair that sat at an angle to Jordan's. Todd's baseball cap was hanging on the back of it. It was turned enough that he could look Jordan pretty much in the face and still see the TV.

Maddie sat in the chair on Jordan's other side and made some comment about the show. It was about polar bears. There were a couple of cubs rolling around in the snow.

Jordan's eyes were definitely looking at the TV. Ethan saw the corner of his mouth quirk, as if he was about to smile. Ethan searched for something to say, but felt more stupid making a conversation by himself this time than when he'd first seen Jordan at the hospital. That first day, it was different; it was temporary. Now...it felt like an alien had taken over his friend's body. It felt like Jordan was really gone for good.

Maddie laughed. "Oh, Jordan! Did you see that? Those cubs crack me up."

Jordan's lips moved slightly.

"Yeah," Ethan said, trying to sound as normal as M, "just look at that little guy jumping all over the big one's head."

Jordan didn't say anything, nor did he look directly at them, but there was something different in his eyes. He seemed less...plastic.

* * *

MADISON SAW THE TINY SHIFT in Jordan's demeanor. She decided to step out for a while and see if Ethan had more success talking to him without an adult around.

"I'm going to get a cup of coffee. You boys visit and I'll be right back." She looked at Ethan, giving him a nod to continue talking.

Panic bloomed in his eyes. She held his gaze and said, "I'm sure you boys have plenty to talk about."

Ethan managed his first sentence, sounding only a little shaky. She cast him an encouraging smile and left the room.

She stood in the hall for a few minutes, debating on whether or not to actually leave and get that coffee. She decided to hang close, just in case Ethan needed her.

Leaning against the wall beside the door, she listened to the muted narration of the television, occasionally joined by the murmur of Ethan's voice. She sent up a silent prayer that this alone time would allow the security of friendship to coax Jordan closer to communicating.

Suddenly, Ethan's voice rose, panic lacing it. "What? What's wrong?"

Madison pushed the door open, hurrying in and closing it behind her. If Jordan was talking, she didn't want a nurse to burst in here and interrupt.

Jordan's horrified gaze was on the television. The theme of the program shifted to polar bear survival. The screen was filled with a kill, the brilliant white snow showing a large crimson stain.

A thin whine came from deep in Jordan's throat.

He looked straight at Ethan and started to yell, "He didn't mean to do it!"

Ethan had pushed his chair backward, away from Jordan. His face held nearly as much horror as Jordan's.

AFTER MADDIE CAME RUSHING IN, she looked at the TV and then at Jordan.

"He didn't mean to," Jordan cried more softly. "It was an accident...an accident . . ."

Madison didn't seem afraid; she leaned closer to Jordan. "Who didn't mean to, Jordan? Are you talking about your stepdad? Are you talking about Steve?"

Jordan drew his feet up on the chair, pressing his knees to his chest. "It was an accident...ohhh...Stop!" he shouted. "Stooooop!" His face was twisted with fear as he yelled.

Vanessa came bolting through the door. "What happened?" She headed straight for Jordan, who had buried his face against his knees.

Ethan couldn't make any words come out of his mouth.

Maddie said, "We were watching the Discovery Channel. When the scene changed"—she nodded toward the TV where the bear feast continued—"I didn't get to the remote fast enough."

Ethan could hardly believe his ears, M was lying. She hadn't made a move for the remote.

Vanessa placed herself directly in front of Jordan. "Shut off that TV," she said to Ethan, then began speaking softly to Jordan.

She asked Maddie, "Did he say anything, or just scream?"

Ethan watched M's face as she said, "Just started screaming." He couldn't even tell she was lying by looking at her. She'd always been all about truth and trust. He couldn't believe it.

Jordan was quieter now and had stopped screaming. He kept his face hidden and continued to cry.

Vanessa turned to Madison and said, "I'm afraid I'm going to have to ask you to leave. This looks like a breakthrough. I'll page his doctor right away."

"Of course." Maddie motioned for Ethan to follow her out.

He took one last look at Jordan. He wanted to say something to make him feel better, something to help him not be scared.

He just wished he knew what that could be.

When they stepped out into the hallway, they ran into Todd and Mrs. McPherson.

Mrs. McPherson looked angry when she saw them. "What are you doing here?"

"We were just visiting Jordan," Madison answered.

Kate McPherson cast a worried look toward Jordan's room. His muffled cries drifted into the hall. "What did you do to him? He was doing so much better!"

Her accusing glare felt like a knife through Ethan's gut. He stammered, "Nothing . . . we—"

"*You*"—she jabbed a finger at him, making Ethan take a step back—"shouldn't be here!"

Todd put a hand on Kate's elbow. "Take it easy, Kate. I'm sure they didn't do anything."

She jerked her elbow away.

"Todd's right; we were just watching TV with him." Maddie looked as surprised as Ethan felt.

But Mrs. McPherson wasn't looking at Maddie. She was looking at Ethan—and it appeared that she wanted to tear his head off.

Why was she so pissed at him?

Maddie said, "Kate, Vanessa said she felt like this was a breakthrough. Jordan *is* getting better."

Mrs. McPherson jerked around to face Maddie. "You! None of this would have happened if you'd stayed up north where you belong!"

Todd put his arm around her and pulled her away. "Let's go see Jordan."

"I don't want them near him. Never again."

"Shhh," Todd said. "We don't want to upset Jordan more."

As he took her into Jordan's room, he looked back and mouthed, "Sorry."

"What was that all about?" Ethan asked Maddie quietly as soon as Mrs. McPherson was out of sight. "Why was she so mad at me?"

"Let's get out of here." The fact that she'd lied back in Jordan's room, coupled with that tone in her voice, started the wheels in his head turning.

At that moment it clicked...and he was scared shitless.

Chapter 15

ETHAN HAD SURVIVED by his abilities to read people and situations. He was a remarkably astute kid—which could sometimes be a real pain in the ass. On the drive home he had repeatedly tried to get her to say out loud what they were both thinking. And Madison had repeatedly avoided saying it.

As soon as they walked into the house, she said, "Go on up to your room. Finish your homework."

He gave her a stony glare. "Come on, M. Stop treating me like a kid."

"You are a kid. Go do your homework."

"I don't have any." The *take-that* tone of his voice set her further on edge.

"Then go take a shower."

"I know what everyone's thinking," he said gruffly. "Stop trying to pretend you don't."

"Ethan." She gritted her teeth. "Just go upstairs for a while. I need some time."

With a huff, he stomped up the stairs, muttering, "Why would this be different? Everybody always blames me...."

She closed her eyes and wished Ethan was suffering from normal teenage skewed perception. Unfortunately, in this case she was becoming frighteningly aware that his assessment was dead-on.

She needed to think; to formulate a plan.

The realization that Kate McPherson had somehow gotten it in her head that Ethan was responsible for her husband's death and her son's mental state had hit Madison with the force of a speeding bus.

Had Kate taken the offensive—either knowingly or subconsciously—realizing that sooner or later her husband's abusive attitude would come to light? Was she on the attack to prevent her own son from being accused? A mother's instinct to protect was a force of nature.

Madison paced between living room and kitchen until daylight began to fade. As the corners of the room gathered gloom, her mood followed suit. She needed to take a lesson from Kate. Be proactive. Get a handle on this before the situation grew a life of its own.

How best to do that? That was the question she'd really been avoiding, because the answer was as glaring as if it were written in neon letters. And it meant putting at risk any possible future relationship with Gabe Wyatt.

She had made the firm decision to keep her association with him casual and professional, at least until this entire situation resolved itself. But with the ground shifting beneath her feet, she decided, for Ethan's sake, she had to take advantage wherever she could.

She picked up the phone and dialed Gabe's number.

Once that call had been made, she called Ethan downstairs.

He came dragging down the steps, looking as if he'd been asleep. Sleeping or not, she could see the edge of anger was still running strong.

"All right, I've called Ga—Sheriff Wyatt. I want you to tell him what happened to Mr. McPherson."

"Okay." He looked at her with confusion. "But Jordan can't back me up."

"I know. But the best way to contain what could very easily get out of hand is to tell the sheriff everything now, before he has to come with a subpoena to get it."

"'Out of hand'?" His sarcasm was sharp. "Looks to me like things are already there."

She took a deep breath and tried to focus on what mattered, that Kate's reaction wasn't based on truth. "We're still outsiders here. Believe me when I tell you, people will go a long way to prove their assessment of a person's character isn't wrong; particularly in a small community like this—and especially if you *married* that person." She held his gaze. It was clear he understood. "Everyone knew Steve McPherson; the general impression of him was that he was a great guy. The people in this town *don't* know us. When push comes to shove, I want the law on our side.

"But before the sheriff gets here, I want to make certain you've told me everything—you haven't left anything out, no matter how insignificant you think it might be."

"I told you everything." His posture stiffened. "You don't believe me?"

"I do. I just need to make sure I have all the facts. Especially with Colin's accident now."

"What does Colin's accident have to do with it?"

"I don't know that it has anything to do with it. But you can be sure the police are going to be looking for a link. Good investigators don't believe in coincidence. And public opinion won't need facts to create a link."

Ethan looked away and blew out a breath that puffed his cheeks. He took a swipe through his hair. "Maybe Jordan will be able to tell his doctor what happened. That would fix everything. The lady said he was having a breakthrough."

"Ethan"—she stepped closer—"just because he remembers and can talk, doesn't mean he'll tell. It's going to be hard for him to admit what he did. He's going to be afraid."

"But if Mr. McP was hurting him—"

"Yes, well, Jordan's the only one who'll be able to corroborate that, isn't he? And I'm not sure his mother will be receptive to that line of thinking."

He had a sharp intake of breath. "That's why you didn't tell Vanessa that Jordan had talked! You're afraid his mom will—"

"We can't be certain of all that's going on in Mrs. McPherson's mind right now. She's grieving. Not thinking clearly. But it's important we tell the sheriff *everything* today."

Ethan nodded nervously.

"You've told me everything?"

He paused, as if going over the entire thing in his mind. "Yes."

"All right, then. Get yourself something to eat. Sheriff Wyatt will be here in a half-hour."

As she watched Ethan go into the kitchen, Madison thought about Jordan's outburst. She'd gone over the scene forward and backward a thousand times. One thing kept sticking in her craw. Jordan had said, "*He* didn't mean to do it." *He,* not *I.*

Madison hoped with all of her heart that he didn't repeat that phrase to anyone else.

GABE ALWAYS REFUSED TO GO TO BED before dark—no matter what kind of night and day he'd had. That was why he'd been sound asleep on the couch in the living room when Maddie had called him on his cell phone. He'd been so far gone that it had taken him a moment to realize where he was and what had awakened him.

The second he'd heard the troubled tone in her voice, he'd snapped fully awake. She'd been cryptic enough that his worry was now growing each minute as he traveled to her house.

The somber picture she presented when she opened the door did nothing to quell his rising concern. Her undisguised anxiety, so uncharacteristic of her, made him reach out and take her by the shoulders.

"What's happened?"

He felt her lean slightly forward, as if momentarily giving in to a need for comfort, before she stepped back out of his reach.

"Ethan wants to tell you what happened on the mountain." Her grim expression made him want to turn around and walk back out the door.

"All right," he said, his voice rasping in his suddenly dry throat.

After this, he thought, there would be no turning away from his suspicions, no avoiding conclusions because he didn't have solid evidence. And Maddie looked grave enough to tell him that this was not going to be good.

The three of them sat down at Maddie's round glass-topped kitchen table. Gabe listened without interrupting as Ethan explained why he'd formed the theory that Steve McPherson had been mentally and perhaps physically abusive toward his stepson. He gave more details, fleshing out what Maddie had already told Gabe at Killroy's.

The picture Ethan painted certainly didn't fit the Steve McPherson Gabe knew. But he wasn't a fool; things weren't always what they appeared to be.

Then Ethan went through the events of Saturday afternoon on the mountain. Again, Gabe held his questions until the boy had finished. It appeared to be painful in the telling. Ethan's hands fidgeted nervously the entire time and his voice cracked when he described the scene he returned to after walking back from his climb up the falls.

Finally, he finished. He'd given just enough detail, without elaborating so much as to appear he'd been fabricating. He hadn't worked to convince, simply walked Gabe through the events.

It appeared the boy was telling the truth—or he was a very skilled liar.

Gabe asked, "What route did you take back to the falls?"

"I went south and looped around."

"Why south?" It was longer and more difficult. "You had to go up before you could come back down. It would have been easier and a whole lot faster to go north."

"I didn't want to get too close to camp. I didn't want Mr. McP to know I'd been climbing when he'd told us not to do stuff like that." The kid's answer came quickly and sincerely.

"And how long were you gone, leaving Jordan alone?"

Ethan chewed his lip for a moment. "Maybe twenty or thirty minutes."

Gabe questioned him about the whereabouts of the other two boys.

"I guess they were in camp the whole time. After I found Mr. McP, I ran halfway back there yelling and that's the direction they came from."

Twenty or thirty minutes would have been more than enough time for one or both of the other boys to have made it to Black Rock Falls and back to the campsite. But that left the question of what possible motive could they have had to kill McPherson?

Gabe had to admit, Jordan acting in self-defense was sounding pretty credible. Both Colin and J.D. had said that McPherson was angry when he left camp to look for Jordan and Ethan.

"When you found Jordan, did he have a rock or anything in his hand he could have used to hit his stepfather?"

Ethan shook his head slowly. "He had blood on his hands...but he wasn't holding anything." He paused. "He never would have done anything like that unless he was protecting himself. He was afraid of everything; he can't even kill spiders."

Maddie had been silent the entire time. Gabe looked at her. "You have anything to add?"

She shook her head. Strain showed in the corded muscles of her neck. Her hands were grasped so tightly together that her fingers blanched. He resisted reaching over and putting a hand over hers, unclenching those fists and soothing the tension in her neck.

Things were going to get a whole lot more uncomfortable before this was put to rest. No one in this town was going to want to believe the man they'd trusted with their kids was capable of abusing his own stepson. And unless Jordan recovered and admitted everything, it was going to be a hard public sell. Both Ethan's and Maddie's lives were going to be very unpleasant and difficult for the foreseeable future.

"Ethan, I'll need you to come to the office tomorrow to make a formal statement."

"Okay. Can M be with me?"

"I'd prefer it. That way there will be no question afterward about how the information was obtained."

Maddie recoiled slightly, her gaze cutting him like a whip. She was worldwise enough to know the game—as well as the stakes.

Gabe added, "And you can have a lawyer present if you choose."

"Why would I need a lawyer?" Ethan asked in a panicky voice.

"It would only be for your comfort. All we'll be doing is recording everything you told me today."

"Okay."

Maddie remained silent.

Gabe said, "Is there anything about Colin that you'd like to tell me now?"

Ethan's head tilted slightly. "What do you mean?"

"Does Colin's accident have anything to do with what happened last weekend?"

"I don't know anything about Colin's accident. Period."

Gabe laced his fingers together on the table in front of him. "Now's the time to step up with anything you think could be relevant."

"Nothing. There's nothing." There was just enough hesitation in Ethan's response for Gabe to note it. Was there something? Or was Ethan simply searching his memory to be sure?

"Thank you, Ethan." He stood and offered a handshake. "You've done the right thing."

Ethan shook his hand, but looked miserable...like a boy who'd betrayed a friend's trust.

Gabe said, "I'd like to talk to Maddie for a bit, if you don't mind."

The boy left the room with obvious relief.

Gabe sat back down.

Maddie looked at him. "So?"

Gabe massaged the back of his neck. "I'm going to have to do some work on this. It's hard to believe a kid like Jordan could take down a man the size of Steve McPherson. There may be some of the forensic studies that'll help corroborate it, but I'm not holding my breath."

The temperature in the kitchen dropped about ten degrees. Maddie's cold hostility and tense posture said more than words ever could.

"You think he's making this up?" she finally said.

"No. I'm saying he didn't actually witness the murder, so, given the characters in the scene, it's going to be hard to make this scenario fly." He paused. "Unless, of course, Jordan confirms everything."

Somewhere, whispering deep in Gabe's mind, was another scenario. One not so far from the picture Ethan had painted—and yet drastically different. Gabe feared that if this was anyone but Maddie's son, he'd be listening a whole lot more intently to that whisper.

"How likely do you imagine that's going to be?"

"When those boys came off the mountain, they said Jordan said it was an accident. Maybe he believes it was. With his current mental state—"

"He's improving. We saw him today. Maybe you'll be able to question him this week."

"That would be a welcome miracle. Still, an accident is one blow, not a dozen. A dozen is rage." He ran a finger across his lips, trying to align the facts. "Which could be consistent with defense against long-term abuse." He sat in silence for a moment, then asked the question that had to be asked. "Is there anything in Ethan's past that will crop up and work against him?"

Her gaze sharpened. "What do you mean?"

"Like I said, all we have is Ethan's supposition about what happened. No witnesses. No evidence to speak of. You know the crap that crawls out from under the carpet in cases like this. Is there anything to impugn his testimony?"

"You mean other than having been poor and homeless and from up north? Not the pillar of the community that Steve McPherson the child beater was?" Sarcasm lanced her words.

"Watch it. You're letting your emotions cloud your vision of this situation."

The rigidity drained from her and she pushed her hair from her face. "I know. I know."

He brought up another subject that needed airing. "We also need to look at Colin Arbuckle's accident. Where does it fit in all this?"

"I've been looking at that one myself," she said. "Drowning his guilt in Budweiser you think?"

"Could be. Maybe he knew more than he admitted to when I questioned him. And maybe it's pure coincidence."

She raised a brow. "If you believe in coincidence, you're the first investigator I've come across that does."

"I don't. But that doesn't mean it doesn't happen."

They sat in silence for a moment.

The lull dragged on long enough that Gabe stood and said, "I suppose I should go." He didn't want to. He wanted to stay here and assure her everything was going to work out; that he believed her son without a doubt. But neither of those things was true.

She didn't get up. But she didn't rekindle the conversation either.

He'd made his way to the kitchen door when she said, "You know no one in this town is going to believe Ethan without Jordan or Kate admitting that Steve abused his stepson. I've seen what public opinion can do to pressure a DA and pollute a jury pool. I don't want it happening to my son."

"This isn't about public opinion. It's about evidence and facts—wherever they lead. Don't underestimate me, Maddie. I might be a country boy, but I know how to do my job."

She looked up at him. He wished she hadn't. There was no trust in her eyes.

Chapter 16

MADISON WATCHED ETHAN walk into the high school from where she'd dropped him at the curb. She didn't like what she saw. He'd fallen back into the closed-off, don't-mess-with-me posture it had taken her two years to banish. As he passed, groups of girls leaned their heads together, their eyes casting skittish glances his way. A couple of guys gave him a wide berth at the doorway.

God, she hated this. All of the hurtful attitudes she had hoped were gone from his life forever had returned with a vengeance. She wanted to get out of the car and slap those gossiping girls silly, to grab those boys by the shoulders and shake them until their teeth rattled.

Of course, she didn't. She gritted her teeth, put her car in gear, and headed to work.

Pausing at the glass door before entering the newspaper office, she saw Judy standing beside Jennifer the receptionist's desk. When Madison pulled open the door, their

conversation stopped abruptly and their guilty glances
shot her way.

"Good morning, ladies," Madison said brightly. "Don't
let me interrupt your conversation." She walked on past.

From their blushed cheeks and startled looks, she realized she'd broken yet another ironclad Southern rule:
When you catch someone gossiping about you, you go to
great lengths to pretend you don't have a clue.

*Dear Lord, all of these social customs could suck the
energy right out of a person.* And today she was far too
stressed and tired to apply herself.

"Since you seem to be finished," she said dryly, "Judy,
I want you to cover everything having to do with Colin
Arbuckle's accident—interview the authorities, family,
friends, whoever. And Jennifer, call Donnie and see if he
went out and got any photos during the search and recovery." Photographer Donnie Roudebush did freelance work
for the paper, relying on his police scanner for hot scoops.
"If not, have him go take some of the scene, preferably
looking from the creek up toward the bridge. Oh, and call
the family for a recent photo of Colin."

Both women nodded. Judy followed Madison into her
office. "I—I already interviewed the Arbuckles.... I figured ... well, I mean ... considering everything—"

"For goodness' sake, spit it out, Judy." Madison continued to put her tote beneath her desk and powered up her
computer.

Judy looked as startled as if Madison had just poked
her in the eye. Chalk up one more social gaffe by the resident Yankee.

After a moment of recovery, Judy said, "I assumed you

wouldn't want to be covering this...with the boys being so close and all."

"Colin and Ethan weren't close. But thank you for your consideration." Madison could almost hear the *whoosh* as the cynicism passed directly over Judy's head.

"Um, okay then." She started to back toward the office door.

"And Judy"—Madison looked up from her desk—"stick with provable facts—no speculation. If there aren't facts, say so, and that we'll print details as we receive them from the sheriff's department."

"Of course."

"Please close the door on your way out."

As soon as the door latched, Madison slumped back in her chair and rubbed her temples. This was going to be one freakin' long day.

After a moment, she dug out her PDA and looked up the number of the private investigator she'd used back in Philly. She'd never called upon his services for a personal matter. For some reason, doing so made her feel oddly vulnerable—in a way she didn't care for at all.

But it had to be done. She had her hands full here and could hardly run all over creation digging up details. Plus, she'd gotten the feeling that time was going to be of the essence. This guy could do in a couple of days what might take her a week or more.

Once that call was completed, she closed off her personal life and escaped into her work, gearing up for her next article on teenage steroid use.

First she dug into today's stack of mail. Not surprisingly, there were multiple letters to the editor slamming her for her continuing articles about local teens at risk.

Reading one after the other, there didn't seem to be anything new or different...until she reached the next to last letter in the pile.

> If you're interested in what a girlfriend has to say
> about steroid use, ask Shelly Mitthoeffer.

No signature. No return address.

Shelly Mitthoeffer—the girlfriend of the now-incarcerated brother of J.D. Henry.

Madison leaned back in her chair and smiled. *Thank you, Julia.*

GABE HUNG UP from talking to the forensic lab. He'd pleaded his case, stressing the age of the victim. Lucky for him, the technician he'd spoken to had teenage children of her own and promised to personally take care of processing the beer cans and get back to him about the fingerprints by Wednesday.

Now all he had to do was figure out who might have put their hands on those beer cans. With no suspect, there would be nothing to match.

The other pressing item on his agenda was to get some background on Steve McPherson and his stepson. Kate would be his last interview, after he'd gathered what he could from others who'd had contact with Steve and Jordan. That way perhaps he'd have enough leverage to get her to admit what was going on.

Bobby Gray was near the bottom of his list, too. He wanted less-partial views first; opinions that would give him guideposts through all of the conflicting emotional bias both Kate and Bobby were sure to have.

He decided to start with Jacob Roberts, the man who'd coached Little League alongside Steve McPherson.

Luckily, Jacob was easy to locate; he was a firefighter housed three blocks from Gabe's own office. The unusual cool snap that had locked in for the past week had finally moved out. Gabe walked those three blocks in the warm sunshine.

When he arrived at the fire station, Jacob was cutting the scrap of front lawn around the flagpole. He shut off the mower when Gabe approached.

"What brings you by the firehouse, Gabe?" Jacob wiped his brow with his T-shirt sleeve.

"Can you take a break for a couple of minutes? I'd like to talk to you about Steve McPherson."

Jacob looked puzzled. "Sure. Okay." He led Gabe inside the open overhead door to the garage, then through a passage door into the living quarters of the station. "Something to drink?" He motioned Gabe toward a dining table surrounded by six chairs.

"No thanks." He pulled out a chair and sat.

Jacob retrieved a bottle of water from the refrigerator and sat opposite Gabe. "Damn shame about the Arbuckle boy. I sure went out there hoping for a better outcome. He was a real good ballplayer." He gave a sad shake of his head. "You find out who he was meeting?"

"Not yet. You hear any rumblings from your kids… who they suppose it could have been?"

"No. I've been talking to them, but then they're very selective in the news they broadcast at home. They're not gonna admit to me they know how to get beer."

"I know it's tough to parent kids these days," Gabe said sympathetically.

"Yeah, it can be a real bitch—teenagers especially." Jacob uncapped the bottle of water and took a swig. "So, what do you want to know about Steve?"

"I'm just looking for some input. You spent quite a bit of time with him and his stepson, Jordan, right?"

"Yeah. The kid didn't play, but Steve brought him along—trying to get the boy up to speed; play in a few practice games."

"How did Jordan act when he came along?"

Jacob gave a half-laugh. "Aw, you know kids. He spent most of his time moping around, not paying any attention to what was going on. Didn't have a lick of interest in sports. Was real awkward around the other kids."

"And how did Steve try to get around that?"

"The way most dads—and coaches—do; he pushed. Sometimes that's what it takes to get a kid like that out of his shell. He tried to make Jordan feel like one of the team—yelled at him like he was anybody else when he screwed up. Which was pretty damn often."

"Did you ever see him get physical with Jordan?"

Jacob sat up straighter in his chair. "Where are you heading with this, Gabe?"

"I'm just asking all of the questions that come to my mind, gathering facts. I'm trying to solve a murder here."

"You *can't* be serious." Jacob shook his head. "That puny kid couldn't have given Steve a good bruise, let alone murdered him. You're lookin' in the wrong place."

"I didn't say I thought Jordan killed Steve. I said I was asking questions. You have any ideas where I *should* be looking?"

Jacob leaned back in his chair, pushing the front legs off the floor. "Well, I don't like to carry tales, especially unreliable ones I hear from teenagers." He let the chair legs back down on the floor with a thump. Setting his forearms on the table, he looked Gabe in the eye. "But since you're just gathering information, I'll tell you what I heard from my kid."

Gabe's legs flexed, instinctively ready to launch himself into a run...away from something he was sure he didn't want to hear. Only his rigid will kept him in the chair.

"Apparently there's talk around school that Ethan Wade threatened some kids at the skate park some weeks back."

"What's that got to do with Steve and Jordan?" Had he sounded as neutral as he should? Or had his voice carried the edge he felt?

"He threatened those kids because they were giving Jordan Gray a hard time." Jacob's blue gaze sharpened and he tilted his head slightly. "My kid says if anybody messes with Jordan, that kid from up north is all over them."

"Are you telling me you think Steve was hurting Jordan?"

"Can't see it. But he could get pretty in-your-face with the kid. Maybe something happened up there that made the Wade kid think Jordan *might* be hurt. Long as you're asking questions, it's worth looking into."

Gabe wished he could just stop asking questions.

MADISON CAUGHT SHELLY MITTHOEFFER on the sidewalk outside the video store on her smoke break.

"Shelly?" she said as she approached.

"Yeah?" Shelly's voice was rough and raspy; even

though she couldn't be more than nineteen, she and cigarettes had already had a long and intimate relationship.

"I'm Madison Wade. I'm working on some research
about ster—"

"I read the paper." She shifted her weight from one
pencil-thin leg to the other.

"I was wondering if you had anything you'd like to
share with me."

She gave a coarse bark of laughter. "Seriously." She
pumped her thin arm. "I really look like I'm doping."

Madison played along and offered a chuckle. "I was
thinking more about your old boyfriend, the one in jail."

Shelly put one arm across her midsection. Resting her
other elbow on top of it, she held her cigarette to the side
and flipped off the ash. "What about Jeffery?"

"He's in jail because he assaulted you."

She turned her head, giving Madison a view of her
fragile profile. "Yeah, so? That was a long time ago."

"Was he taking anabolic steroids?"

Shelly glanced through the front window of the video
store. "Listen, I gotta get back to work." She stubbed her
cigarette out on the brick window ledge.

"I just want to find out who's selling this crap so no
more kids in this town die…and no more girlfriends get
the shit beat out of them."

"Yeah, well, good luck with that." The girl hurried
back into the building, but didn't turn away so quickly
that Madison didn't see what she was looking for.

Shelly knew. She knew who the supplier was. It was
written all over her face.

Now Madison just had to figure out a way to get it out
of her.

* * *

WHEN GABE RETURNED TO THE OFFICE, there was a voice mail from the counselor at the high school requesting that he call as soon as possible.

He almost wished he hadn't come back in. New problem; or another stick on the pile of old ones?

He dialed and then entered the counselor's extension.

"This is Mrs. Whitfield."

"Sheriff Wyatt, returning your call."

"Oh, Sheriff, I'm so glad you got back to me so quickly. I've had several students in here today—you know, two student deaths like we've had have been really hard on our kids."

"It's hard on everyone in a community like ours. I'm sure you've had your hands full."

"Yes, we have. And I don't know if there's anything to this, but two of my students came in with something I thought you should know. It's about Colin Arbuckle and Ethan Wade...."

Chapter 17

A T FOUR-THIRTY THE DOOR to Gabe's office abruptly opened, swinging wide enough to slam against the file cabinet sitting to its side.

His startled gaze snapped up. Kate McPherson stood there, fury painting every line of her body. "I want you to arrest that boy!"

"Kate?" Gabe now saw Bobby standing a step behind her.

"Ethan Wade tried to kill my son!" she shouted. "I want him arrested!"

Gabe rose from his desk and moved to close the door behind them, looking at Bobby, seeking some rational explanation.

Bobby's expression was a mix of mystification and pain. "Jordan took an overdose of sedatives yesterday afternoon."

"He did not!" she yelled. "Someone drugged him! He couldn't have gotten those pills by himself. All medications are kept in a locked cabinet."

"How is he?" Gabe asked.

Bobby looked grave. "They caught it in time. He should be okay...or at least as okay as he's been."

"He was getting *better*," Kate snapped. "He said his first words yesterday; on the road to recovery. Now this . . ."

These two people were suffering in ways Gabe couldn't imagine. For the second time in one day, he'd been reminded of what a rough road it was being a parent. Then he thought of Maddie, doing it completely alone. Kate's accusation was going to affect her, whether it was true or not.

"Why don't we sit down?" he suggested calmly, motioning to the two chairs on the opposite side of his desk. "Can I get you something to drink?"

"No, thanks," Bobby said as pulled the chair out for Kate to have easier access.

Kate sat and gave a jerky shake of her head. "All I want is for you to arrest that boy before he kills someone else."

Gabe sat and folded his hands on his desk. As he did, he realized they were trembling.

He didn't waste his breath arguing that Ethan hadn't *killed* anyone. Even if her wild accusation about the pills was true, Jordan was alive. And although he had no authority where the alleged crime had taken place, he didn't want to turn her out of here and let her serve as a bellows to the rumors already smoldering around town.

"Let's back up just a bit," he said. "Explain to me what happened."

Sliding forward to the edge of her seat, Kate tapped her fingernail on Gabe's desk, emphasizing every word as she said, "Yesterday Ethan Wade visited my son. Whatever he did or said had Jordan hysterical. They asked us to leave, the doctor was on his way. Thirty minutes later, the nurse found Jordan unconscious. No one at the stress center can explain how he got the pills, or why he would have taken them himself. They're *very* careful with their medications. No unauthorized persons can access them; they're kept in a secure locked cabinet."

Gabe could hear the corporate rhetoric in her last lines. There were plenty of instances where medications were given in error or left unattended; any number of things that could result in something like this. Last year, County Hospital had just such a situation that resulted in a nasty lawsuit. The first line of defense for the facility had been to circle the wagons. Gabe imagined it was the same everywhere.

"What makes you think that Ethan Wade had anything to do with Jordan taking these pills?"

"Who else? He was the only visitor yesterday...he and his mother. He probably forced Jordan to take them. That's why Jordan was hysterical."

Christ, what else could go wrong for Maddie?

"Did the facility call the police to report the incident?" Gabe asked.

After a pause, she admitted, "Well, no."

Bobby said, "They're checking into things themselves first."

Kate's face hardened and she lowered her voice. A fevered gleam came into her eyes. "Of course, they don't know the whole story. I've been thinking"—she paused—"nothing else makes any sense. I'm sure that boy killed Steve, too."

"Whoa." Gabe raised a hand. "Accusations with no facts or evidence won't help matters here."

"*Who else* could have done it?" She leaned forward. "We've known those other boys all their lives. They adored Steve." Settling back in her chair, she crossed her arms over her chest. "Nothing like this ever happened around here until that boy and his mother showed up." She paused. Her lips were pinched tight when she said, "You know he was adopted—and not that long ago. Lived like a wild animal most of his life. Who knows what he's done in the past. That's probably why they moved from up north in the first place—gettin' away from what he's done."

For a moment, Gabe sat quietly, reassessing his perception of Kate. He'd never seen this meek, weak-willed woman so vehemently assertive. Given the atmosphere in town right now, she could stir up a real hornet's nest.

Maddie had said there was nothing in Ethan's past to cause issues. He just had to keep things focused on the facts.

Bobby said, "If there's a chance in hell that it's true, that he killed Steve, you have to do something. If he's a murderer, he probably had something to do with the Arbuckle boy's death, too."

Something in Bobby's tone plucked Gabe's intuition. Why would he take such a leap? Gabe hadn't questioned Bobby yet about the possibility of Jordan being abused; hadn't spoken to him at all since last week at the insurance office. That didn't mean Gabe had eliminated him as a suspect in McPherson's murder.

"What makes you say that?" Gabe asked, keeping his tone neutral. This was exactly the kind of wildfire he didn't want to see started. Especially if it was being set to throw the focus off the true murderer.

"Like Kate says, who else? A kid with a past like that,

he's sure to know how to get all the illegal crap he wants. Beer wouldn't have been a problem at all. He probably got Colin drunk and shoved him off the bridge to shut him up."

"Shut him up?" Gabe kept his mind trained on the idea that Bobby was working him and tried not to think of the Eagles cap he'd found on the bridge.

He'd held that piece of evidence here in the department's evidence room. He hadn't sent it to the lab with the beer cans because there was no way to directly link it to the crime scene. It could have been lying around for weeks, or dropped by anyone. DNA testing was expensive and often inconclusive. Now he had to ask himself, was all of that simply justification? Had the real reason been that he was afraid they'd prove it indeed belonged to Ethan?

Now it looked like testing that cap was going to be necessary, possibly to protect Ethan.

"'Cause Colin saw him kill Steve," Kate said.

"He told you this?" Gabe's gut felt like a churning cesspool. "Colin said *to you* that he saw Ethan Wade kill Steve?"

"Well, not to me," Kate admitted. "But Carrie Jacobs said her son said that Colin had said to someone at school that he knew what happened up there."

At school. Mrs. Whitfield's conversation bounced around in Gabe's mind. The first sparks had already been set to tinder. "I questioned Colin more than once. He was very clear in his statement. He did not witness what happened to Steve. He and J.D. Henry were *together* in camp at the time, a ten-minute walk from the falls. J.D. gave the same story as Colin—*independently*. Neither boy saw what happened.

"I'm afraid the Buckeye grapevine is sprouting new

fruit as it grows. I can assure you," Gabe continued, "we're doing everything we can to catch whoever killed your husband. There is no evidence that points to any particular suspect at this time." He locked gazes with her. "*Any* suspect."

"What about what happened to Jordan? That boy is trying to kill my son, too!" Kate remained unmoved by Gabe's logic, swinging her focus back to her original accusation.

He stood. "Why don't you let me ask some questions and see if I can help sort this out." Not that he had any authority at the stress center, and until he had a better handle on what was going on, he sure as hell wasn't going to urge her to contact the police in Knoxville. "Meanwhile, it's always best for those involved not to talk publicly about ongoing investigations."

Her eyes widened slightly. "Oh, I see."

Gabe walked around the desk and put a hand on her shoulder. "Can I count on you both to keep this between the three of us for the time being?" What a tangled web we weave.... But people in this town were already worked up; mob mentality could become a problem in a hurry. He assured himself he would take this stand for anyone in Ethan Wade's shoes.

"Of course," Kate said as she and Bobby stood.

"I'll be in touch as soon as I have any new information," Gabe said, opening the door.

Bobby stopped to shake his hand on the way out. "Thank you."

As Gabe shook his hand, he felt like a first-class heel. He should have simply told them it was out of his jurisdiction and their complaints needed to be made to the Knoxville police department.

Watching them leave the outer office, Gabe hoped like hell that Madison had been in the room with Ethan and Jordan the entire time yesterday.

EVERYONE LEFT THE NEWSPAPER OFFICE AT FIVE. An hour later, Madison finished her final proof. This article on steroid abuse focused on the investigation into Zach Gilbert's death. Gabe had sent the boy's computer to the state lab for their geek squad to search for any information that could expose the source of the illegal drugs. She made it clear that a good percentage of the time, it wasn't some nameless, faceless Internet address, but someone in the community.

She had gone on to state that Zach Gilbert wasn't the only boy in Buckeye to use steroids. She stopped short of naming names, since all she had at this point were rumors and suppositions. But the more this topic was out there, the more in-your-face she could make it, the more likely it would be that someone would spot something suspect and report it to the police.

She could hardly wait to see the mail response she got after this one. She could take the heat; in fact she was beginning to look forward to it. It brought back memories of the good old days. Besides, it'd all be worth it if it made these kids wise up, or even better, caught the creep who was dealing.

She shut down her computer and her office lights with a feeling of satisfaction.

Packing up her things to leave for the day, she chuckled as Gabe's words came back to her. *Put the paper down for a nap.* He was smart enough to know he was butchering the phrase. That was one of the things she liked about him, his willingness to be the butt of the joke. It was rare to find a man, especially one in a job like Gabe's, who didn't take himself too seriously.

Too damn bad they were standing on opposite sides of the river looking at one another. And she didn't see a bridge being built anytime soon...not until McPherson's murder was solved.

Today, she'd become much more aggressive about that subject herself. In addition to setting her old PI friend to work, she'd done a little digging on her own.

Steve McPherson had lived in Ann Arbor, Michigan, prior to moving here. Madison had been very curious about his first wife's death. She could hardly wait to tell Gabe what she'd discovered. In fact, she decided, she'd swing past his office on her way out of town. Maybe she'd catch him still there.

As she drove past the grade school, she saw several boys playing basketball on the outdoor court. There were also several standing around watching. One of those was J.D. Henry.

Considering Shelly's inadvertent confirmation that Jeffery Henry had been using steroids, this opportunity was too good to pass up. Madison stopped and got out of the car. She didn't walk over to the court. Instead, she stood, leaning against the fender, and watched for a while.

Traffic was still a steady flow behind her, people on their way home for dinner. From what she knew of J.D.'s mother, there most likely wouldn't be a hot meal waiting for him at home.

She was just about to give up and leave—it would be positively fruitless to walk up and try to engage J.D. while he was with his friends—when J.D. turned, said something to the kid standing next to him, and started to walk away.

Madison walked casually over and met him at the edge of the sidewalk. "How are you doing, J.D.?"

"Fine, ma'am." After a short pause, he said, "My mom said I'm not supposed to talk to the newspaper about what happened to Colin."

"I see." *Ma'am. Southern boys, even when they're blowing you off, they're polite about it.* She shifted her weight and lifted her chin to look at him since he was slightly taller than her. "Good thing I don't want to talk about Colin then."

"You don't?" The surprise in his voice told her that was all anybody had wanted to talk to him about.

She shook her head. "No."

"I don't know anything about the other, neither."

"The other?" she asked.

"You know . . . Mr. McPherson."

She couldn't tell if he was looking at the ground to avoid looking her in the eye, or bowing his head in respect for the dead.

"Ethan said you didn't," she said. "Know anything about what happened to him, that is."

"He did?" His face brightened perceptibly. He squinted slightly when he asked, "Did he say the same about Colin?"

"Yes." She studied him closely as that brightness drained away. She realized how busy the tongues in Buckeye had been over the past couple of days. She supposed if Gabe had made that leap and come to question Ethan, so would everyone else.

She took a breath and tried to corral her temper. "I'm curious about your brother."

"Jeffery? What about him?"

"I understand he's in jail."

"Yeah." J.D.'s chin came up, defiant. "Ma says it's bogus."

"The charges against him, you mean?"

"Yeah."

"What do you think?"

He shrugged.

"Jeffery good at sports? Does he work out?" she asked.

"Oh, yeah. He can bench-press one-seventy-five."

"Seriously? He must have been dedicated to lifting."

"I guess. He has a bench and weights in his room."

"Do you think maybe he was taking something…you know, to bulk up?"

J.D. cut her a sideways glance. "Like doping, you mean?"

"Yeah, like doping. I was thinking, maybe it wasn't really his fault…with the girlfriend and all. You know steroids can cause violent behavior. His actions might have been out of his control. It doesn't seem fair for him to be locked up when the person who got him to take the stuff is walking around free."

"Yeah, well, life ain't fair." He started to walk away. "I gotta get home."

"Do you think Jeffery would talk to me?"

J.D. stopped dead. He turned around and said, "No way."

As she watched him walk away, she became aware that the scuffle of feet and the bouncing of the basketball had silenced. Turning, she saw most of the kids on and near the court were standing still, watching her.

She gave a smile and a wave. Dear polite Southern boys, a good number of them waved back, even as they looked at her like they'd love to pick the meat from her bones.

When she got back in her car, she saw it was nearly seven. Fat chance that Gabe was still at the office. She swung by anyway, but his Jeep wasn't in the lot. Damn. She'd really wanted to share what she'd learned.

It was probably just as well, she needed to get home. Ethan had checked in after school and she'd told him she'd be home by seven at the latest.

WHEN GABE'S PHONE RANG, he glanced at the caller ID.

Maddie. He couldn't help the rush of pleasure he felt at the prospect of talking to her. Especially after the day he'd had. Would he tell her about Jordan—about Kate's accusation?

Not tonight, he decided.

"Hello."

"Is this Sheriff Wyatt?" Not Maddie. Ethan.

"Yes." He hoped to hell the kid wasn't calling to drop another bombshell.

"This is Ethan. Ethan Wade," he added, as if his first name wasn't enough to identify him in the current circumstances. "Is M...my mom with you?" He sounded put out.

"No. I haven't seen or spoken to her today." Much to his disappointment. "I assume you tried her office."

"Yeah, every fifteen minutes for the past two hours. She's not picking up her cell either."

The first prickles of unease descended Gabe's spine.

Ethan continued, "She was supposed to be home by seven. If she's not with you..." The pique in his voice shifted to concern.

Gabe looked at the clock. Eight-thirty. That unease deepened. The first shot of adrenaline tingled every nerve ending. Maddie wouldn't just not show up at home when Ethan was expecting her.

"I was just about to run to the store," he lied, not wanting to fuel Ethan's worry. "I'll swing by the paper and make sure she's not still there—"

"She's not. She's been all over me about keeping in touch, so she wouldn't just *not* answer the phone."

Gabe thought of her flat tire the other night. "I'll drive past anyway. If I don't see her car there, I'll drive out to your house, just in case she's had car trouble along the way."

"If it was car trouble, why wouldn't she use her cell, or at least answer it?"

"Maybe the battery is dead." Gabe was itching to get off the phone and into his car.

"She has a car charg—"

"Listen, Ethan, the sooner I get going the sooner I'll find her. I'll call you as soon as I do."

"Give me your cell number, in case I need to call you."

Clearly the kid was thinking things through. Gabe gave him the number, then hung up.

As Gabe got into his Jeep he thought, *There have already been three*; Grandmother's rule of three had been fulfilled. Three deaths. It was done.

Please, dear God, let it be done. Let Maddie be safe.

Chapter 18

ETHAN WAS RIGHT. The newspaper office was dark when Gabe drove past. Maddie's car wasn't parked anywhere within a three-block radius.

He pushed back panic, for the first time realizing what a tall order that was when he asked it of others in his capacity as sheriff. How tough it must have been for Kate, sitting there, waiting by her son's hospital bed to hear her husband's fate.

Fighting the urge to blast through speed limits, he cruised past the drugstores and the groceries. No Saab in any of the parking lots.

Driving up and down every street in town didn't make sense. The most likely place to find her if she had experienced car trouble was between the newspaper and her house. He swung his Jeep back around and took that route.

It was fully dark, so he drove slowly, looking not only for a car at the side of the highway, but also for skid marks or signs that a car had gone off the road.

No car was stalled on the side of the highway. No evidence of an accident. He reached the turnoff for Turnbull Road.

The intersection was on a curve, making it dangerous. He stopped, shining his searchlight all around, making sure he didn't miss a car in the ditch. Then he started up the road, fighting off encroaching panic. His heart was beating faster than it should and his mouth had turned dry before he'd even left his house.

What if he didn't find her? Where would he look next?

One step at a time, he told himself, just as he always told everyone else.

If he had to lay money on the most likely place for trouble along this road, it'd be at the railroad overpass. At least once a year there was an accident there, either between two cars head-on or someone rounding the curve prior to the narrow underpass and slamming into the bridge supports.

Each time he blinked, he saw Maddie's red Saab folded accordion-style against a stone support. He forced himself not to hurry along to that spot. She could be anywhere along here. Most of the road had a side drop-off of some degree. He shone his light from side to side as he went, looking for broken branches or scarred tree trunks.

As he drew closer to the railroad overpass, fear tightened the bands around his chest, and his breathing grew shallow.

Next curve, he thought.

He found himself leaning to the left, trying to see around the bend more quickly. When his headlights struck the stone abutments, he finally drew a steady breath. No crumpled car. No injured Maddie.

His relief was short-lived. On the other side of the underpass, the S curve curled back around. As he drove under the railroad, his headlights illuminated broken saplings and freshly peeled bark.

She'd driven straight off the edge.

THE TELEPHONE RANG. Ethan sprang from the couch as if catapulted by an electric shock, pushing the ON button as he did.

"M?" Every muscle in his body remained tensed.

For a long while there was only silence on the open line.

"M! Are you okay? Where are you? Talk to me!" His throat was so tight and dry he could hardly form the words.

Nothing but dead air.

Ethan strained to hear any noise in the background that could tell him where she was.

There was a click. Then music filtered through the telephone, soft at first, then louder, as if the source was getting closer. After a few seconds, he recognized it: the theme to last summer's slasher film, *Bloody Dawn at Spirit Lake*.

"M! Are you there?" Even as he said it, he knew this wasn't M. He walked quickly to the front door and turned the deadbolt. Then he eased one eye to look through the sidelight. He scanned the front yard. It was dark—way darker than it ever got in the city. He couldn't see shit.

He hurried around the downstairs, making certain the windows were latched and the kitchen door locked. It was stupid; if somebody wanted in, all it would take was a rock—the place was about one-third glass. He'd slept on dangerous streets and his gut had never twisted with fear quite like this.

Then a raspy voice began, "Admit what you did. Admit it and I'll kill you quickly." The music swelled. "Don't look out there. Your mommy can't help you now."

Ethan ended the call and threw the phone onto the couch.

He knew that scene. Someone was playing the sound track from the movie into the phone. But why?

"Your mommy can't help you now."

Oh, shit. What'd happened to M?

He grabbed the phone again and dialed Sheriff Wyatt.

On the sixth unanswered ring, he got off the phone, grabbed a flashlight and his baseball bat, and ran out the front door.

THERE WAS NO PLACE on the tight S curve to pull off the road. Gabe switched on the red-and-blue emergency lights and moved as far to the side as he could. Before he got out of the Jeep, he aimed the spotlight into the area where the car had crashed through the vegetation. There was no way to get it angled down the slope; it ended up illuminating a lot of trees.

Sickness swelled in his stomach. About fifty yards down that sloping ravine there was a sheer thirty-foot drop into a creek bed filled with boulders and huge chunks of fallen rock.

Grabbing his flashlight, he opened the Jeep's door. As soon as he did, he heard music—rock music with a heavy bass line. It was loud enough that if he'd had his window open, he'd have heard it before now.

He ran around the car and stared into the dark ravine.

The music was coming from down there. Sweeping his flashlight beam from left to right, he caught the red reflection of taillights.

A tiny ribbon of relief threaded through his fear. At least she hadn't gone plunging off the cliff and into the creek.

Maddie's Saab sat about forty feet down the steep slope, nose down. No lights. No movement. Just that throbbing music.

She had to be injured—please, just let it be an injury.

He scrambled down the dangerously rough embankment, his feet skidding and slipping as he descended at an insanely unsafe pace in the dark.

All logic, all of his training seemed to fly out of his head. He had to get to Maddie.

He called her name, but got no response.

That damn music was so loud.

His foot caught on a fallen branch. He pitched forward and rolled the last ten feet, stopping only when he ran into the back of the car. His flashlight hit the trunk with a loud snap.

For a split second he held his breath, worrying he'd set the car in downhill motion again.

It remained still.

The music stopped.

"Maddie!"

"Gabe? Oh, thank God!"

He got his feet back under him and moved to the driver's door, steadying himself on the car as he did.

Maddie reached out the open window—around a tree trunk that was jammed against the door.

Grasping her hand, he said, "Are you hurt?" He aimed the flashlight to look at her.

She squinted and turned away from the light. "You're blinding me."

He didn't move the beam, studying her face, looking for trauma. Her left cheek was badly bruised, most likely from the air bag. There was blood on her forehead. Reaching in he felt it; sticky, crusted at the edge, not a fresh flow.

"I'm okay. I just can't get out. Seat belt's jammed. I couldn't reach my phone."

The car was sitting at about a forty-five-degree angle; the pressure of the belt against her shoulder had to be painful.

"I can't get this door open. I'm going around."

She didn't let go of his hand. "Do you have any idea how freakin' dark it is out here? I didn't think anyone would find me tonight."

"So you cranked up the stereo." He couldn't keep himself from leaning down and kissing her hand. It felt cool under his lips. It wouldn't get dangerously cold tonight, but when he considered shock into the equation, he was very glad he'd found her before she'd spent an entire night out here. "You're one smart city girl."

"Figured there was a better chance someone would hear it than see lights all the way down here. Didn't want to waste the battery on both." Her grip was reassuringly strong.

"You're gonna have to let go, Maddie, so I can go around."

"I thought you were holding on to me."

He laughed, relief flowing through him like a cool waterfall. "I am." He squeezed her hand and let go.

After climbing up and around the rear of the car, he shone the flashlight on the passenger side. It was jammed against a sheer slab of rock that had been heaved out of the earth eons ago. He didn't want to think about the odds of this car wedging between the rock and the tree—because that was probably all that prevented it from careening on down the slope and off the rock face into the creek.

Climbing back around to the driver's side, he said, "Neither one of these doors are going to open."

"Try the windshield," she said. "It's already got a hole in it."

Gabe shone the flashlight on the windshield. The glass was a mass of spiderweb cracks surrounding a six-inch hole just below and to the left of the rearview mirror. "What—"

"I think it was a rock, a big one; must have come off the railroad overpass."

His stomach turned at the thought of that rock hitting just a little farther to the left.

He handed her the flashlight. "Shine this on the windshield. I'm going to get on the hood." Inching around the tree, he held on to its rough bark, then used it to pull himself up on the hood. Although the car canted severely downhill, the hood was buckled, preventing it from acting like a slide and sending him off the front.

He took off his shirt and wrapped it around his hand, then grasped the hole. "Cover your face."

"Stop!" she shouted.

"What?"

"You're gonna cut your fingers off. Won't it be less dangerous to just kick it the rest of the way in?"

"It'd probably hold together, but I don't want to take the

chance of pieces flying at you. I'll try pulling. Cover your face in case shards pop loose."

He couldn't get any leverage with the angle of the car and his precarious position.

"Just kick it, Gabe."

It didn't look like he had any choice. He unwound his shirt from his hands, shook it to make sure it wasn't harboring broken glass, and handed it around to the driver's window.

"Use this. Keep your face down and head covered."

She took the shirt. A moment later she said, "Go."

He lifted his foot and slammed the heel of his boot against the cracked glass. With his limited range of motion, it took three good kicks to knock the windshield free. He hoped the shatterproof coating had kept the fragments to a minimum.

"You okay?" he asked.

"Yeah."

He heard tiny bits of glass falling as she moved.

"Hand my shirt back. I don't want to slide across this without it."

She handed it out the windshield. "Use those fancy cutters you heroes have and get this belt off of me," she said with a smile in her voice. "It's locked up so tight it's hard to breathe."

Her humor was reassuring; it backed up her claim to be uninjured.

"Sorry, firefighters get all the cool tools." He shook his shirt to rid it of glass particles, then put it back on. Lying on his belly and pushing against the raised crumple of the hood, he crawled headfirst across the dash.

"Us poor sheriffs have to use low-tech gadgets." He

held up his pocketknife as he lay there facing her. The blood on the right side of her forehead appeared to come from a gash at her hairline. Closer inspection reaffirmed that she wasn't still bleeding.

"I don't like to look a gift rescuer in the mouth, but are you sure you don't want to call the guys with the cool tools? I mean, I'm pretty attached to all of my parts, and that's one bitchin' knife."

"Why, this is just a puny thing for a Southern country boy." He turned the three-and-a-half-inch blade; its broad side glinted as she shone the flashlight beam on it. "I'm almost embarrassed to pull it out in public." He smiled and reached for the belt, testing to see if there was any give at all. "Trust me."

"Do I have a choice?" She drew her chin toward her chest, keeping a wary gaze on the blade.

"Sure, you can wait for the next guy to come looking for you."

She stopped recoiling from the knife and asked, "How *did* you know to look for me?"

"Ethan called, said you were late."

"My cell's been ringing every few minutes. He must be worried to death. Get my phone and call him, tell him I'm okay."

"First things first." He eased the wide blade between the front of her shoulder and the seat belt. "Can you brace your feet on the floorboard and push against the steering wheel with your left arm, ease some of the weight off this shoulder?"

She moved, but it was still difficult to get any motion in the knife.

"Careful with that thing, buster," she muttered, keeping her head perfectly still. "You do know the carotid and the jugular are both pretty vital."

He felt her tremble with the effort of pressing herself up and leaning away from the knife simultaneously. He cursed the webbing manufacturer, wondering why in the hell these things had to be so tough. In his next breath, he was thankful for its strength; without it Maddie might well be dead.

It took several minutes before the last thread snapped. When it did, Maddie pitched forward. He barely jerked the knife out of her path in time to miss her neck.

Her breath huffed out as she hit the steering wheel and the deflated air bag.

"Okay?" he asked.

"Depends. Am I spurting blood?"

"Jugular and carotid both intact, ma'am."

"Then I'm okay."

"Can you hand me the flashlight?" It was gripped in her right hand. She held it up.

He wedged it between the bent metal of the left side of the car and the tree.

As he helped her crawl out, she said, "You're not gonna peek up my skirt are you?"

He chuckled. "You're one amazing woman." Most women he knew would be an emotional wreck after going through what Maddie had just endured.

"Does that mean you *are* going to peek up my skirt?"

Tiny bits of glass falling off her hit the metal of the hood, sounding like hailstones.

Once he had her through the windshield, he got off the hood first, and then assisted her off the car.

The instant her feet hit the uneven ground, her knees buckled. As she went down, she pulled him to his knees.

"*Sonofabitch.*" She sucked in air between her teeth. "My legs are numb. How can they hurt so bad if they're numb?"

"Lie down," he said.

"Gravity already took care of that."

"I mean all the way. Put your head back." He retrieved the flashlight and laid it on the ground beside her. "We'll just wait until your blood learns its way around again."

The skirt of the suit she wore was one of those short skinny ones. His momma would skin him, but he couldn't help but appreciate the fact that it was hiked up well beyond decency.

He knelt at her feet and began massaging her calves.

"Ouch! You're supposed to be helping me."

"I am. I'm making the painful part go a little faster."

"A real hero would make it go away altogether."

A real hero wouldn't be enjoying the feel of her legs under his hands under these circumstances. But damn, he was so glad she was basically unharmed that he felt light enough to float. "Again, you confuse me with a fireman."

"Ugh." She moaned. "Stop that. I'll take the slow pain."

"Your choice." He ran his hands up and down the length of her legs one last time. "I'm going to get your shoes out of the car."

"Shoes? I'm not wearing my shoes?"

"This might take longer than I thought. Try to keep moving your feet." He took the flashlight and climbed in across the dash again.

He found her shoes under the brake pedal. As he pulled

them out, he shook his head. The red four-inch heels were stripper hot, but she'd be better off to climb back up the slope barefoot than in these. "Do you have any other shoes in here?"

"Oh yeah, my entire wardrobe is in the trunk." She paused. "Bring my tote, too."

He shone the light around the interior of the car. The right side of the driver's headrest had a two-inch tear in the leather. He searched for the rock that had come through the windshield and found it lying in the middle of the backseat. It probably weighed three pounds, was wickedly jagged—and it wasn't one of the stones used to support the railroad.

That rock certainly didn't fly off that rail overpass by itself. His heart did a double-beat. He wanted to get his hands on whoever had hurled it. The question burned in his mind: Was this a random act of teenage stupidity, or was Maddie targeted?

The answer to that was just going to have to wait until he got Maddie checked out at the hospital.

He left the rock where it was and grabbed the straps of the tote that was jammed under the dash on the passenger side. "This thing weighs a ton. Let's let the tow truck pull it up with the car."

"No!" There was a thin note of panic in her voice...the first he'd heard tonight. "Don't leave it in there. It has my laptop in it."

"Good reason to let the tow truck bring it up. It's gonna be a tough climb. We might break it."

"I'll take the chance. I can't leave it here." The determination in her voice told him further argument was worthless.

Once he was back by her side, he said, "Any feeling coming back?"

"Feels like my legs are being eaten by piranhas."

"Progress."

"Easy for you to say. Get my cell phone out of the tote. I want to call Ethan."

It was at that moment that Gabe realized he'd been so recklessly frantic, he'd left his own cell phone in the Jeep.

"It's in the outside pouch," she said.

He set down the flashlight and the tote, then pulled out one of those fancy gadgets that looked more like a calculator than a phone.

She pushed herself to a sitting position and took it from him. After dialing, she waited. "No answer. Where could he be?"

"Let's go see." He put her heels in the tote. "No sense in trying to climb with these on. Do you think you can stand?"

She nodded.

He put her tote on his shoulder and handed her the flashlight. Taking a wide stance on the slope, he reached down and grasped her forearms, pulling her up. She wobbled and weaved, then steadied.

He hooked his left arm around her back. Her right arm went around his waist.

"Let's go," she said. Her voice was strained enough that he knew her legs still hurt.

"Keep the flashlight on the ground. I'll try to guide you into places easy on your feet."

"I may be a city girl, but my feet are Tennessee all the way. Never wear shoes unless I have to."

As they struggled to climb the slope, the distance

seemed to increase. The downward trip had only taken Gabe seconds; up was another story. By the time they reached the road, he was sweating and Maddie was trembling so hard the flashlight beam bounced along the ground ahead of them.

He let the tote slide to the ground, opened the passenger door, and backed Maddie inside. The flashing emergency lights on top of the Jeep cast her face in pulsating shadows.

"Okay?" he asked, resting his hand gently along the line of her jaw.

She looked up at him, her brown eyes welling with tears. There was such an unexpected look of vulnerability in them that it hurt his heart.

Before his better sense kicked in, he leaned down and kissed her.

Chapter 19

Madison locked her hands behind Gabe's neck, clinging to him, returning his kiss with all she had within her. Suddenly, nothing else in this world mattered. She would meld herself completely into his being if it were possible.

He straightened, pulling her back to her feet, wrapping his arms around her waist. The solid feel of his flesh under her hands affirmed that she really was safe.

She'd managed to hold back her fear as the hours had passed and the sun set. It had become much harder after darkness descended. If there was a moon, not a single beam made its way past the thick trees. The only time she could recall being in any place darker was when she'd been in a cave and the tour guide had turned out the lights. Absolute darkness, the man had said, pitch black. And he'd been right. That's when she'd discovered something frightening about herself.

Absolute darkness suffocated her. It tore the breath

from her lungs and reason from her mind. It made her want to run blindly, searching for light.

And even though tonight she had not been plunged into pitch blackness in a nanosecond as she had in that cave, even though night had fallen in its natural way, the feeling of being smothered had been the same. She'd fought the urge to scream, to flail, to struggle toward unseen light.

Once she'd turned on the car's interior lights, but that had just made her surroundings that much darker. Besides, she'd wanted to save her battery, as no one was going to see her lights down there. Sound was a better solution— but when to use it? Hardly anyone traveled that road after eight in the evening on a weeknight.

Then she'd heard the bobcat cry and she'd just about lost it. No one had prepared her for how awful that sound was; chilling and threatening and morbidly frightening. A thousand times worse than the tomcat romancing her neighbor's Persian. Compounded with the darkness, it was more than she could stand. She'd turned on the stereo. Although she would never admit it to Gabe, she'd done it as much to drown out the far-from-the-city night sounds as to attract the attention of a passerby.

But now all of that fear seemed so far away. Gabe breathed breath into her lungs. His wonderful voice instilled calm. His arms gave her strength. And his heart brought light to her own. Gone was the urge to run. She wanted to remain right where she was and not move— maybe ever.

All too soon, Gabe eased away. He traced his thumb along her lower lip. "I hope I didn't hurt you."

"That was the first thing all night that hasn't hurt. Do it again."

His smile was sweetly lopsided and the color of his face vacillated between red and blue in the lights. "I've never met a woman like you."

She stretched up and kissed him lightly. "I suppose you prefer a woman with Southern charm instead of Yankee frankness."

He shook his head. "I never knew how much I liked Yankee frankness—or maybe it's just when it comes from your lips."

Oh my, the way he said those words made warmth bloom in her belly. Good God, he could charm snakes with that voice.

He leaned slowly closer until his lips grazed her neck. Then he whispered in her ear, "We need to get you to the hospital."

"No." She reluctantly leaned away from him. "I'm fine. I want to go home."

"Maddie—"

"I just climbed out of that ravine, didn't I?" He didn't look persuaded. She said, "It's ten o'clock. Ethan didn't answer. I *have* to get home."

He placed a hand on either side of her head, then kissed her forehead. "All right. But I'm checking you over when we get there."

A delicious little thrill went through her at the prospect of having those hands roaming over her body, even if it was to inspect for injury.

He eased her back into the passenger seat. Putting his hands behind her knees, he swung her legs into the car as if she were an invalid. He buckled her into the seat belt before he closed the door.

As he walked around the front of the Jeep, he stopped dead. She couldn't see anything beyond him in the flashing red-and-blue lights.

Then Ethan appeared running straight for them. The strange light accentuated the terror on his face. He had a baseball bat at his side.

Gabe raised a hand in the air. "She's okay!"

He directed Ethan to the passenger side.

Ethan yanked open the door and fell to his knees beside the Jeep. "When I saw the lights...I thought"—His voice locked in his throat. Tears shimmered in his eyes.

"I'm fine. A rock fell off the railroad overpass and crashed through the windshield of my car and I went off the road." She put a hand on his head. "I was stuck and couldn't reach my phone." Pushing the hair away from his eyes, she said, "I'm so sorry to have worried you."

He bowed his head; she knew it was so she wouldn't see his tears.

"Climb in and we'll go home," she said. "I'm starved."

When he lifted his head, he had a grateful grin on his face and he blinked his tears away. "Me, too."

She didn't question him about the baseball bat. A kid with a past like his didn't go out to meet trouble unarmed.

AS MUCH AS MADISON WANTED TO LEAN ON GABE, to have his reassuring touch, she deliberately put space between them after he'd given her a hand out of the Jeep. She walked up the steps to the front porch slowly, but under her own power. Ethan was standing there, patiently holding the door open for her.

Gabe followed her through the door. "I'll give Earl

Whetzel a call in the morning to pull your car out of the ravine."

Ethan said, "I'll do it." There was just enough of a protective tone in his voice for Madison to notice.

"Will you two stop treating me like I'm broken? *I* can make a phone call."

Gabe took her by the elbow and led her closer to the lamp in the living room. He stood in front of her with his hands on either side of her head, turning her face toward the light. "I don't think that cut needs to be stitched. Let's clean it up, just to be sure."

She could almost feel the heat of Ethan's glare as Gabe handled her.

"I tell you what," she said, pulling her head from his grasp. "I'll take a shower, then if I think it needs attention I'll go to the emergency room."

"That'd be fine, but you don't have a way to get there," Gabe said. "Besides, I need to ask you some questions about the accident. You go ahead and shower. Ethan and I will make something to eat."

Glancing at Ethan, she could tell he wanted Gabe out the door. This unfamiliar dance was making her uncomfortable enough that she almost wished him gone, too. But she knew Gabe wasn't leaving until he was satisfied she wasn't in need of medical attention.

"All right." She headed toward the stairs, moving more stiffly by the step. It felt like every muscle in her body had suddenly decided in unison to seize up. "You two remember, any mess you make, you're cleaning up."

She heard Gabe chuckle behind her.

Ethan made a sound of teenage exasperation and clomped toward the kitchen. "I don't need help."

* * *

GABE WAITED UNTIL HE HEARD THE SHOWER start upstairs, then went into the kitchen. Ethan was cracking eggs into a mixing bowl and flipping the shells into the sink.

"Now that Maddie's out of earshot," Gabe said, "why don't you tell me what happened."

Ethan continued to crack eggs and didn't turn around. "What are you talking about?"

"What happened to make you run a mile down the road with a baseball bat?"

"I was worried about M." Ethan's voice was steady. He tossed another eggshell into the sink without turning to face Gabe.

"You were worried about her earlier when you called me, but you didn't go tearing around in the dark with a bat. In fact, you were very clearheaded and rational."

Ethan stopped what he was doing and finally turned. Bracing his palms on the edge of the counter behind him, he said, "I called your cell and you didn't answer. I got *more* worried."

Gabe didn't believe that was everything, not by a long shot. He'd seen the terror on the kid's face. Something had convinced him that his mother was in real danger.

Gabe just stood looking at the boy, trying to force the truth from him by simply outwaiting him.

The seconds dragged on. Neither one of them spoke. Gabe remembered then that Ethan was no ordinary teen; most of the tricks Gabe used to get kids to spill their guts probably weren't going to work on him.

There were lots of things he wanted to squeeze out of Ethan Wade—like the complete and absolute truth about what went down at Black Rock Falls, and why Jordan

Gray was in his current emotional meltdown. But Gabe wasn't going to get those things unless he developed some new tactics.

His conscience niggled. Questioning Ethan about any of those things without Maddie's knowledge was a breach of trust.

But you wouldn't hesitate to do it if it was anyone else's kid and you thought it would get you closer to solving the crime.

He couldn't deny it. Whatever he squeezed out of a kid might not be admissible in court, but it went a long way to getting the truth out in the light of day.

"You did the right thing, calling me. Maddie might have been stuck down there all night if you hadn't."

The guarded look in Ethan's eyes didn't lessen. "Yeah, well, I knew you'd work harder at finding her than anyone else." The tone in his voice said that wasn't a particularly welcome thing.

"Listen, I don't see any reason to bullshit you. I like your mom—a lot. But things are really complicated right now, so you can smooth down your hackles. Her first concern is you, as it should be. I'm not the enemy here."

"But you don't trust me." Ethan never broke eye contact.

Gabe held back the automatic denial that tried to come out of his mouth. "My job is to ask questions. I can't let my personal feelings keep me from doing that. My guess is you don't trust me either."

A slight smile of confirmation crossed Ethan's face. "You want some eggs?"

It was clear that the kid appreciated the head-on approach. He was enough like Maddie in that respect to be her biological child.

"Sure."

"The plates are in that cabinet over there." Ethan pointed. "And the silverware in the drawer under it."

Gabe stepped to the sink to wash his hands. "You went to see Jordan yesterday?"

Ethan had his head in the refrigerator. He held perfectly still for a moment. "Yeah."

"How was he?"

Pulling out a carton of milk, Ethan returned to the bowl of eggs. He set the milk down and looked at Gabe. "It was weird, you know. He was still out of it, but after a while it seemed like he was at least hearing what was going on around him. Then he just went nuts, crying and stuff, almost like up on the mountain."

"Really? Anything in particular set him off, you think?"

Ethan hesitated just long enough to signal he was deciding just how much he wanted to say.

"Not that I could tell," he said, turning to pour milk into the eggs.

"What did your mom think? Was she in there, too?" Gabe nearly held his breath as he opened the cabinet, praying for the answer he wanted to hear.

"She couldn't figure it out either. The lady at the place said she thought it was some kind of breakthrough. Sure didn't look like that to me."

Gabe noted that Ethan had skated around directly answering the second part of his question.

Before he could ask again, Maddie came into the kitchen. "I've given myself a clean bill of health."

Gabe turned to look at her. She had on the oversized orange University of Tennessee sweatshirt and gray sweatpants. Her hair looked nearly black when it was wet. She had it pulled back in a ponytail.

He stepped closer. She dutifully tilted her face toward him so he could inspect the cut on her forehead. She was right; it was long, but not deep. Judging by the slash in the driver's-side headrest, he imagined the jagged rock had nicked her as she reflexively dodged out of the way.

"How about everywhere else?" he asked.

"Got a hell of a bruise on my right shoulder and across my chest from the seat belt, and when I move I feel like I'm about a hundred and ten, but other than that, I'm good."

"You take some aspirin?"

"Three." She stepped away from his scrutiny and peeked over Ethan's shoulder. "How long? I'm starved."

AFTER THEY FINISHED EATING, which was a matter of a few mostly silent minutes, Madison asked Ethan to go upstairs.

"I need to clean up the dishes," he said. "You said so before you took a shower."

Gabe smiled at Ethan, and Madison saw what she thought to be genuine fondness in his eyes. "You cooked," he said. "And very well, I might add. I'll clean up."

Ethan slid a disgruntled look from Madison to Gabe and back to Madison again.

Madison said, "I'm sure Sheriff Wyatt has some questions about my accident."

The look Ethan gave Gabe reflected anything but fondness. "She needs to rest. Can't you ask tomorrow?"

"Seriously, I'm fine," Madison said. "Stop worrying and go get your homework done."

Ethan picked up his plate and set it on the kitchen

counter with a clatter. He cast one last glower toward Gabe before he walked out of the kitchen.

"He's worse than a disapproving father," Gabe said.

Madison's smile was cut short when the pain in her left cheek kicked in. "Hey, I'm all he's got." Then she added quietly, "He was really scared tonight."

Gabe reached across the table and took her hand. "He wasn't the only one."

In a normal tone, his voice moved things deep inside her. His words now were delivered with such husky tenderness that she felt as if molten lava was ready to erupt right out of her pores.

Her skin beneath his touch sparked with life...and need. It was the need that crippled her, stole her reason, and her breath. She'd never *needed* like this.

His gaze held the same longing that strangled her words in her throat. The gravitational pull of his nearness had her moving from her own chair and settling herself on his lap.

When he caressed her injured cheek, his touch was feather light and the look in his eyes showed more pain than any of her own physical injuries.

"Maddie," he breathed her name. "When I thought you—"

"Shhh." She lowered her lips to his. If she revealed the thoughts that had gone through her mind while she'd been trapped in the dark in that ravine...well, she just couldn't. Not even to Gabe.

What had been an act to silence quickly turned into something else. Her lips sought to devour his. She breathed in his exhaled breath, feeling the sweet hot flow of it all the way to the bottom of her lungs.

Gabe's one hand slid up her back, beneath her sweatshirt, while the other cradled her head. When his mouth moved to her neck, she slid half off his lap, then straddled him. Her most intimate place rested against the ridge of his erection.

And she wanted more.

As his lips played along the sensitive skin of her collarbone, a hunger unlike any she'd ever experienced engulfed her; a hunger of the soul. She yearned to draw Gabe completely within herself, absorb every cell of him into her being, meld their bodies and their spirits into one.

When his hand moved to her breast, she moved against him.

He quickly grabbed her waist, stilling her. "Dear God in heaven, woman."

She kissed him again. Once she'd completely robbed him of his breath, she said, "I suppose if you can't stand the heat, we could get out of the kitchen...."

Heavy steps thundered overhead as Ethan moved between his bedroom and the bathroom. A door slammed.

Maddie closed her eyes, rested her forehead against Gabe's, and took a deep breath.

"Or not." Gabe's tone was a peculiar mix of desire, disappointment, and humor. "The kid knows how to do his job—better than a disapproving father, in fact."

Maddie's mouth drew into a smile, appreciating to her very core Gabe's gentle tolerance of her situation. She threw her head back and blew out a long breath, trying to get her own body to pull back a notch or two. "Probably the most effective birth control I've ever had."

"Is he too old to leave with a sitter?"

Laughter broke free. A person just had to love a man

with a sense of humor in a sexually frustrating situation like this.

Gabe cupped her face. "Seriously, Maddie, I'm so glad you're safe—and sorry I didn't get to you sooner."

She dropped an innocent kiss on his mouth. "I'm glad you were clever enough to find me at all. Thank you." She slid off his lap and back into her own chair. Her good sense was slow in returning. She had to fight the urge to go back to him, to pretend there was nothing in the world that separated them.

Oh, to be in another place and time.

When had she turned into such a foolish dreamer?

She watched as Gabe took a long drink of ice water.

She followed suit, hoping it did the trick to cool her off.

He leaned back in his chair, rubbing his palms on his thighs. After clearing his throat a couple of times, he said, "Better get down to business; just in case Ethan is listening at the air ducts." He winked. "Tell me what happened, what you remember before you went off the road."

"It all happened so fast. I was driving under the overpass and suddenly there was a rock crashing through my windshield. I ducked…maybe I even pressed on the gas when I did it…the next thing I knew, I was headed downhill, crashing through the trees. Lots of branches were slapping at the car, then I guess I hit something hard enough to set the air bag off and stop the car. Like they say, it's not the fall but the abrupt landing that'll hurt you."

"Did you see anyone on the overpass?"

"I wasn't looking up there. You know how dangerous that curve is. I've learned not to take my eyes off the road for a second." The implication hit her. "You think someone threw that rock at me?"

"The rock in your backseat wasn't a piece of limestone from the bridge. And it was bigger than a football, with jagged edges. It doesn't seem likely that it was sitting on the center of the overpass and just happened to fall off."

He shifted in his chair. "We've occasionally had trouble with kids throwing rocks off overpasses at cars. But not there; they usually pick something more heavily traveled."

Madison stretched her memory, trying to remember if she'd seen movement up there in her peripheral vision. But she'd been so intent on the curve and watching for oncoming traffic that nothing else had registered.

"I really don't recall seeing anyone. But it's not like I haven't pissed plenty of people off lately."

Gabe's green gaze snapped to hers. "What do you mean?"

"Seems I've ruffled feathers with my articles on teen steroid use. Folks are taking it as a personal assault on the community's morals."

"And how are they displaying this displeasure?"

"Now you're hurting my feelings. Don't you read the paper?"

"I've been busy lately. What's happened?"

"There have been some pretty ugly letters to the editor."

"I want to see them. Anything else?"

"Well, Mr. Whetzel said there wasn't anything wrong with my tire that was flat the other night. Somebody let the air out."

Gabe looked intrigued.

"That night, there was some guy loitering around the front door of the newspaper. I thought he was just ducking in to get out of the rain...but maybe it was the person who deflated my tire."

His eyes narrowed. "You mean there was somebody hanging around the newspaper when you were the only one there...and you didn't tell me when you saw me minutes later?"

She just couldn't admit that she'd been spooked enough to call 911. With a shrug she said, "I said I assumed it was someone getting out of the rain."

His mouth was tight when he said, "No more assuming, not after tonight."

With a nod, she said, "Okay. You're right. I'll be more careful."

"And tell me whenever something happens: letters, threats, shadows, creepy feelings...."

"All right. I get it." She chewed her thumbnail. "You know, I think I'm right about a local dealer."

"What do you know?"

"I talked to Julia Patterson about her boyfriend's steroid use. At first she wanted to talk, but then she backed off. Now she seems scared out of her wits. But I received an anonymous note that had to have come from her, telling me to ask Shelly Mitthoeffer about being the girlfriend of a steroid user. I caught Shelly at work. She blew me off, but I'm not giving up yet."

"So this could be trouble from disgruntled townsfolk *or* an act by the dealer to scare you off?"

She gave him a slow grin. "Maybe." As much as she hated being a target, she liked the idea that it confirmed she was on track in her investigation. "Or," she said, thinking realistically, "maybe it was just some stupid kid's prank."

"Maybe. I'll go up there at first light and look around."

"You know, I swung by your office on my way home." She paused, listening to make sure Ethan hadn't come back downstairs. "I discovered some information today that I thought you'd find interesting."

"About?"

"Steve McPherson's first wife."

Chapter 20

W ELL," KATE SAID TO HER COUSIN OVER the phone, finally getting to the meat of why she'd called Christie in the first place, "I'm not at liberty to discuss details. But since you're family and all, let's just say some people are born bad."

"Jordan?" Christie sounded shocked. "I can't believe that."

"Not Jordan!" Christie had never been the glossiest leaf on the family tree, bless her heart. "Jordan is a *victim*—and he's not the only one."

Kate just had to vent to somebody. Bobby was too preoccupied with his precious appointments. If only Todd were home, he'd understand what she was going through. But he wouldn't get off work at the video store until eight.

Really, Kate didn't have to worry about Christie ruining Sheriff Wyatt's investigation; the girl couldn't hold a thought long enough to repeat it to anyone. Nobody paid any attention to what came out of her mouth in any case.

"Who else is a victim?" Christie sounded completely clueless.

"Think about it," Kate prompted. Sometimes she had to lay breadcrumbs all the way to the front door before Christie found the house in the forest. "What other horrible thing has happened lately?"

Kate heard Christie's sharp intake of breath. "Oh, dear."

"We never had anything like this happen until that newspaper woman and her son moved here," Kate said. "She adopted that boy. You know what they say, blood always tells."

"Oooh." Christie paused. "Somebody should do something. Did you tell the police?"

"They know. I just want you to take care of you and yours until this is all done. We don't want to lose anyone else while the police dillydally around."

"Don't you worry. I'll make sure to keep a close eye on Melinda Sue."

"You do that."

"You'd think a woman with a kid like that would lay low and not stir up all this nonsense about drug use around here." Christie made the most astute statement Kate had ever heard come out of her mouth.

"Maybe she's using all that hoo-ha to keep everyone looking the other direction," Kate suggested.

"I reckon it's possible. People like that shouldn't be allowed to live around decent folks—should stay up in the city with their own kind."

"We just have to make sure they don't get away with it...." That's when Kate realized there was more than one way to skin a cat.

* * *

ETHAN THREW HIMSELF ON HIS BED. He looked at the history book sitting on his nightstand. What was the point?

He shoved the book off the table and onto the floor, then rolled onto his side.

Life had been so much simpler when he didn't give a shit. Before he'd met M, he couldn't remember the last time he'd cared—about anyone, even himself. His life had been reduced to what his science teacher called "basic instincts," which boiled down to staying alive. After finding M, he realized staying alive wasn't enough. He wanted more.

And he almost had it.

Now everything was going to shit. It had been better when he hadn't known the difference.

Rolling onto his back, he laid his arm over his eyes. He ignored the wetness he felt there.

The image of Mr. McP dead on the ground was always there when he closed his eyes. It had begun to fade, the brilliant colors of blood and bone against emerald green ferns paling. But tonight it had come back in all its bloody glory.

It had not been Ethan's first encounter with death. He'd had two others—not that he'd be telling anyone that little detail. Shit, people looked at him like he was a murderer already.

If he was smart, he'd split. It would be better for M. She didn't deserve to have this crap happen to her just because of him. She and Sheriff Dude had been all quiet about the details of what caused her wreck; a rock had "fallen" off that overpass at just the moment she'd been driving under it. Yeah, sure. Ethan wasn't stupid. Someone had waited for her and thrown it. People hated him, and now they hated her.

He rubbed his eyes furiously to scrub away Mr. McP. Then he wished he hadn't. Although the image of Mr. McP's bloody head was gone, another had taken its place—one from long ago.

He'd come home from fifth grade and found his mom, her face blue-white, her body cold, her dark hair matted and uncombed, with a needle still in her arm.

It was different than with Mr. McP. Because when his mom died, in addition to the shock and sadness, he remembered feeling—relieved. That feeling shamed him. He rarely admitted it to himself. But it was true; something he'd been bracing himself for had finally happened.

For as long as he could remember, on the days he'd been brave enough to come home after school, he'd stopped with his hand on the doorknob to their apartment. He had taken a deep breath, which in the hallway of their apartment building was hazardous in itself, and wondered if that was the day he would find her dead, or doing some dude for drugs, or just...gone. He supposed dead was better than gone in some ways. He hadn't had to wonder if she was coming back.

If something happened to M, it would be so much worse. There would be no relief, only guilt. With M, he hadn't had to take the few scraps of good along with the boatload of bad. With M, it was good. Period. Even when she pissed him off.

Had he read too much into that weird phone call? Had it just been some kids screwing around?

He wanted to think so. But shit, that line about Mommy had nearly given him a heart attack.

He never should have allowed himself to hope that his life was going to be like a normal kid's. He should never have gone on that camping trip.

GABE WAS MORE THAN INTERESTED in hearing about McPherson's first wife. Checking into McPherson's life in Michigan was his first priority tomorrow morning. This would give him a leg up. He pushed his plate away and settled his forearms on the table. Dishes could wait.

"What did you find out?" he asked Maddie.

"After you said that McPherson didn't like to talk about his first wife's death, it made me wonder why. I mean, grief is understandable. But to have lived here all these years and remarried even, it seemed odd that nobody knew exactly what had happened to her. Most everyone I spoke to assumed as you did, that she'd had cancer or something.

"But that isn't the case. She died after falling down the stairs—at home. *Supposedly* alone. Todd came home from baseball practice and found her. He was only ten."

Gabe kept his response neutral. "Damn. Poor kid. No wonder he's so protective of Kate."

She looked at him as if he was missing the point. "Don't you find it significant that a man who we suspect was knocking his stepson around had a wife who died like that?"

The point hadn't been lost on him. But he was having a difficult time not discussing with Maddie more than he should about this case. He couldn't deny he was personally invested in her. Plus, she was intelligent and had an investigative mind; she could help him think things through. But she was also involved on a level that precluded such conversations. It was a hell of a line to straddle.

He said, "I'll contact the authorities in Ann Arbor and see what the investigation revealed. I can't imagine it'll be enough to confirm abuse... I mean, the guy wasn't charged."

"You're right, he wasn't. But maybe they had suspicions without enough evidence for a case." She cast him a piqued look. "Did *you* do any checking into his background after we talked?"

Her question rankled. "I wasn't aware I was required to report to you about every step of *my* investigation."

Maddie's offended gaze shifted away from him and she sat up straighter in her chair.

He doubted she'd want to hear what Jacob Roberts had had to say. What if her theory about Steve's abuse turned out to be true, but led to another scenario altogether about the last moments of his life?

She wanted the truth, but only the parts that worked to clear Ethan of suspicion.

And things were not stacking up in Ethan's favor at the moment.

Madison wasn't going to want to hear that there were kids who'd reported to the school counselor that they'd witnessed Ethan threatening Colin Arbuckle in the hall at school the day before he died—because Colin was mouthing off about knowing what went down on the mountain. She wasn't going to want to hear the stories of Ethan naming himself Jordan Gray's personal protector. And she sure as hell wasn't going to want to hear Kate's latest accusation.

Hell, he hadn't wanted to hear any of those things either. But there they were.

He was desperate to unravel this and find that all of those things had been products of coincidence and gossip.

Because if he didn't, he wasn't going to have any choice but to share all of those facts with the DA—who'd begun making daily calls to check on Gabe's progress. So far he'd avoided laying out what he'd discovered using the excuse of waiting for lab results, hoping to buy enough time to come up with a more likely suspect. But Forrest County wasn't a place accustomed to murder and unexplained deaths and everybody was getting edgy.

God, Gabe didn't want *any* of this to be happening.

"Maddie, I can't make the fact that Ethan is still a person of interest in this case go away. As much as I'd like to, I can't do it."

Maddie sat in rigid silence. Her gaze was fixed on the remnants of the scrambled eggs drying on her plate. She clenched her hands in her lap and her mouth was pinched with anger. The sound of her ragged breathing filled the room.

"As long as I've already pissed you off," he finally said, "I have a couple of questions for you."

Her jaw was tight as she turned to look at him. "Of course my son and I will cooperate fully with *your* investigation." Her tone was cold and formal.

"Damn it, Maddie, you're making this harder than it has to be." He wished they were back to the point where the only thing standing between them was her belief that she had to choose between being a woman and being a responsible mother.

She glared at him. "Your questions?"

"Did you and Ethan go see Jordan yesterday?"

"Yes."

"Were you with them the entire visit? Was there a time when they were alone together?"

She rubbed the side of her neck—a sure sign that she didn't want to answer. If she did that in front of the district attorney, she was sunk. That man could read tells better than any police interrogator Gabe had ever run across.

"Why?" she asked. "What difference does it make?"

He nailed her with his gaze.

She raised her chin. "I was there."

Gabe would have been relieved if he hadn't heard the instant of hesitation in her voice or seen the flash of indecision in her eyes.

He stood and picked up their dirty plates. "All right, ma'am. Thank you for your cooperation. I'll be finishing my chore, then get on my way." He gave her a dose of her own medicine, sounding just as stiff and standoffish as she had.

He set the plates down so hard on the kitchen counter that the silverware resting on them clattered.

Lord Almighty, this woman ignited his passion and challenged his patience. Everything about her provoked extremes.

He turned on the water and the garbage disposal, then scraped the plates, making more racket than necessary.

He was so hot under the collar that he could snatch her up out of that chair and shake her. Didn't she know he was trying to help her? Hiding things from him—his thoughts stumbled right there.

If she revealed things to him that might be damaging to her son, he wouldn't be able to ignore them; he'd already told her as much. He couldn't expect her to confide in him as a friend and a partner in solving this mystery if he was going to act like an officer of the law. He couldn't have it both ways any more than she could; there was no separating the job from the man, or the mother from the woman.

When he turned around after putting the plates in the dishwasher, she was sitting right where she'd been when he'd left the table. Her back was to him, but the rigidity had left her shoulders; her posture told him just how exhausted she was.

What kind of bastard was he? The woman had had a rock thrown through her windshield, driven off the road, and been trapped in her car in the dark for hours. This heaped upon all the rest of the recent trauma and public speculation.

He stepped behind her and put his hands lightly on her shoulders. "I'll call you after I check out the railroad overpass tomorrow; let you know if I find anything."

She didn't say anything, but nodded once.

"Can I do anything for you before I leave?" Although they were beyond taking a giant step backward to those moments after he'd helped her out of that ravine, he tried to convey his regret for the loss with his voice and platonic touch.

She kept her face forward as she took her left hand and patted his where it rested on her right shoulder. "Thank you for rescuing me."

They were both torn, bloodied, and wounded. It seemed best to leave it there.

He gave the same response he'd given her several times before. "My pleasure."

Then he left. As he got in his Jeep, he looked back at the house. Ethan was silhouetted against his upstairs bedroom window, watching him leave.

Chapter 21

GABE'S CELL PHONE RANG EARLY the next morning while he was on his way to check out the railroad overpass. He was still in a funk from a sleepless night spent digging up details he wished he hadn't—details that painted an entirely new picture of Ethan Wade. Sluggish as he was, he answered his phone without checking caller ID.

"Hey, little brother."

"Hey, Grant," Gabe said. Why hadn't he checked before he answered? "Before you start ragging my ass, I already did the Chamber of Commerce thing." Grant was their father's campaign manager, a job he took very seriously—unlike his slacker little brother.

"Good. That's not why I'm calling."

"Oh?" Grant never called for idle chitchat.

"I want to know what the hell is going on over there. Can't make it a freakin' week without hitting the news? Christ, you're killing Dad's 'Safety in Our Cities' platform."

Gabe's jaw tensed. He'd been interviewed once by the local TV news, but had been too busy investigating deaths to actually catch a broadcast. Who knew what kind of picture they were painting? "Buckeye isn't a city."

"Exactly. If you can't keep your sleepy little town clean, what does that say about places with big problems?"

"You think I'm having people offed in my county just to upset the campaign?"

Grant took on his big-brother stop-being-so-damn-preposterous tone when he said, "All I want is for you to tell me you're getting close to an arrest."

"I could tell you anything you want to hear. But that won't change the fact that it's still early in the investigation."

"Damn it, don't give me that public statement bullshit. How many goddamn suspects can you have in that backwoods county?"

"Just because my haystack is smaller than most doesn't make it any easier to find the needle. Did Dad ask you to call?" It wasn't like his dad to initiate this kind of pressure tactic, but since he was slipping in the polls he might be feeling desperate.

"You want me to push the state lab for results? I have a few friends there." The fact that Grant ignored Gabe's last question answered it; Dad had no idea.

"I've got it covered, thank you. Even us hicks know how to use a phone and a little finesse."

Grant ignored his comment. "I'm hearing it's some crazy kid from up north."

Jesus. Gabe closed his eyes for a second and pressed his lips together to keep from yelling the curses that shot through his mind. The last thing he needed to do was to tweak Grant's interest in the subject. If Grant put himself to the task, he'd discover the same thing about Ethan that Gabe had last night. Once it was out in the open, it would start a wildfire.

He said calmly, "And what *official* gave you that information?"

"I have my sources."

"I see. Since I'm heading up this investigation and have made no comment on persons of interest, let alone suspects, I can only imagine your 'sources'. If you and Dad begin judging people guilty based on gossip and public opinion, how's that going to look to the citizens of the great state of Tennessee?"

"Don't lay that crap on me. I'm the one watching Dad's back here. Get that mess cleaned up... and fast. I can only manage so much damage control."

Gabe ended the call.

Sometimes just hearing Grant's voice pissed him off. Sanctimonious, image-conscious bastard. Gabe had no doubt that Grant would sleep like a baby if Gabe arrested an innocent person, as long as it resulted in a positive media spin.

If what he'd discovered became common knowledge... Public opinion could indeed bury Ethan Wade, just as Maddie had feared—unless Gabe could zero in on another suspect, and soon.

He stopped his Jeep about a quarter of a mile from the railroad overpass. It was the closest safe place to leave a vehicle.

Before he got out and walked to the railroad, he called the lab and asked for Barbara, the one who had promised to have the prints from the beer cans processed by tomorrow. He'd already received a report on Colin's blood alcohol level. No surprise; it was three times the legal limit.

When Barbara got on the line, he said, "This is Sheriff Wyatt in Forrest County. I know you said Wednesday—"

"I was just about to call you. I stayed late last night and ran the tests."

Of course, this information wasn't going to do Gabe much good until he had prints to try to match. He would have to take Ethan's and J.D.'s—with the hope that at the very least, he could clear them both of being the one who gave Colin the beer.

Barbara continued, "You're not going to believe this."

"Oh?"

"There were only one person's prints on *all* of those cans—the victim, Colin Arbuckle."

"You mean only one clear set—"

"No, Sheriff, I mean only one set. Not a trace of any other person's prints. And with the plastic six-pack loops still on some of the cans, we know they didn't come out of a box."

"That is interesting." The only way for that to be possible was if they'd been specifically wiped clean before Colin held them. Stockers, sales clerks, somebody had to have touched those cans before Colin Arbuckle drank them. "Do all of the cans have prints?"

"Yes. All the victim's. I'll fax this report to you."

"Thanks for the rush job, Barbara."

"No problem."

Gabe put his phone away and sat there for a minute, massaging his aching eyes with his thumb and forefinger. Whoever had purchased that beer for Colin must have had some idea that there would be a reason for the cans to be tested.

Which meant someone had known Colin was going to die.

AS GABE WALKED TO THE RAIL OVERPASS, he mulled over possibilities. He didn't like where the trail in these deaths, meager and circumstantial as it was, was leading. It was nearly impossible to consider Colin Arbuckle's death wasn't in some way connected to Steve McPherson's.

There was no way around it. Gabe was going to have to send the hat and button he'd picked up on the bridge to the forensics lab. Again, meager and circumstantial. Yet those small pieces of circumstantial evidence were growing into a substantial collection.

Had Colin Arbuckle seen what happened to McPherson? Had he witnessed a murder, then kept his mouth closed about it?

Gabe had trouble believing that was the case. There had been nothing in Colin's initial interview that gave Gabe the slightest vibe of anything except the truth. Plus, his facts were in complete agreement with J.D.'s story. Neither boy had acted as if they'd been threatened or were in any way afraid.

If Colin had kept what he'd witnessed secret for the first four days, due to threats or some other unknown reason, why would he have started making such a public statement and *not* informed the police or his parents—people who could protect him?

It didn't make sense. Gabe had discovered that Colin liked to be the center of attention. Had his mouthing off been nothing but bluster? Had that fabrication drawn a killer down on him?

As Gabe reviewed what J.D. had told him after Colin's

death, one thing stood out: Colin had called J.D. to go out there with him on Friday night, had specifically said J.D. had been "invited" by whoever got the beer.

Were all of the boys targets?

Right now, the idea of Ethan being a target held slightly more appeal than the alternative.

He quickened his pace. He wanted to get finished here and go talk to J.D. again.

The only things Gabe found on the rail overpass were old broken bottles and several cigarette butts. When he laid eyes on the first one, he felt a little thrill of excitement; it was a Marlboro, just like those near where McPherson was killed. Good news: They were just like the ones on Bobby Gray's desk. Bad news: They were just like those in Ethan's jacket.

As he looked further, he found butts from several other brands.

He bagged them all, useless as they were likely to be.

Just as he was climbing down from the overpass, he heard the approach of the grinding diesel of Whetzel's tow truck. Gabe met the man as he climbed down out of the vehicle.

After the good mornings, Gabe said, "There's a big rock in the backseat. Just leave it where it is and don't touch it."

"Don't touch things inside people's cars." Earl shifted the toothpick from one side of his mouth to the other, took off his ball cap, and scratched his mostly bald head. He raised a questioning brow. "Mischief makers?"

"Most likely."

"The lady must be hittin' some raw nerves." Earl walked over to the winch and started to unwind the cable.

"You hearing things you want to share?"

"Nothin' that you prob'ly ain't heard yourself. General talk 'bout folks bein' unhappy that she comes in here and starts criticizing the way we raise our young'uns." He paused and looked at Gabe. "That flat of hers wasn't no accident."

Gabe nodded, then looked at the passenger side of the truck and saw it was empty. "You come alone?"

"Bruce called in sick."

"Here." Gabe wasn't about to let the old guy climb down that steep decline. He reluctantly took the cable hook and started down the ravine.

Questioning J.D. would have to wait.

WHEN GABE PULLED UP at the high school to have his chat with J.D., Madison was getting out of a white Taurus with a green Enterprise Rent-a-Car sticker on the rear bumper.

He parked his department SUV in the emergency lane at the curb and walked toward her as she got out. It took only one glance to see she was furious, even through the purple bruise that covered most of the left side of her face.

She stalked toward him. "Why didn't you tell me that Jordan tried to kill himself?" Before he could open his mouth, she cut him off. "I already know you knew before we talked last night."

"I wasn't going to deny it." In their circumstances, he figured the occasional lie of omission was to be expected. But it stung that she thought he'd lie outright to her. He held her gaze, refusing to say more.

"You really do piss me off!" she said with a clenched fist. "You tried to trick me into incriminating my own son. You aren't even looking at anyone but Ethan for any of this, are you?" She took a step closer and poked him in the chest with her index finger. "There's a killer out there. He's going after all of these boys...*including* my son, and you're not looking for him!"

He raised his palms. "Slow down. First of all, what makes you believe Colin was murdered? It appears to have been an accident." For all anyone but him knew, at least. "And as far as I can tell, the only person who sees a villain in Jordan's suicide attempt is Kate."

"Come on! Colin. Jordan. J.D.'s afraid to leave his house. And Ethan got a threatening phone call while I was in that ravine—that's why he panicked and left the house last night." Her mouth tightened. "And sometime last night, someone trashed Ethan's locker—including putting photos of Colin and Jordan with red Xs across them in it."

"Is that why you're here?"

"Yes. The city police have already been here and gone. I'm taking Ethan home."

"How do you know J.D.'s afraid to leave his house?" Even as he played devil's advocate, his skin tingled with apprehension.

"The principal told me when she called about Ethan's locker." Her gaze was accusing when she added, "*She* obviously thinks there's reason for concern."

His fuse finally ignited. He took her roughly by the arm and marched her to the passenger side of his Jeep. "Get in. We need to talk."

For a long moment, she stood there, defiance in her eyes.

"I'm breaking my own rules here," he said curtly. "Get. In." He yanked the door open.

There was no resignation in her face as she climbed in the car. She slammed the door shut before he could close it.

By the time he was in the driver's seat, he'd regained some of his composure. He said, "Tell me about this threatening phone call Ethan received."

After taking a deep breath and exhaling loudly, she said, "It was a little past nine o'clock. First there was silence, just an open line. Then some creepy music started to play. Ethan said it was from some horror movie that was out last summer on DVD."

"Did anyone ever say anything?" Creepy music hardly qualified as a threatening phone call.

She shook her head. He noticed she was gentle about it and he wondered how much pain she was in. After the wild ride she'd had last night, she had to be sore. He felt like a heel for manhandling her toward his car.

"Nothing at all?" he prompted.

"No one on the phone said anything. But Ethan said the dialogue from the movie said, 'Your mommy can't save you now,' or something like that. That's why he freaked out. He thought someone had done something to hurt me."

"Someone had. Someone had thrown a rock big enough to kill you through your windshield. You're pissing people off with your articles."

"You think that phone call was related to my hate mail and not anything going on with the boys?" She looked at him as if it hadn't occurred to her as a possibility before now.

"Most likely. The implied threat was to Mommy, not to Ethan."

"But it said Mommy couldn't *save* him. I think it was a threat against Ethan. And with what happened to his locker—"

"Why did you lie to me?" he interrupted. He wanted to get this all out in the open now, before she started down the trail of Ethan being a victim.

The look on her face seemed to ask, *Which time?*

For a woman who proclaimed to be all about frankness, she was turning out to be a contradiction of deceit. He clarified, "When I asked you if there was anything in Ethan's past that could come out and bite him on the ass, you said no."

She rolled her lips inward as if measuring her response before she said, "I didn't exactly say no. I believe I deflected the question."

Recalling her exact words, *You mean other than having been poor and homeless and from up north? Not the pillar of the community that Steve McPherson the child beater was?* he supposed she was technically right. He'd taken the leap and considered it a negative response.

"Is that the way you want to play this? Semantics and vagaries?" His temper was flaring again.

She faced him. "I don't want to play this at all."

"Too bad."

"You can't drag in things that happened years ago to build your case. You have no proof that Ethan has done anything, other than being at the wrong place at the wrong time."

"I have enough to get a warrant," he said coldly. He wanted her to know how deadly serious this was. In reality, if the suspect had been anyone except Ethan, he probably would have taken this to the DA already.

She paled. Even her bruise faded in color.

He said, "You should have told me he'd been questioned in a murder case before." Of the things he'd discovered about Ethan in last night's research, that was the most damning.

"Why? So you could do what you're doing now and judge him solely on that?"

"So I could have prepared. What if I wasn't the one who uncovered this first? It'll look really bad for Ethan if it crawls out on its own. You couple the previous murder investigation with the fact that his father is in prison for manslaughter...."

Her gaze snapped up.

"Yes, I found that out, too. And don't say it never crossed your mind to tell me. I asked specifically about his biological father when we were discussing Ethan's adoption."

"His father was *never* a part of Ethan's life, so guilt by association can't even apply. And if you read about the murder investigation, you know Ethan wasn't charged, simply questioned. He was detained because he had no home and no guardian."

"Yes, but that case was never solved. Which means the killer is out there walking around free. It could be Ethan as easily as anyone else in that investigation."

She looked as if he'd slapped her.

"I'm stating the reasons why this is a problem for Ethan, not what I believe," he said. He just wished he knew exactly what *to* believe. Had he been blinded by his admiration for Maddie and not seen the boy for what he was?

Her anger bubbled in every word when she said, "That

murder wasn't solved because the victim was a homeless old man, murdered in the middle of winter for his shelter, blankets, and food. Nobody cares about people like him. The police did a cursory investigation then filed it away in the cold case room. Ethan was eleven years old, for God's sake. Feel free to question him about it yourself."

"I will. And stop looking at me like that. I'm only trying to cover all of the angles, because believe me, things are not looking good for him at the moment." He paused. "Here's the part where I'm breaking my own rules. I should never discuss a case with someone associated with a suspect, but I want you to be prepared. There may come a time when it's out of my hands. The DA is already getting pushy. If he knew half of what I know, you can bet there'd be a warrant for Ethan tomorrow."

"Why Ethan?" she asked. "Why not J.D.? He was the one with Colin on the mountain during the murder. It makes more sense that J.D. killed McPherson than Ethan, especially with Colin's death."

"J.D. didn't threaten Colin in the hallway at school the day before he died. And I didn't find J.D.'s cap on that bridge."

"Ethan and I both told you his cap didn't come home with the rest of his stuff. Maybe J.D. had it. Maybe he planted it to make it look like Ethan was the one. What kind of threats are you talking about?"

"Kids said Colin was telling them that he knew what happened on the mountain, he knew how McPherson died. Ethan came up and slammed his fist against the locker right next to Colin's head."

"That's all?" Was Gabe mistaken, or did she sound relieved?

He said, "In the circumstances it's enough to raise suspicions—especially when you compound it with the laundry list of other things. Besides, J.D. was sick that night."

"So was Ethan. And if you think Ethan could muster up the energy to go throw Colin off a bridge while he was sick, why not J.D.? All you have is J.D.'s word. Christ Almighty, his brother's in prison for beating a woman. That sounds a lot more incriminating than Ethan's father being in jail—a father whom he hasn't seen in fourteen years.

"Listen," she went on, "I'm almost certain J.D.'s brother used steroids, which can cause mood swings and violent behavior. That could account for the assault on Shelly. Look at J.D.'s size. He plays football; maybe he's using them, too."

He didn't want to dismiss that theory out of hand. In fact, everything she'd said about J.D. being a probable suspect had grounds. But he also didn't want to let her shift the focus of this discussion. *Maybe because you're more upset that she kept this from you than you are concerned about the case?*

She pressed on. "My point is, J.D. makes as likely a suspect as Ethan.

"*Ethan's* locker was trashed. Whoever did it was making it clear that Colin and Jordan were his victims—that Ethan was next. Why couldn't it be J.D.? Who, by the way, hasn't seemed to have received a threat and is lying low at home."

Gabe sat in silence for a few minutes. Why *hadn't* he looked harder at J.D.?

The answer came fast and clear. Because his gut told him J.D. was telling the truth. In his heart, he believed that Colin Arbuckle had told the truth, too. He believed neither of those boys saw what happened on that mountain. Not to mention the most obvious and investigation-sound reason; lack of motive.

But Ethan had held back; he'd kept most of his story to himself until he *needed* it. And his motive could be found in his protective attitude toward Jordan, and his suspicion that McPherson was abusing his stepson.

They sat in silence for a few moments. Then Maddie sighed. "I think someone we haven't considered killed McPherson for reasons we don't yet know. Someone who is getting nervous that he didn't get away as cleanly as he'd first thought, and now is tying up those loose ends."

"You think someone climbed that mountain to beat the man to death?"

"The murderer assumed it would be viewed as an accident. If that didn't fly, he assumed no one would consider anyone other than the four boys who were with McPherson."

Maddie had just echoed one of his own possible theories, one that he hadn't found a scrap of evidence to support. He reminded himself that she had also been the one who tried to direct Gabe's attention toward Jordan's being the killer. Was she grasping any straw that pointed away from Ethan?

After a moment, he asked, "Does Ethan have any Diesel-brand clothing?" Gabe asked.

The distrust in her eyes nearly pierced his heart. "Why?" she asked.

"It's a simple question, Maddie." Had he asked it for the right reasons? He'd as much as given her fair warning to get rid of it if Ethan did have any.

"No. He's not into brand stuff. He's just thankful to have clean clothes," she said sharply.

"There are kids who notice and care about that kind of stuff," he said. "Kids who remember what everyone else wears."

"Listen to me." She shifted to look squarely at him. "I'm not so stupid as to lie about something like that. If I hadn't wanted to answer, I wouldn't have. I'm trying to cooperate with you and all I get is a raft of shit. Maybe I should take the safe route and have Ethan and me speak to you only with an attorney present."

He felt a fraction of satisfaction in the hurt he saw in her eyes; it was just a little bit emotionally satisfying to know his distrust hurt her as much as hers had cut him.

"That's your right," he said. "But if I was trying to trap either you or your son into an incriminating statement, I wouldn't have laid my cards on the table like this. I'm doing this because I care about you."

"But you don't believe Ethan is innocent." Her voice was cold enough to frost his ears.

It slashed him to the bone that his confession went unheard. God, he did care about her. More than he'd cared about a woman for a very long time. "I don't believe he's *guilty*." Could she see the difference? "But I have to follow *wherever* the evidence leads."

"It won't be to my son. Good God, why would he have killed Steve McPherson? He barely knew the man!"

"I think you've already answered that, back when you were supposing it may have been Jordan acting in self-defense." Shit, talk about blowing your own case.

Unwelcome realization dawned on her face. "You think

Ethan killed McPherson because he thought the man was knocking Jordan around?"

"I don't have a solid suspect at the moment. But that is a theory I can't dismiss. Colin and J.D. said McPherson left camp angry because the boys weren't back yet. Hell, maybe McPherson went after Ethan, too, if he tried to step in and protect Jordan."

"If Ethan was that protective of Jordan, it blows your theory that he tried to kill the kid with sedatives, wouldn't you say?"

"I think Jordan is a very troubled boy. Until there is a complete investigation into how he got the drugs, we can't say anything at all about that piece of the puzzle."

"Ethan had nothing to do with McPherson's death. The fact remains that the man was murdered. Out of the four boys on that mountain who could possibly have witnessed it, one has had a nervous breakdown and made a suicide attempt, one is dead, one is hiding, and my son is getting threats. I'm very worried that Ethan is this guy's next victim. It's scaring the crap out of me. Find the sonofabitch."

She opened the car door and got out before he could reply.

Chapter 22

MADISON SPOKE PRIVATELY with the principal before she went to the counselor's office to pick up Ethan. "I want to see his locker."

Mrs. Gibbons said, "There isn't much to see. The police took almost everything."

"I still want to see it."

"All right, then." The principal stood, looking only slightly resentful for Madison wasting the woman's time. "I'll take you."

As they walked down the hallway, their high heels clicking in unison, Mrs. Gibbons surprised Madison by saying, "Are you planning more articles on drug abuse?"

"Yes, I am," Madison said firmly. "Unpopular as the topic is around here at the moment, I still feel it needs to be addressed."

Mrs. Gibbons stopped and faced her. The woman was at least five inches shorter than Madison, but carried herself with an authority that commanded respect. "Good."

Madison tilted her head. "Good?"

"Yes. No matter what people say, educating yourself on these subjects can't do anything but have a positive effect. Knowledge is power, as they say."

"I'm glad to hear you feel that way. I think people's objections have more to do with the messenger than the message. If I had had one of the staff who is a long-time resident take on this topic, it might have been better received."

A small, knowing smile crossed the principal's face. "You're learning fast." She started walking again. "Here we are."

They stopped in front of a locker whose door had a sharp bend right at the latch. Pry marks marred the paint on the frame. Whoever broke in wasn't trying to be sly about it.

"You can just swing it open," Mrs. Gibbons said. "I've had Ethan remove his personal things and put his books in another locker. The police have the photographs and other articles that were left here."

Madison hesitated. "What other articles?"

A look of distaste crossed Mrs. Gibbons's face. "A dead rat. An empty beer can. A handful of some kind of pills. And a rock." The principal didn't seem to have any problem seeing the significance of these items.

Madison said, "Being an outsider in this town carries a heavy prejudice, wouldn't you say?"

For the first time, Mrs. Gibbons did not meet her eyes. Madison couldn't tell if it was because she agreed with the implications of the message, or if she was ashamed that her community was so shallow and quick to judge.

"Are there video surveillance cameras in and around the building?"

"We've never had the need for such a thing." There was just enough accusation in her voice that Madison decided to stop asking questions.

She took one finger and pulled open the locker with her breath held in her chest.

Mrs. Gibbons said, "As I said, the police took everything except Ethan's books."

The inside of the locker was empty. Madison realized her tension came from picturing the moment her son opened this door and discovered the hateful message. She released her breath, but not the anger welling inside as she closed the damaged door.

They returned to the office in silence. Ethan had come out to wait at the front counter with his backpack sitting at his feet.

Madison's heart squeezed tighter. He looked so defeated, so broken. "Ready to go?"

He nodded and hefted his backpack to his shoulder.

"Ms. Wade?" the principal said before they got out the door.

"Yes?"

"I think it'd be best to keep Ethan home for the next few days."

The "suggestion" was made in a tone that didn't reveal the reason for it. For Ethan's safety, or because she thought Ethan was a threat?

GABE PULLED UP OUTSIDE J.D. Henry's duplex and shut off the engine. He was waiting on hold for the ME to come to the phone. The sun was beating through the windshield; he opened the window and rested his elbow on the door.

From the moment Madison had gotten out of his Jeep this morning, her fury had eaten at his insides like acid. He was in one hell of a mess. Investigative logic led him down one path, while his gut diverted to another. And as much as he tried to be objective when he asked if that gut's instinct was being swayed by his heart, he wasn't coming up with an answer he wanted to acknowledge.

He was ignoring his obligations; his responsibility to the people of this county being only one. Family loyalty was another. What if Gabe's missteps blew the bottom out of his father's political boat? It was one thing to stand fast to his gut convictions if he was right. What if he was wrong? He could be taking his father down with him. And although he and his dad differed on many subjects, his father was the best choice for governor of this state.

There were questions Gabe had been avoiding asking himself. It was time to drag them out into the light.

Was Ethan much smarter and more devious than either Gabe or Maddie suspected? Gabe had studied plenty of cases where a psychopath blended right in, never once arousing suspicion of even those closest to him. How much did Maddie know about Ethan's early years, the ones that shape and mold the human psyche?

Because Ethan had managed to avoid child protective services, there would be no psych evaluations, no counselor's recommendations, no records. Maddie could only know what Ethan chose to divulge. If he'd been physically and emotionally abused himself, it could account for his heightened protective instincts for Jordan.

Damn it. If not for his feelings for Maddie, Gabe knew

full well who he'd have in his sights as his most likely suspect.

He pushed ahead along that path, making himself look at things as he would if he knew nothing except what he'd discovered since McPherson's death.

The key to the entire thing lay in the motive. Why would anyone kill Steve McPherson?

Considering Jordan's peculiar fears at home and the fact that McPherson's first wife's death was an unusual—and unwitnessed—accident, abuse could be a motive. As soon as he got to the office, he'd call Ann Arbor about the accident investigation.

If revenge or self-defense from abuse was the motive, did Jordan have the strength to carry out such a brutal beating?

Even if the answer to that question was undoubtedly yes, the kid had been locked up in the stress center since then. He couldn't have had anything to do with Colin's death.

Gabe forced himself to keep marching down that path. If Jordan couldn't have had anything to do with events this past week, it meant someone else had set Colin up for his "accident."

Did Ethan fear that Colin had actually seen the murder? Regardless if it had been Jordan or Ethan who committed the original act, Ethan could be the one cleaning up the mess.

As for the locker, Ethan could have trashed it himself in order to throw off suspicion. What better way in these circumstances than to hide behind the mask of a victim himself?

And what a perfect sign of a psychopath.

Had Ethan made up the phone threat? Or did he receive it and use disgruntled citizens taking issue with Maddie's public view of their community and twist it into his own defense?

Gabe hadn't asked if Ethan had received that call on his cell or the home phone. Gabe would have to find out, and confirm a call had been received at that time. If not, it would be clear Gabe had backed the wrong horse. If there was a call, perhaps it would lead him to whoever threw that rock through Maddie's windshield.

He'd have to go to the judge for a subpoena—which meant he had to tell the DA everything.

If Gabe was operating with a clear head, he wouldn't shy away from the prospect.

His fear boiled down to the worry that the DA would buckle to the pressures of public opinion (this was an election year), and take a case forward on less than solid grounds.

It was Gabe's job to investigate and present what he discovered to the DA—and it was pretty damn clear he wasn't doing his job.

Christ.

Blowing out a long exhalation, he ran a hand through his hair.

The phone line clicked. "I'm sorry to keep you waiting, Gabe," Dottie Zinn said. "What can I do for you?"

You can tell me there's no doubt that Colin fell off that bridge all by himself. "I was wondering what your preliminary findings on the Arbuckle boy are telling you."

"You already know he had enough alcohol in him that he couldn't tell up from down. Cause of death thus far appears to be a broken neck. It was instantaneous."

"Anything suspicious...defensive wounds and the like?"

"Nothing conclusive. The poor boy fell thirty feet and landed on a bed of rocks. He was wearing two sweatshirts and a T-shirt, lots of padding against possible defensive marks on the forearms. I was just going over his hands again when you called. I recovered some fibers from under the fingernails on his right hand. It's going to take a couple of weeks to get them processed."

Two weeks. If Maddie's theory was right, by then all four boys could be dead. If Kate's theory was right, at least three of them could be.

"No skin under the nails?" he asked. DNA would take weeks, but it might be the only near-conclusive thing they had in this case.

Would it exonerate Ethan, or incriminate him?

"Nothing I can detect visually. I've taken scrapings from all ten. Again, until the lab gets back to us, I don't have a thing for you to work with. Sorry."

"Use the age of the victim as leverage and see if you can get a rush on that lab work."

"Already placed the call," she said. "I'll let you know as soon as I have anything."

"Thanks, Dot."

"Oh, Gabe?" she said as he was about to disconnect.

"Yeah."

"You might want to know our young DA came scratching around here like the cock of the walk earlier today. He mentioned that he'd told Kate McPherson—who apparently has initiated a telephone campaign to put pressure on him—that he'd look personally into her husband's murder investigation. He expressed concern over our 'lack of progress' in the case. I set him right straight. *Lack of progress* . . . ," she said with a sneer in her voice. "We've managed to cut the wait time in a quarter for most of the stuff we've needed processed. I told him that if he'd had *experience* with murder cases, he would know that a week is a drop in the river. He didn't much like it. But he went away."

Gabe couldn't help but smile through his frustration. He'd loved to have been a fly on the wall when Dottie "set him right straight."

"Thanks for the warning." Again, Kate surprised him with her aggressive tactics. Apparently he'd underestimated the woman. He hung up and went to question J.D.

After knocking on the front door three different times and getting no response, Gabe walked around the outside of the duplex. All of the drapes were closed tight.

As he approached the back door, he stopped. Something black and about the size of a toss pillow was jammed just above the threshold between the screen door and the passage door.

He climbed the four steps to the back stoop.

Leaning close to the screen, at first he thought it was one of those fake fur pillows. Then he saw it was a black cat—a dead one.

A message left for J.D.? Maddie's theory of someone after all four boys took on more credence . . . unless Ethan had been the messenger. Gabe realized this new clue was just another question with no answer.

He left the screen closed and thumped on the door frame. "J.D.?" he yelled. "Mrs. Henry? It's Sheriff Wyatt."

The back door opened on the other half of the duplex. A stooped old woman with a deeply lined face peeked out. "They's long gone, honey."

Gabe went down the steps and stood at the base of the neighbor's steps. "Do you know where they went?"

"No, sir. I just heared lots of yellin' this mornin'—which ain't so uncommon, mind you. Today she wuz carryin' on somethin' 'bout her cat. Shortly after that, I seen her and the boy leave with suitcases." She drew her face into a disapproving frown. "It's a school day, too. That boy's gonna end up bad as t'other, way she's goin' 'bout raisin' him."

"Do you know what time they left?"

"Yes I do. It wuz during *The Price Is Right*."

Gabe could check the television listings if it became an issue. "Thank you, ma'am." He started to step away, then paused and asked one of the questions he'd come to ask J.D. "Um, do you happen to know if J.D. is a smoker?"

She blew a breath through her prune-like lips and waved an arthritic hand in front of her face. "Lordy, who could tell? That young'un always smelled like it. But could be from his momma. There's always so much smoke over there, it comes right through the wall. Shameful the way she's raisin' them boys."

After thanking her again, Gabe returned to his Jeep. He put on latex gloves and pulled out a fingerprint kit and a garbage bag, then went to retrieve the dead cat.

He wondered how Dot felt about working with animals.

Chapter 23

WHEN GABE RETURNED TO HIS OFFICE, it took four phone calls to track down the officer in charge of the investigation into the death of Cheryl McPherson in Ann Arbor ten years ago. Once Gabe identified himself and why he was interested in the case, Detective Fiore (now Captain Fiore) couldn't talk fast enough.

"That case has nagged me every day for ten years. I was never completely convinced that Cheryl McPherson's death was an accident. But you know how it is when there just isn't enough evidence to back up your gut instinct."

Gabe almost admitted that he was dealing with that problem for the first time; gut saying one thing, evidence another. Instead he asked, "So what exactly was your gut telling you?"

"No doubt she died from a fall, but I think she had help falling down those stairs. Maybe they were in a tussle resulting from an argument; maybe it wasn't intentional. Or maybe he just came up behind her and gave her a huge shove. Whatever, it appeared she took a flying leap over the first steps. The signs of her fall began at the sixth step. And those treads were hardwood, not carpeted."

"When you say 'he,' I assume you mean her husband, Steve?"

"Yeah. Couple of the neighbors suspected something wasn't right in that house. Of course, they couldn't testify to anything specific, just that Cheryl seemed nervous, edgy—a couple even went so far as to say she seemed frightened."

"And this was a deviation from her normal behavior?"

"According to everyone I interviewed, including her own family. Still, no one had witnessed anything that could identify why. Everyone insisted that Steve was such a great guy that the idea of abuse was ludicrous. You know as well as I do, more times than not that's exactly the way it plays out."

"Any indications of either partner having extramarital affairs?"

"Not one. If either of them had, they were extraordinarily careful about it. Mr. McPherson said his wife had been depressed in the months before the accident, even went so far as to suggest she might have thrown herself down those stairs."

"Hmm. Insurance policy?" Gabe asked.

"No. Not even a small one to cover burial costs. If there had been a sizable policy, I might have had something to base a case on."

"Steve McPherson take a polygraph?"

"Yeah. Volunteered even. It was inconclusive. His alibi was weak, but he did have one, at least during the most likely time of death. He was at the bank applying for a loan. Seems they were switching the boy from public to private school the following fall."

"Really? They have a reason?"

"It wasn't all that unusual. Lots of folks were switching to church-based education right around then...you know, school shootings and all were making parents nervous."

Captain Fiore went on. "After the bank, McPherson went to lunch and then to work. There was plenty of slop in the timeline, but with nothing else to go on..."

Gabe had been hoping for more than the same problems he was having with his own case. He took one last stab.

"Any forensic evidence worth running again?" There had been huge strides in DNA processing over the past ten years.

"No. Nothing under the victim's nails. No signs of assault at all. Everything pointed to an accidental fall."

"Except your gut."

"And that ain't admissible in court," Fiore said dryly.

Gabe thanked the captain and hung up. For several minutes he sat there staring at the wall, fearing that ten years from now *he* was going to still be gnawing on *this* case.

Then he got up and headed out to pay Bobby Gray an overdue call.

SHELLY MITTHOEFFER STOOD BEHIND THE COUNTER at the video store and watched him watch her. She knew he had no reason to be here now. But it was just like it had been every day for nearly two weeks; he was here just to let her know he was watching.

He'd become more aggressive about it since the day

she'd talked to the newspaper lady. It hadn't mattered at all that she'd blown the woman off.

Shelly was beginning to understand how those people in Nazi Germany felt.

He stared at her over the rack of videos as he talked to another customer. Even though the cold look he gave her made her insides turn liquid and her knees want to buckle, she stood tall and held his gaze.

She always made a show of not being afraid of him. But she was. Deathly afraid. There was something deep inside warning her not to let him see that fear. He was the kind to pounce on any weakness and use it in whatever way he felt necessary to get what he wanted.

He didn't stay long. He didn't check out a movie.

As he left he smiled and gave her a cheery wave. "Y'all have a great day."

She smiled in return, holding back the bile climbing in her throat.

GABE KNEW HE SHOULD HAVE CALLED FIRST. Not that the Gray Insurance office was that far from his own. But right now he didn't have time to waste and Bobby wasn't at his desk.

The lovely gray-haired receptionist told Gabe that if he'd like to wait, young Mr. Gray was due back shortly.

Gabe shifted his gaze for a second, deciding. Brooks glared at him from where he sat talking on the phone at his desk. If looks could kill... He decided not to wait.

As he turned to leave, he heard someone coming up the creaky staircase. Sticking his head around the corner, he saw it was Bobby—who didn't look any more pleased to see Gabe than Brooks had.

Gabe gave Bobby the gift of not having this conversation in front of his secretary... and himself the benefit of not having to do this in front of Bobby's overprotective brother.

Gabe stood at the top of the stairs and asked, "You have time for a cup of coffee?"

Bobby glanced at his watch. "A quick one. I have an appointment in an hour."

"I promise not to take long."

Bobby did an about-face on the stairs. He held the door that opened onto the sidewalk open for Gabe to follow him out. He gestured down the block and said, "Smoky Ridge?"

"Sure."

As they walked, Bobby asked, "You find out anything from Pleasant Hill yet about their investigation into Jordan getting those pills?"

"I'm working on it. These things take time. Institutions like Pleasant Hill don't like bad publicity."

"You *really think* Jordan got those pills himself and took them?" There was a fresh edge to Bobby's tone.

"It's a possibility that we can't dismiss."

"He wouldn't do that. No way," Bobby said adamantly. "*Someone* forced him."

"I know it's hard to look at the possibility, but Jordan is suffering from incredibly difficult circumstances. We can't know for certain what happened until he tells us. Is he anywhere close to being able to do that?"

Bobby put his hands in the pockets of his slacks and looked at the sidewalk beneath his feet. "The doctor said he's making progress, but he wouldn't discuss specifics over the phone. We have an appointment with him tomorrow, before we see Jordan. We're allowed to visit Sundays and Wednesdays now."

"That's a good sign—the increased visitation, isn't it?"

"Maybe. The doctor seemed to think more contact would be better for him. Kate said Todd's started sending Jordan a card every day."

Bobby stopped in front of the café and opened the door for Gabe. He confided, "That kid really rubs me the wrong way, but I gotta give him credit for trying to help Jordan."

They took a seat at a booth near the back and ordered coffee.

Bobby leaned back and crossed his arms. "You checked into the Wade kid any more since we talked?" He seemed less agitated about Ethan than he had when he'd been in Gabe's office with Kate. It made Gabe wonder who was the instigator of that visit.

"I'm checking into several things at the moment," Gabe said evasively. "That's why I have more questions to ask you. Keep in mind, I'm simply looking for several missing puzzle pieces."

Bobby gave a nod. "All right."

"What do you know about McPherson's first wife?"

"Only that she died when Todd was in grade school."

"Any idea how?"

The waitress delivered their coffee. Bobby waited until she was gone to answer. He looked puzzled himself. "I guess I don't. I always got the impression she had cancer or something. She would have been pretty young."

"How would you describe Steve's relationship with Jordan?"

Bobby's eyes narrowed. "Why?"

"Puzzle pieces."

Bobby lifted a shoulder. "I suppose they got along okay. He always wanted Jordan to be like Todd...like him. Those camping trips were a prime example." His hands wrapped around the coffee mug. The knuckles of his right hand were scraped and there were a couple of razorlike slices on the tips of his fingers.

Gabe wondered if perhaps the injury could be from prying open a metal locker—or hefting a rock off a railroad overpass. Bobby was a long way from being knocked off Gabe's suspect list.

"You would never have taken Jordan camping?" Gabe asked in a casual tone.

Bobby blew out a dismissive breath. "I'm not like Steve the Mountain Man and his son. I go huntin' with my dad and brother, but it's just for the company. I probably couldn't find my way back home without them." He went on, "McPherson pushed too hard, tried to make something out of Jordan that he isn't." He raised his gaze to meet Gabe's. "I'll admit it right here and now that I didn't like it. If that puts me on your suspect list, even though I was hunting at the time, so be it."

He seemed to be waiting for Gabe to tell him he wasn't on that list. When Gabe remained silent, Bobby said, "The best way to describe how Jordan seemed around Steve is intimidated."

"Intimidated?"

"You know, uneasy, afraid to disappoint, maybe a little scared even. Jordan is a quiet kid. He never wants to talk about much of anything—let alone the particulars of his home life with Kate and Steve. It was all reading between the lines, you know? Steve was a big dude; I don't think he realized how he came across to a kid like Jordan."

Gabe took a sip of coffee and thought Bobby was weighing his words very carefully. Unwilling to speak ill of the dead? Or for some more self-serving reason?

"How'd you hurt your hand?" Gabe asked offhandedly, motioning to the scraped knuckles.

Bobby glanced at his hand, then tucked it in his lap. "Working on that old motorcycle I bought last spring— you know, the one that sat out in front of Whetzel's for nearly a year with a FOR SALE sign on it." He shook his head. "I might never get that thing finished and on the road."

"You were working on it last night?"

"Yeah."

"When?"

Bobby's brow creased. "I dunno. I went out to the garage right after work…a little before six, I suppose. Came in and ate a bowl of cereal and took a shower around ten."

"You were in your garage between six-thirty and eight then?"

"Yeah."

"Alone?"

"Yeah. What's this about? What do you think I did now?"

"Just gathering puzzle pieces, remember?"

"I don't understand where I fit into this puzzle."

"Neither do I." Gabe got up and left a five on the table.

Chapter 24

Bobby sat next to Kate in Pleasant Hill's lobby, nervously waiting for their appointment with Dr. Brinegar.

"I wish they'd shut off those damn fountains," he said quietly.

"I think they're supposed to be restful," Kate offered.

"All that splattering is getting on my nerves. We'd probably have to pay a lot less for this place if they cut out some of the bullshit."

Kate's admonishing glare cut his way. "It's always about the money with you—"

The receptionist called them before she could finish. Just as well, Bobby thought, they didn't need to get into that old argument right now.

He followed Kate into the small, well-appointed conference room.

Dr. Brinegar was already seated at the table, alongside Vanessa, Jordan's counselor. There were several manila folders on the table in front of them. They both stood and shook both Bobby's and Kate's hands before being seated again.

Dr. Brinegar said, "I've asked Vanessa to be here with us because she's the person who has spent the most time with Jordan. I hope you don't mind."

Bobby shook his head and from the corner of his eye saw Kate do the same.

Vanessa said, "Even though we've had this setback, Jordan is improving. He's even talking a little. But he's still extremely wary and reserved."

"Oh, good. He *is* getting better," Kate said, relief in her voice. "After what happened Sunday, I've asked that no visitors other than immediate family be allowed to see him."

Bobby's gaze cut to her. For as long as he'd known her, she'd looked at the world though polarized lenses, ones that only allowed what she wanted to see to pass through. Here she was again, filtering out all but what she wanted to hear.

Dr. Brinegar cleared his throat. "Yes, about Sunday. Our investigation showed our inventory of several different sedatives to be a total of twenty pills short. With only one or two pills missing from various bottles, it didn't flag up immediately."

"I thought your drugs were all kept under lock and key!" Kate leaned forward in her seat.

"Our pharmaceuticals are kept under strict security. Reviewing the meds log, not all of the drugs showing a shortfall were out for distribution at the same time. And not all of the drugs removed from Jordan's stomach were distributed on Sunday. Mrs. McPherson, I think we have to look at Jordan's act last Sunday as a well-planned, pre-meditated suicide attempt."

"No! It was *that boy*. He came in and somehow got all of those pills—he can probably pick a lock, for heaven's sake. Then he forced Jordan to take them." She turned to Vanessa. "You saw how upset Jordan was with Ethan in there. My poor baby was terrified."

Bobby put a hand on Kate's arm. "Let's hear what the doctor has to say, then maybe we can figure this all out."

Bobby knew Jordan was in need of help, but the suicide attempt had taken him completely by surprise. He was very interested in anything the doctor had to say that might shine a light on the reason why—and what they could do to prevent it from happening again in the future.

"After the incident, we ran additional psychological tests on Jordan. And to be perfectly honest, the results are slightly baffling. We see no clear indicators that would lead us to believe Jordan was at high risk for suicide—"

"That's because he didn't try to commit suicide!" Kate said. "Someone tried to kill him—"

"Kate, please," Bobby said quietly. He was so anxious to hear what those tests told about his son's psyche that he was sitting on the edge of his chair. All of Gabe's questions about Steve had gotten him thinking—pulling out old memories that standing alone didn't flag anything, but when assembled as a whole showed the possibility of a trend.

The doctor continued, "Our tests do indicate that Jordan feels bullied, intimidated, unsafe in his own environment."

Intimidated. Bobby had used that very same word yesterday when talking with Gabe.

"That's ridicu—"

Bobby cut Kate off. "Do your tests show where this bullying is coming from?"

"I'm afraid our tests aren't that specific. That's where the counseling part comes in. We use the tests to discover psychological characteristics that a person might mask, either consciously or unconsciously, in our therapy sessions. In Jordan's case, he's very repressed in this area. My opinion is that the intimidation has been long term and is ongoing; not just a recent attitude developed from a social situation at school, for example."

After a meaningful pause where Bobby could easily read what was coming, Dr. Brinegar said, "With the recent violent death of his stepfather, there could be a link. Usually in these situations it's a male relative, or a male close to the family...."

Kate shot to her feet. "What are you saying? My husband did not abuse my son! He always went out of his way to make Jordan feel included."

"Sit down, Kate." Bobby's tone was sharp.

She dropped back into her chair.

Bobby's thoughts were fast and angry. First Gabe, now the doctor with the same suggestion. Jesus, had McPherson bullied his son to the breaking point? How had Bobby missed something so critical?

He asked, "But if that threat is gone, why would Jordan try to harm himself now?"

"A very good question, Mr. Gray. And one we're trying to answer. It is going to take some time—these things are often painfully slow to unravel."

Kate got up. "I don't need to listen to this ridiculousness anymore." She stormed out of the conference room.

Bobby didn't follow her. If he did he might do or say something he'd regret. Jesus Christ, she'd brought that man into their son's life. She'd allowed Jordan to be psychologically beaten down for years. Bobby's hands clenched in his lap and he tried to breathe slowly to calm himself. Anger wasn't going to help Jordan; in fact that was what had done the damage in the first place.

After a moment, he asked, "So where do we go from here?"

"I suggest that at least for the next month, we continue inpatient treatment."

"And then?"

"And then we see. There may be months and months of outpatient treatment. If we can get to the root of the problem, your son should have a good prognosis."

Bobby got up to leave before the doctor said more. What if a part of the root of the problem was that Jordan had been there when his stepfather was killed?

BOBBY SAT HUNCHED OVER, his elbows on his knees and his hands steepled in front of his chin, watching Kate chatter to Jordan. Bobby had to admit, even with the suicide attempt, his son appeared more relaxed, more focused on what his mother was saying. He even gave an occasional single word response.

He thought back over the years since Kate had married Steve, looking for clues that he'd missed. Bobby and Kate shared custody of Jordan, dividing his time equally between them.

There had been times when Jordan had begged to stay with Bobby and not go home with his mother. But not often enough to make him think there was a serious problem. He'd attributed it to the fact that he made a point of always doing something special when Jordan was with him. He knew it was selfish of him to want to make their time together exceptionally happy; he knew he'd been making up for the fact that he wasn't able to be there for Jordan every night and every weekend. Kate had actually accused him of trying to sway their son away from her. And maybe she'd been right—or maybe Jordan's reluctance to go home with her had nothing to do with Bobby at all.

Shit. Why did things have to be so much more clear in hindsight? Why did it have to get to the point where the wheels were falling off before you noticed all of the warning signs that trouble was brewing?

He hated the fact that he'd failed his only child. Hated the soul-searing fear he'd witnessed in his son over the past weeks.

The sound of Jordan's laugh jerked Bobby back to the present. It was fleeting, the first hint of there still being the boy Jordan used to be buried inside that defensive shell. His face appeared more natural; the plastic-looking mask he'd worn since his arrival here seemed to be dissolving.

Bobby looked at Kate. She was looking back at him and grinning the same way she had when Jordan had uttered his very first word. Emotions kicked up, swirling like a cyclone in Bobby's chest. He was just about to get up and walk over to her when the door opened.

"How's my little brother today?" Todd said brightly as he entered the room.

Jordan had looked so normal a few seconds ago that Bobby looked toward his son, almost anticipating an equally cheery response.

But Jordan had reverted to hollow eyes and plastic features.

Bobby watched carefully as Todd approached the chair where Jordan sat.

Kate said, "Jordan's so much better today."

Todd leaned close. "Is that right?" He put a hand on Jordan's shoulder and Bobby could swear he saw Jordan flinch. "Why, you'll be back home before you know it."

Jordan blinked, but kept his eyes fixed straight ahead.

Had the glimmer of normalcy been just a passing moment?

Todd was big, like his father. In Jordan's current mental state, was he confusing the two?

The doctor's words came back. *"With the recent violent death of his stepfather, there could be a link. Usually in these situations it's a male relative, or a male close to the family...."*

Bobby sat back and continued to watch.

ETHAN SAT IN A CUBICLE just outside Madison's office, his head resting on his folded arms on the desktop. He'd been quiet and taciturn all day, not that she could blame him. His life had been turned upside down yet again, just when she'd begun to see a real spark of hope for the future in his eyes.

Not for the first time in the past week, she wondered if she'd made a mistake in coming here. There had been dangers in Philly, for sure—the brotherhood of gangs and old habits constantly beckoning. She'd known there had been a distinct possibility if they'd remained in that city that the lure of no rules and complete freedom might have won out over living with her once the newness had worn off.

But were those things any worse than what was happening now? She'd traded familiar risks—those for which he'd established adequate defenses and coping abilities—for hazards with which he had no idea how to cope.

In her naiveté, she'd thought a slower-paced small town would be an easier place for a teenager to build a new life. But a small town held complications she'd never considered. Maybe she should have sought out a larger metropolitan area, one where a person could start over without all of his baggage arriving on the next train right behind him.

Of course, that baggage might have stayed on the train and chugged on through town if all of this McPherson crap hadn't happened. Things would be so much easier if she'd just listened to her gut and refused to allow Ethan to go on that camping trip.

She studied him through the doorway—the exhausted line of his back, the nervous bounce of his knees; he was full of contrary emotions and fatigued energy. And she felt totally inadequate to help him.

He hadn't wanted to come to work with her, but there was no way she was leaving him out there in that house alone. Not with all of the threats still looming.

Here under her own nose, in the company of her co-workers, he might be bored out of his mind, but he was safe. He'd finished his schoolwork by ten a.m. When he asked if he could go for a walk around town, she'd nearly bitten his head off. She didn't want him out of her sight—not until the murderer was caught.

It was only Wednesday, his first full day away from school. How were they going to make it through the rest of the week? Maybe she'd figure out a job he could occupy himself with around here for a few days—

When her cell phone rang, she realized it was nearly five o'clock. She'd been sitting there staring at him for longer than she'd imagined.

She picked up the call, dragging her thoughts away from her son. When she heard who was on the line, those thoughts rocketed right back where they'd been for the past twenty minutes.

MADISON DISCONNECTED THE CALL, her insides buzzing with excitement. Her PI had given her what could be the key to this entire situation. She wanted to pass it along to Gabe immediately.

Everyone in the office was getting up and leaving for the day, an activity that brought Ethan back to life. He rubbed his eyes, then looked hopefully at her.

She smiled and held up her finger. "Just one minute," she said loudly enough for him to hear.

He rolled his eyes and slumped over on the desk again.

She dialed Gabe's office number, only to find he'd left for the day. Then she tried his cell. It rolled right to voice mail.

"It's Madison. I have some information you really need to hear. Call me on my cell as soon as you get this."

Chapter 25

GABE SAT IN Coach Lawrence's office, ignoring the phone vibrating on his belt. He listened as sophomore Cory Woodbine inched closer to divulging the local source of the steroids.

Gabe had come to the high school personally, taking precious time away from his murder investigation, because he was concerned for Maddie's safety. He supposed from a law enforcement perspective, he should thank her for her gritty determination to expose this danger to the youth of Buckeye no matter how unpopular or how nasty the local response got. Whoever thought she would be altered from her course by threats and close calls didn't know Maddie.

She wasn't going to stop. So Gabe had to stop whoever was going after her. The thought of someone out there stalking her—someone whose tactics had recently taken a direct and violent turn—made Gabe sick, and interfered severely with his concentration.

Cory Woodbine offered the first positive step Gabe

had had in that direction. Moved by teenage deaths and fear of discovery after Maddie's articles, Cory had come forward and confessed his own steroid use to his football coach. When Coach Lawrence had called Gabe, Gabe had assured him that there would be no legal action against this boy if he told where he'd gotten the drugs.

Cory's fingers drummed on the arm of the chair and his eyes kept darting to the small window in the door to the coach's office.

Gabe said, "Coach Lawrence locked the outer locker room doors. No one can get in."

Cory shifted in his seat, then looked at Gabe. "Coach said I won't get in trouble."

"That's right. As long as your parents know about your use, nobody else has to."

The boy's eyes snapped up. "You're gonna tell my parents?"

"No. You are. That's the deal. Take it or leave it."

Drawing in a deep breath and releasing it noisily through his nose, Cory nodded.

"And I want your assurance that you're not using any longer."

"Hell, no!" He stopped himself. "I mean, heck no. I'd only started a few weeks ago. I just wanted to bulk up for football season. I didn't know they could kill you."

The boy looked scared enough that Gabe believed him.

Cory licked his lips. "I don't know the dude's name— the one who gets the stuff. It's all done without contact. You drop a DVD case with your name and cash inside at the video store. You're supposed to Scotch-tape the case closed. The next day, you pick up your stash and your case at the drop point."

This was one smart dealer. None of his customers could ID him.

"Where's the drop point?" Gabe asked.

"Everybody has a different one. That way no one can lift your drugs."

"Does your dealer know you've stopped?"

Cory shook his head. "He's not expecting another order from me until next week."

"Would you be willing to place that order and tell me your drop point?"

"No way, dude—I mean, sir. He'd know it was me who ratted him out."

"Do you think he works at the video store?"

The boy shrugged. "Doubt it. He's way too secretive and smart. Probably has somebody there who passes stuff along."

There was a knock at the door. Cory nearly jumped high enough to hang from the ceiling.

"It's okay. It's Coach with your parents."

Cory sprang from his chair, horror on his face. "You brought my parents!"

"Would you rather I had driven you home in my department vehicle and escorted you to the front door?"

"No. But why'd you have to bring them here? I said I'd tell them."

Gabe gave the boy a half-smile. "I was a teenager once myself, *dude*." He got up and let a very angry-looking Mr. and Mrs. Woodbine into Coach Lawrence's office.

"THERE'S NO FOOD IN THE HOUSE; you want to stop at Augustino's for pizza?" M asked as they finally left the newspaper office.

"Can we carry out?" Ethan asked.

"Let's eat there. We need to stop at the store on the way home or there won't be any milk and cereal for breakfast in the morning, either."

They got in the rental car—a reminder of how much everyone in this town hated him.

"If we're stopping at the store anyway," he said, once they were inside the car, "why don't we get something to fix for dinner, too?"

M gave one of those annoying sighs. "Because I'm tired and hungry and don't want to cook and clean up the kitchen. What's the big deal? You love Augustino's."

The big deal was that it was Wednesday night. Augustino's was always packed on Wednesday night. Ethan didn't want to sit around and be everyone's entertainment. Didn't M know that everyone was talking about him? He'd just been thrown out of school, for Christ's sake.

"I *used* to love Augustino's," he corrected. "Now I don't like anything about this town."

She made a sympathetic sound. "I know it's hard. But this is all going to be straightened out soon and we can go on with our lives."

Jesus, even she didn't sound like she believed that line. He slumped down in the seat and stared out the window. Maybe someday she could forget all of this, but he never would—and nobody in this town would, either. His one chance at a normal life was shot. And if he stayed around here, he'd just bring M down with him.

M pulled into the parking lot at Augustino's. Ethan thought about refusing to get out, but what did it matter now?

As they were walking in the door, a horn honked

behind them. Ethan turned to see Sheriff Wyatt pulling to the curb and getting out of his Jeep Cherokee.

M said, "I have something to tell the sheriff. Why don't you go on in and order for us? I'll be right behind you."

Now she was sending him to face the crowd alone. He didn't argue, just went on and opened the door. Several people were waiting for tables. As he walked past them to put their name in with the hostess, Ethan heard his name mentioned more than once.

He ground his teeth to keep from yelling at them to shut up and mind their own business.

After finding out it would be a twenty-minute wait, he hunched his shoulders and headed toward the bathroom. At least there he could lock himself in a stall and wouldn't have to hear the whispers or put up with the looks.

Before he even made it inside a stall, someone behind him said, "Ethan!"

He turned to see Jordan's brother, Todd, slipping inside the door to the men's room and locking it behind him.

For a split second, Ethan's muscles tightened, ready to face a fight.

Then Todd smiled. "I'm so glad I ran into you, man."

Ethan kept a wary posture. "Yeah?"

"Yeah. I wanted to warn you."

"Of what?"

"My stepmom has this crazy idea that you killed my dad. I can't get it out of her head."

"And you don't?" Ethan asked.

"Hell, no. Why would you? You're getting the shaft just 'cause you're not from around here."

Someone was finally seeing the logic of the truth. Ethan didn't respond, waiting to see what else Todd had to say.

"Anyway, she's crazy. She's been making phone calls to the DA and all kinds of crap. I can't get her to listen to reason. But she's finally gone too far. Jordan started talking—and she's convinced him to say you're the one who killed Dad. It's only a matter of time. If I were you, I'd be taking off tonight."

"Why do you give a crap if they fry me?" Ethan asked.

Todd looked at Ethan as if he suddenly thought Ethan had turned stupid. "Because that'll mean the *real killer* got away. I want whoever murdered my dad to pay." He briefly put a hand on Ethan's shoulder. "And because you're Jordan's friend. My brother needs you."

Ethan didn't say anything.

"They're gonna railroad you, dude."

"If I take off, they're just gonna come looking for me."

"Yeah, but you're good at staying out of sight when you need to. You wouldn't have made it all those years without being stuck in foster care otherwise.

"If you go, it'll give me time to push them to look for the real murderer. Shit, if I was you, I'd have been long gone already just out of fear that the murderer was gonna take me out like he did Colin. You know, J.D. took off yesterday."

Ethan thought about the photos in his locker. Whoever killed Mr. McP probably *was* gunning for him. If he stayed here, that'd put M at that much more risk of being hurt in the process. She'd already had a close call because of him. What if she really got hurt or worse next time?

"Thanks." He walked past Todd, unwilling to give up anything, unwilling to put full trust in Todd's motives.

Once Ethan reached the door, Todd said, "I'm just trying to help. If you want a ride somewhere so they can't

start tracing you right away, meet me out by the bridge on
Settlers Road at two tomorrow morning. It's the least traveled road that'll get you to the highway, so use it—with,
or without me."

Ethan turned the lock.

"I'll be there," Todd said. "You show or not, it's up to
you."

Ethan walked out the door without answering.

GABE WAITED FOR ETHAN to enter the pizza place before
he said, "I was just pulling up your number to return your
call, then I looked up and there you were."

The second he'd laid eyes on her, he'd felt like a little kid
looking at a carnival; his eyes mesmerized by the motion of
the brightly colored lights, his pulse racing with anticipation, and his insides bracing themselves for excitement. For
that brief second, it didn't matter that he and Maddie had
parted badly. It didn't matter that this case was like a giant
anchor around both of their necks. It was a rush of pure,
untainted emotion. He wanted to grasp it and hold tight.

But he wasn't a little kid. Life wasn't a carnival. And
this case might just kill any hopes of ever having a relationship with this woman.

She stepped away from the door, drawing him with
her to the side of the building away from the parking lot.
There was such an excited spark in her eyes that Gabe felt
a rush of gladness. He saw no trace of the cold tension of
their last meeting.

After taking a single look over his shoulder to make
sure no one could see them from the street, he stepped
very close and looked down at her. Their bodies were just
short of touching and he could feel it in every one of his

cells. She was like a magnetic pull that his physical being had no power to resist.

Not that he wanted to resist.

For a long moment she smiled at him, looking as if she held the answer to his prayers.

Before responsible thought intervened, he leaned down and pressed his lips to hers. She didn't draw away, as responsible thought would have dictated. Instead her mouth welcomed his and her body pressed closer.

Dear God in heaven, how could a simple stolen kiss reach right to the center of his being and set him on fire?

This had to stop. What if someone saw them? They were on a tightwire here, and Ethan was the one who would suffer if either of them took a misstep.

As if Maddie's reason returned in tandem with his, she pulled back. Her lips were rosy and moist from their kiss. His thoughts slipped right back to their irresponsible ways and he mentally listed the places he'd like to feel those lips on his body.

She caught her lower lip between her teeth, as if keeping excited words from tumbling out too quickly. Grasping his arm with one hand, she said, "I've got good news. My private investigator just called me with information that backs up our theory that McPherson was abusing Jordan."

Gabe felt just a little deflated, realizing the delighted gleam in her eye wasn't there because of passion he'd stirred.

She looked as if she was dangling the bait in front of the tiger.

He brushed off his bruised male ego. This is what made her tick; the challenge of the hunt for information, the thrill of little victories when she discovered what she was after. It was why she was so good at her job.

"And?" he finally prompted.

"One of the McPhersons' Ann Arbor neighbors still lives across the street from their old house. They told my guy that they were suspicious something wasn't right in the McPherson house for months before the Mrs. died. Cheryl seemed exceptionally withdrawn and skittish those last weeks."

Gabe held himself back from snatching her off her feet and spinning in a circle. He had to be reasonable, examine with an impartial eye. "It's always easy for people to say stuff like that after the fact. They read things differently in retrospect."

"I thought people always said the opposite. You know, the serial killer next door was such a nice, quiet guy, they never imagined he was a monster."

"Yeah, that, too. My point being, general statements like those, made *after* something has already happened, don't carry a lot of weight. Did any of these people report their suspicions to the police *before* Mrs. McPherson died?"

She crossed her arms over her chest and looked sharply at him. "Seriously?"

"I'm just saying..."

"I know what you're saying. And believe me, I've had enough experience to get it. But *my* point is this is yet another straw on that camel's back. My guy also discovered that Todd was institutionalized for three months after his mother's death. He couldn't get the health records, but it was a stress center...a facility much like the one Jordan is in now. Quite the coincidence that both of McPherson's kids needed psychological treatment."

"Any kid who came home and found his mother dead at the bottom of the stairs might need some help."

"No kidding. Especially if that kid had also witnessed his dad knocking his mom around before that."

"This still isn't helping us find a suspect other than Jordan and Ethan," he said gravely.

"Not yet. We're just not able to put this patchwork together into a coherent pattern. But we will. My guy is still digging. Maybe McPherson picked on somebody else along the way. Somebody who struck back. It opens up the door to all sorts of possibilities."

Gabe shook his head. "I'm not seeing it. Who would climb up there and hunt the man down? Who would take a chance on having the opportunity to get the guy alone and make it look like an accident?"

He could see the excitement drain from her, one muscle fiber at a time. "You know Ethan *did not* do this!"

The only other suspect that fit into the murder motive being the Jordan-being-abused scenario was Bobby Gray. Gabe hadn't eliminated him completely. Bobby *said* he couldn't find his way around the mountains, but that could just be smoke.

Gabe didn't jump in and immediately agree. And with that pause, that hesitation, he saw something shift in her eyes. He was no longer on her team. His insider privileges had just been revoked.

He reached out to put his hands on her shoulders. "Maddie—"

She jerked free. "I have to go." She walked away.

It would be so easy to call her back. To tell her what she wanted to hear; utter the words that would bring her closer. But he didn't want a momentary fix with Maddie. He wanted the basis for a long-lasting relationship. He wanted trust.

Chapter 26

GABE SAT ON HIS COUCH, putting his stocking feet up on the coffee table, taking a few minutes for himself before he started returning missed calls. Two were from Bobby Gray and one from the DA. Luckily it was too late to call the DA back until tomorrow morning. If there had been something really urgent, dispatch at the department would have contacted him by radio.

Bobby Gray's multiple calls said he obviously had some bee up his butt. Most likely put there by his ex-wife—and even more likely to be a plea to arrest Ethan. Bobby had said they were meeting with Jordan's doctors today. Who knew what that had stirred up? Probably the call from the DA.

Gabe leaned his head back and rolled his neck, trying to unknot his muscles. Then he returned Bobby's call.

There was no answer.

He wasn't disappointed. He wanted to spend this evening sorting out what he'd gathered about the steroid dealer. This situation nagged him more than professional reason dictated. But Maddie was at risk. When she'd been missing, her fate unknown, it had felt like a bullet in the gut. He could not let anything happen to her.

Too bad Cory's attack of conscience hadn't gone so far as to allow him to let Gabe stake out his drop point. Gabe wasn't ready to put the squeeze on the kid to do it; because what Cory had said was true, it would put him at risk.

Shame on Gabe for listening, even briefly, to that little voice inside that said, "Better Cory at risk than Maddie."

Solving this case would go a long way toward easing Maddie's way in this town. People here might not like it, but they'd have to admit that she had been right.

The video store was his closest link to the dealer. Maddie had questioned Shelly Mitthoeffer, who worked there and had an ex-boyfriend who was a likely user. That was his next step.

Gabe got off the couch and found his shoes. He was going to see if he could do what Maddie couldn't; get Shelly Mitthoeffer to crack. Maddie just hadn't had the right tool at her disposal. Gabe did.

If he could get one witness, he could go for a warrant, make an arrest.

Maddie would be safe.

"I'M GOING TO BED," Ethan said.

Madison looked up from the book she was trying to read in her effort to make things feel more normal. The stress was wearing on her; it had to be eating Ethan alive. "It's only nine-thirty."

"Yeah, well, who knew being bored out of your mind all day could be so tiring." He gave her a watered-down smile.

She reached out to him. "Come and sit with me for a minute."

Tucking her feet under her, she made room for him on the couch. He shuffled over and sat down. Resting one elbow on the arm of the sofa, he chewed on a thumbnail. He didn't look at her.

Madison said, "I know everything is a big bucket of crap at the moment, but I promise things are going to get better. Jordan is making headway. Once he corroborates what happened up there, the focus can be totally on the search for the person responsible for Mr. McPherson's death.

"Until that person is caught, I'm afraid it's going to be you and me 24/7." She reached over and brushed his hair away from his eyes. "I don't know about you, but I'm looking forward to spending more time together."

She saw his throat work as he swallowed. His gaze remained fixed on a point somewhere in mid-air. He looked as young and emotionally exhausted as he had the first time she'd seen him—the day he'd stolen her heart.

His voice seemed hollow when he said, "Yeah, me, too."

So much for their no-bullshit pact. Neither of them seemed to be living up to it at the moment.

This was why people lied to those they loved; sometimes it was the only way to wrap the knives and daggers of life so they didn't pierce the heart of those you cared for.

"Okay," she said cheerfully, "I've tortured you enough with my mom-talk." She fluttered her hand in the air. "You're free to flee to your room."

He turned his head so slowly when he looked at her that she felt like time itself had slowed down. The light from her lamp reflected in his eyes, revealing tears she knew he wasn't aware of, because he never would have allowed her to see them. He looked at her for a long moment. His lips parted as if to speak, then closed again.

She wanted to say something to erase the pain she saw in his face. And it absolutely killed her to realize it was completely beyond her ability. Maybe if she'd had him for all of his life she'd be better equipped, more in tune with remedies for wounds of the soul. Maybe if she'd prepared adequately before she'd adopted him, she'd have the salve to keep his heart from scarring. But she sat helpless and hurting, completely worthless to him.

He got up. As he walked past her, he stopped and reached out, putting a finger lightly on her bruised cheek. Then he bent down and kissed her forehead. She was too startled to move.

"Good night, M."

Still stunned from his show of affection, she mumbled, "Good night."

She listened to his slow, heavy footfalls up the staircase. When his bedroom door closed, she curled on her side and clasped her book to her chest. She lay there for a long time, thinking she'd open her book again.

But she didn't.

GABE WAS TOO LATE when he arrived at the video store. The lights were off, the doors already locked. He went past the Mitthoeffers' house. The lights were still on and a television flickered in the living room. He rang the doorbell.

The porch light came on. Mr. Mitthoeffer opened the door wearing a plaid bathrobe and a scowl.

When he saw it was Gabe, he grumbled, "Which one is it now?"

The Mitthoeffers had seven kids, most of them troublemakers.

"I apologize for arriving unannounced and so late. I'd like to speak to Shelly. I just have a few questions to ask her."

"She ain't home from work yet. Momma asked her to stop by the 24-hour Walgreens and pick up a prescription for Jenny's earache." He tilted his head, making his double chin sway to one side. "Why you want to talk to her? She done somethin'?"

"No, she hasn't." Gabe stepped away from the door. "Sorry to disturb your evening."

"Ugh." The door closed.

Gabe got back in his Jeep and headed to the drugstore, which was only five blocks away.

He found Shelly back at the pharmacist's counter waiting with her pale skinny arms crossed. She paused chewing her gum long enough to throw him a look of displeasure. After that brief eye contact, she turned her back to him and picked up a magazine from the rack.

Moving to stand right behind her, Gabe said, "I think you and I need to have a little talk."

Her shoulders stiffened. She didn't turn around, continuing to flip pages when she said, "I haven't done anything."

"I didn't say you did—yet. But I do happen to know there's drug dealing going on where you work—anabolic steroids for sure. I'm still uncovering what else."

She spun to face him, her eyes wide. She glanced nervously around at the empty store, then said in a low voice, "I don't have anything to do with that!"

"That's what they all say." Shelly was a tough girl who'd

lived a tough life. Nudging her sense of self-preservation was his best bet.

"I can't tell you anything," she said through tight lips.

"Okay. We'll just go have our talk at the city station. I'm sure Chief Davis will want to be in on this since the video store is in his jurisdiction."

"You can't take me in there." She took a step back. "Everyone will find out."

"If you haven't done anything and don't know anything, it shouldn't matter. You can convince us of that and then go on your merry way."

Her eyes took on the look that Gabe had once seen on a cougar backed against a cliff. "You and that bitch at the newspaper are trying to get me killed."

He made a *tsk*ing noise. "That's not very nice language. Besides, this is Buckeye. I think you're being melodramatic."

"Bullshit! You don't know what he's capable of."

"You know, there'll be a homicide charge along with the illegal drug trafficking charges." She appeared baffled so he cleared it up for her. "With Zach Gilbert's death being attributed to illegal steroid use."

"Oh, no way can you drag me into that." She shook her head in a jerky motion that set her hair to swinging.

"Oh, but I can."

She opened her mouth twice and closed it without uttering a single word.

"I'm going to get this guy one way or the other. My bet is he'll suspect you gave him up regardless. Let me get him now, before he has time to hurt anyone else. Once he's behind bars, you won't have to worry about him ever again."

Looking as though she'd like to rip his head off, she said, "Except I bet you'll need someone to testify."

"Maybe. I can't promise it won't happen. But my guess is this will never make it to trial—once he understands what we have on him. I expect he won't be seeing the outside of the jailhouse for a very long time."

"How can you have anything on Todd—?" Shelly looked like she wished she could swallow her tongue. "Shit!"

"McPherson. Todd McPherson?" The kid was built like a brick wall, was looking to get picked up by a triple-A baseball team. It fit.

"He can't know it was me."

"I'm going to follow you home. Once you're there, tell your dad what's going on and stay there. Do not leave your house for *any* reason. Got that?"

Tears shone in her eyes. Her chin trembled as she nodded.

"It's going to be okay," Gabe said. "He has no idea we know. We'll have him picked up before tomorrow morning. You'll be safe."

And so will Maddie.

Chapter 27

ETHAN TOOK OFF HIS BACKPACK and perched on the railing at the edge of the bridge. As he sat there trying to avoid real thoughts, he listened to the water rushing below and looked up at the sky. It amazed him that a pitch-black sky made so many more stars visible. On a clear night in Philly, the sky was a blanket of gray dotted with the occasional dim-looking star. But here, there were so many stars they looked like they'd been piled one upon the other, glitter flung into the sky.

Even the sound of the water in the creek had a clearer, brighter sound. Everything was different in these mountains. He realized he was going to miss more than just M. But he had to go.

He wondered if M wished she'd never met him; or at least hadn't adopted him.

He tried to imagine what it would be like tomorrow morning when she discovered he was gone. He bet she'd feel a lot like he did when he came home and found his mom dead – sad, but relieved at the same time.

What if she discovered he was gone before morning? That'd really screw up his plan.

After he'd gone upstairs tonight, he'd waited and waited for her to go to bed. But hours went by and she didn't come upstairs. Finally at midnight, he'd tiptoed down and found her sound asleep on the couch. He'd left, holding his breath, fearing she'd awaken—and maybe, if he was honest, there had been a little part of him that had wanted her to.

But she hadn't. He'd made a clean getaway.

She wouldn't go in his room or knock on his door, he assured himself. She never did after he went to bed at night.

He held that thought. Even though he didn't like the idea of anyone knowing what direction he was headed, he'd decided to take Todd up on the ride. Not that he trusted him completely. It was all about calculating the odds and playing them in his favor. And the odds of being caught decreased with every mile Ethan could put between him and Buckeye in the first twenty-four hours.

He'd just have to play it smart. If Todd acted weird in any way when he showed up, Ethan could easily outrun the big guy, lose him in the dark woods.

He looked at his watch; nearly one.

It was getting chilly. He tucked his hands in his jacket pockets, wishing he had his Eagles cap.

His gaze traveled to the center of the bridge. Had that been the place where Colin had fallen to his death? Had he gone over the rail on which Ethan now sat, or the one on the other side?

The official story going around was that it was an accident—Colin had had too much to drink and tumbled over the rail. Everything Ethan knew about Colin said that was damn likely. Even so, Ethan had heard the rumors, had noticed the hushed whispers and sly looks. Everyone thought he'd pushed Colin off this bridge.

After finding those photos in his locker, Ethan thought it was likely that someone had a hand in Colin's death—and it was somehow linked to Mr. McP. Ethan had heard that J.D. was supposed to have been there, too. Would J.D. being there have kept Colin alive? Or would he have ended up dead, too?

Those red Xs on the photos told Ethan that the second scenario was more likely.

Ethan had been convinced that Jordan had accidentally killed his stepdad. And if Jordan's overdose hadn't come on the heels of Colin's death, he might have thought that guilt had driven Jordan to suicide. But Colin dying so close to Jordan's suicide attempt, together with the nasty warnings Ethan had received, painted an entirely different picture.

Colin had had his "accident" the day after he'd started mouthing off to anyone and everyone that he knew what had happened to Mr. McP. The only thing that made any sense to Ethan now was that there had been someone else up there on that mountain; someone who felt like he had to get rid of the four people who might have witnessed the murder.

Maybe Jordan *had* seen what happened.

"He didn't mean to. It was an accident."

Jordan saw. That's why he went nuts; not because he had killed his stepdad.

Ethan tried to piece together anything that might point him in the direction of the killer. It had to be someone in good physical shape and familiar with the mountains. Which didn't eliminate too many of the people around here—almost everyone hunted.

What other clues were there?

Nothing he could recall from the mountain.

What about after, had anything seemed out of place, anyone acted suspiciously?

There was Ethan's hat. Everything else he'd packed for the trip had been with his stuff when he picked it up at Jordan's house. But not that hat.

Then it had turned up here after Colin died.

It had been on the mountain on Saturday for sure; Ethan hadn't even unpacked it. It disappeared sometime between when Mr. McP died and when Ethan picked up his stuff at Jordan's.

Jordan was afraid at home.

Jordan was even more afraid now.

Why? If Mr. McP was the one Jordan was afraid of?

"He didn't mean to. It was an accident."

Jordan was more afraid now....

Todd.

Todd, who'd been in the group who went up the mountain to bring back the stuff they'd left there—and had access to my stuff at his house even after that.

Todd, who'd warned me that Jordan was GOING TO SAY I killed Mr. McP.

Todd, who all of a sudden is going out of his way to help me.

"J.D. took off yesterday."

Had he? Or had Todd done something to him?

Cold beads of sweat popped out on Ethan's skin.

Todd had no intention of driving Ethan anywhere. Todd was tying up loose ends.

As panic rose, Ethan looked up the road for headlights, then looked at his watch; five past one.

Regretting having made the decision to leave his cell phone behind, he picked up his backpack and headed back toward town, staying close to the trees in case those headlights should appear.

Chapter 28

ONCE GABE HAD A WARRANT IN HAND, he left his office to arrest Todd McPherson. It was after one a.m. on a weeknight. He hoped the kid would be home and this could be wrapped up easily and quickly. He had dispatch send a deputy to watch the back of the house. Gabe would go to the front door.

When he pulled up to the modest house on the quiet street, the lights were all off inside the McPherson home, as well as the neighbors' on both sides.

Gabe got out of his Jeep, closing the door softly, then went to the front door and rang the bell twice in succession.

He was just about to ring again when the porch light came on. Kate McPherson's voice called through the door. "Who is it?"

Gabe kept his voice as quiet as he could and still be heard through the door. "Sheriff Wyatt, ma'am."

She jerked the door open, her face ashen. "Something's happened to Todd!" It was a statement full of panic.

"He isn't home?" Gabe asked, noticing through the screen that, even though the house was dark, Kate was still fully dressed.

"No. He's been gone all evening." Her hand nervously clutched the front of the oversized denim jacket she had on.

"May I come in?"

"Oh, yes. Of course." She flipped on the hall light, opened the screen, and stepped back.

"Is it unusual for Todd to be out this late on a week-night?" Gabe asked.

She pushed her mussed hair away from her face. Now that she'd turned on the hall light, it was clear she'd been asleep when he rang. "No, not really. It's just when I heard it was you...Todd didn't answer his cell earlier. I don't know—I just panicked."

"Do you know where he is?"

She shook her head and something that looked like cautious fear flashed in her eyes. "He doesn't like me to ask."

All that fight she'd exhibited the day she'd stormed into his office seemed to have vanished completely. As Gabe studied the woman, trying to decipher exactly what was going on with her, he noticed the jacket she was wearing in more detail.

The second button from the top was missing.

His heart tripped faster. "Is that a Diesel jacket?"

She furrowed her brow and looked oddly at him.

"My nephew." He shrugged. "He wants one for his birth-day. I wasn't sure what I was supposed to be looking for."

"Oh. Yes it is. It's Todd's." Then she looked puzzled again. "Why are you here looking for him in the middle of the night?"

"I was hoping he could help me locate one of his friends...someone we need to question about some vandalism."

She visibly relaxed as she released a breath. "I'll tell him when he gets home."

Gabe pushed open the screen. "Thank you, ma'am."

Once he was back in the Jeep he radioed in to dispatch, giving Todd's name and the license plate number and make of his car. All officers on duty were to be notified of the warrant for his arrest for dealing, as well as being wanted for questioning in a murder investigation. He also asked the dispatcher to alert the city police, and advise them he was leaving one of his patrol officers here to watch the house for Todd's return.

Then he drove around back and told his deputy to stay tucked out of sight and radio him the minute Todd showed up.

The streets were their usual deserted-night selves as he drove back to his office. He'd just pulled in the sheriff's department lot when a figure came running toward his car. Once the person moved into the pool of light near the entrance to the building, Gabe saw it was Ethan Wade.

Ethan didn't slow, nearly plowing into Gabe as he got out of his car. The kid looked scared to death—which scared the crap out of Gabe.

"Maddie? Is she all right?" Gabe asked, his heart on the express elevator up his throat.

When Ethan tried to talk, nothing came out but a raspy squeak between ragged breaths.

"Is it Maddie?" Gabe's hands were on Ethan's shoulders; it took all of his willpower not to try to shake the answer out of him.

Ethan shook his head, still gasping. Even though the night was cool, the boy's hair was wet with sweat. It rolled like tears from his hairline to his jaw.

Gabe forced himself to draw in a breath himself and loosen the grip he had on Ethan's arms.

"Take a minute to get your breath."

Ethan's legs buckled. He sat hard on the pavement. Gabe knelt in front of him.

"T-T-Todd." Ethan dragged in another breath. "He's who Jordan is...afraid of. I think he killed Mr. McP."

Around his rough breathing, Ethan gave Gabe the last pieces of the puzzle. He ended his story with Todd's offer to help him run away.

It was a few minutes before two now.

"You're sure he's coming for you?" That would mean Maddie was safe for the time being.

"Oh yeah. He wants his hands on me."

Todd was as cool and calculating as they came. When Bobby had said that Todd was sending daily cards to Jordan, it had struck Gabe as unusual. Now that seeming act of kindness took on a sinister shadow. It was Todd's way of reminding Jordan not to betray him.

"Do you think you can get him to admit to you he did it?" Gabe asked, a plan falling into place in his mind. "I'll be right there, but out of sight." He figured he could stand just below the bridge and hear everything clearly.

His nervous pulse throbbed throughout his body. It was risky, but he wanted an open-and-closed case. Todd was smart enough and devious enough that, with the right lawyer, he'd be as slippery as a trout.

"Probably," Ethan said with no trace of fear in his voice. "No reason for him not to; he's planning on killing me." Ethan got to his feet. "Let's go. We don't have much time."

MADISON WAS TRAPPED in a dream that made no sense.

She was back in Philly. It was late at night and she couldn't find Ethan. Her heart filled with terror, she ran up and down streets that no woman or child should traverse alone, chased by a giant, squawking bird the size of a Hummer.

She ducked into an alley, trying to lose the bird. Pressing herself against a brick wall, she hid behind a Dumpster that smelled like vomit.

Her feet twitched to keep moving—she had to find Ethan. She couldn't hide here long.

The bird landed at the end of the alley. He turned his head slightly to the side, training one headlight-sized black eye down the alley.

Maddie held her breath.

The bird opened its giant curved beak; instead of the horrific screech it had been emitting, a tiny chirp came out.

No, not a chirp. An electronic beep.

The bird seemed equally surprised.

It flew away.

But the beep continued, tugging Madison away from that dark alley.

She opened her eyes and realized she still clutched her book to her chest as if it were a stuffed animal.

The lights were all off. Hadn't she fallen asleep with them on?

Beep.

She blinked, trying to see in the darkness. Even the

night-light she kept plugged in at the base of the stairs was out.

Her chest tightened as the darkness became as suffocating as a pillow over her face.

Beep.

Just as she was reaching to try to turn on the light, she finally recognized the sound; the uninterrupted power supply on Ethan's computer. The battery backup beeped when the power went out, giving them time to properly shut down the computer.

Turning that lamp switch would do no good.

Her need for light was primal, like the need for air. She stood up, feeling slightly dizzy and disoriented.

God, she hated how dark it got here. In the city, she was never immersed in total darkness—something she never truly appreciated until living on this hill outside of Buckeye. She could see a few of the larger objects in the room, those dark against light surfaces. She walked carefully to the window. Plenty of stars, but no moon.

Beep.

Why wasn't that sound waking Ethan?

She was just a little ashamed when she realized how much better she'd feel with him awake to keep her company in the dark.

She picked her way toward the kitchen, headed to the utility room beyond where the flashlight was. Passing by the kitchen table, she caught her toe on a chair leg, bending it painfully to the side.

"Oooh. Damn it!" Her voice was louder than it needed to be and the chair made a clatter. She paused for a moment, listening for movement overhead indicating she'd awakened Ethan.

Beep.

No footsteps.

How could he sleep with that annoying beeping?

She moved on toward the utility room.

There was a muffled thud. She couldn't tell if it came from overhead, or just outside near the trashcans—Ethan or a raccoon?

Searching with groping hands like a blind woman, she sought the metal barrel of the Maglight she knew was somewhere in the clutter on the countertop. When she'd bought the huge thing, Ethan had teased her, suggesting she wanted it more to use as a club than for light. But she knew the power lines to this house all came in from overhead wires; not the safe, buried lines she was used to in the city. One tree branch—that's all it would take and they'd be without power for who knew how long. She figured the bigger the flashlight, the bigger the batteries, the longer she'd have light. It might have been skewed thinking, but it made her feel better.

She had plenty of candles, too—enough for a seven-day blackout, Ethan claimed. Unfortunately, the lighter was buried somewhere on this same countertop. This had served as a catch-all from the day they'd moved in. She kept meaning to take the time to organize this stuff and put it away. *First thing tomorrow evening,* she vowed.

Finally, her fingers brushed the scored metal of the flashlight handle. It fell over and knocked into something else. With quick hands, she managed to grasp the flashlight before it rolled onto the floor.

Turning on the narrow shaft of light was like having been underwater too long and finally breaking the surface. She was able to take in her first deep breath since she'd awakened.

On the off chance that it wasn't a true power outage, she checked the fuse box, hoping a simple flip of a switch would restore her beloved light.

Nope. No such luck.

Beep.

The whole purpose of the UPS was so Ethan wouldn't lose data and could shut the computer down...so why wasn't he doing it? She started toward his room, secretly glad she had a reason to wake him. Misery loves company, her mother always said.

Always cognizant of his privacy, she knocked on his bedroom door.

Beep.

Louder now that she was close. Loud enough to have awakened him. Ethan was an unusually light sleeper for a teenager.

She put her hand on the knob, hoping he hadn't locked his door.

It swung open. She shone the light toward Ethan's bed and her heart nearly stopped.

Chapter 29

GABE HANDED ETHAN the small tape recorder he kept in his department vehicle. "This will record for thirty minutes." He clipped the tiny microphone to one of Ethan's front belt loops. "Put it in your pocket and press the long button when you see him coming. After that, try to keep your hands away from it and the mic."

Ethan took the recorder and slid it into his jeans pocket, looking at Gabe without a hint of nerves.

"I'll be just on the other side of the railing, tucked right beneath you."

Ethan gave a matter-of-fact nod.

"You're sure you want to do it this way?" Gabe asked. "I can just come out and arrest him the moment he arrives."

"If the tape will help get what's coming to him, then that's the way I want to do it. Nobody around here will take my word about what he says."

Gabe glanced at his watch. Nearly two. He clapped

Ethan on the back and walked around the end of the guardrail.

Maddie would nail his hide to a tree if she knew what they were doing—which was why Ethan had refused to call her. He'd convinced Gabe that short of there being a house fire, she'd never know he wasn't in his room until morning. And by then he'd be home and safe.

Gabe crouched in the undergrowth immediately beside the bridge, where the land fell away toward the creek, his gut twisting with unease.

Ethan sat on the rail above him and slightly closer to the end of the bridge.

The sound of the water rushing twenty feet below gave the night its background. Crickets droned and tree frogs warbled. So much peace surrounding so much tension.

He unholstered his weapon. He'd never had to fire it except in practice, and didn't anticipate needing to tonight. But there was no way he was letting anything happen to Maddie's brave son.

Gabe probably should have called for another unit to back him up. But the terrain made it difficult enough to hide one vehicle and they were running short on time. He had to stay sharp; Ethan's life was solely in his hands.

The boy kept his back to Gabe when he said, "Why d'ya think he did it?"

"I don't know." Had Steve figured out that Todd was abusing his stepbrother? Or had he discovered that Todd was dealing? Maybe he found out Todd was taking performance enhancing drugs himself.

"I mean"—Ethan's voice sounded much more calm than Gabe felt—"he climbed all the way up there—so he had to have planned it, right?"

"Looks that way." Premeditated murder could hardly be attributed to erratic and moody behavior due to steroid use.

As the minutes passed, Gabe continued to think on motive. None of the likely reasons for a person to commit murder—jealousy, love, money, power, revenge—seemed to apply. Perhaps Todd's stint in a treatment facility after his mother died might hold the key. It was possible that Todd suffered from some long-term psychological problem.

Ethan broke the silence. "Maybe he's not coming."

"He wasn't at home." And he wasn't answering his cell. Kate had acted nervous enough to make Gabe think that she felt she had reason to worry. Why else was she sitting in the dark fully dressed?

Where was Todd? Gabe had had dispatch order both department and city officers not to stop him until after two-fifteen a.m.

Gabe had silenced his own radio. He chanced turning it on again. To Ethan he said, "Tell me the second you see headlights."

"Okay."

Dispatch confirmed that no one had called in sighting or apprehending Todd McPherson. Gabe switched off the radio.

"Tell me what he said to you again," Gabe said.

Ethan kept his casual pose on the rail, his attention focused down the road. "He wanted to warn me that his stepmom thought I killed Mr. McP and she'd convinced Jordan to tell everyone that I did. That if he was me, he'd take off right away."

As dead set as Kate had been earlier in the week that

Ethan was guilty, there was no way she wouldn't have had Gabe on the phone the second Jordan said anything of the kind.

Ethan went on, "He said he knew I didn't do it."

"Did he say how he knew this?"

"I didn't have a reason to kill his dad. He thinks I'm getting blamed just because I'm not from around here. He said if I left, he'd have time to convince people that they need to keep looking—he didn't want his dad's killer to go free."

Todd was sounding way too sympathetic; Ethan had been right to get worried. And Todd was clearly very adept at manipulating people. Gabe wondered how much of Kate's conviction that Ethan was guilty had been spoonfed to her by her stepson.

"What made him think that if you left no one would come after you . . . if we're all so convinced of your guilt?"

"He said he knew I was good at staying out of sight when I need to. He also made a big deal about J.D. taking off yesterday, saying the killer was probably coming after me, too." Ethan gave a bitter-sounding laugh. "I guess that part was true."

Todd most likely was planning on killing Ethan and disposing of his body where no one would find it. Ethan's disappearance would then confirm his guilt of the other murders and Todd would never fall under suspicion.

Gabe looked at his watch. Two-twenty.

Why would Todd risk being late? It left open the possibility of Ethan taking off on his own, leaving a loose end—and Todd seemed determined to tie up his loose ends.

An image came to Gabe's mind that made his blood

run cold: Todd sitting in the woods smoking, waiting patiently for his own father to come into killing range.

Gabe thought of the fresh-looking cigarette butts on the rail overpass.

Had Todd waited in the same way for Maddie to drive under the overpass? No loose ends. Maddie was the single person actively pursuing the idea of a local drug dealer.

No loose ends.

Shit!

He pulled out his cell phone and dialed Maddie's home number.

Immediately, he got the fast busy signal that said there was trouble with the line.

Heat washed over his body. Suddenly he was perspiring on this cool night.

Ethan said, "What are you doing?"

"Just a minute." Gabe dialed Maddie's cell number.

After five rings, voice mail picked up and Gabe scrambled up toward the road. "Let's go!"

Ethan didn't move. "Why? We'll miss Todd."

Gabe was sprinting toward where they'd hidden the car a half-mile down the road. "Come on! He's after Maddie, too!"

Behind him he heard Ethan swear, followed by his feet thudding against the pavement.

FOR A MOMENT, Madison stood frozen. Instead of finding her son in his room, she saw the hulking bulk of Todd McPherson standing on the near side of Ethan's neatly made bed.

He was smiling.

"Where's Ethan?" she demanded.

"Oh, I think you've got problems of your own to worry about."

His movement toward her was fast, but she was faster, pulling the door closed and turning for the stairs.

The beam of her flashlight jerked along in front of her as she ran down the steps. She heard the door slam against the wall and heavy footfalls behind her.

She'd made it to the second to the bottom tread when he slammed her from behind with both hands, sending her facedown on the floor so hard that it knocked the wind from her.

The flashlight hit the wood floor, breaking free of her grip.

He didn't immediately fall upon her as she'd expected. Instead she saw his feet come into her field of vision as she lay there helplessly gasping.

"You couldn't let it go, could you?" he said with a surprising degree of calmness. "It didn't have to be like this, you know. You weren't a part of what had to be done."

He knelt down and grabbed a fistful of her hair and lifted her head from the floor. The pain in her scalp sliced white hot, but she didn't have any air in her lungs to cry out.

Where was Ethan? What had this bastard done to him?

"My momma died falling down the stairs," he said. "She didn't have to die either."

He dropped her head. Her cheek hit the floor with a painful thud.

"I just don't understand women," he said with a sigh.

His feet moved away from her, toward the front door. She fought to get a steady breath; to get oxygen to her starved muscles.

Her right hand inched toward the flashlight. Could she reach it without moving too much and drawing attention to her intent?

Her fingers brushed the metal shaft and the flashlight rolled an inch farther away.

Todd picked up Ethan's baseball bat from where Ethan had left it propped beside the front door Monday night.

Turning around, Todd made his way slowly back to her.

She kept her cheek on the floor, holding as still as when she'd been unable to breathe. Her gaze remained on the flashlight; her only hope.

"Bye-bye, newspaper lady."

As the bat came down, Madison rolled quickly to her right, grabbing the flashlight as she did.

The bat hit the floor with a *crack!* that resonated in her bones.

Before he could raise the bat again, she swung the flashlight and connected with his kneecap. It was a sloppy blow, but it drew an animal-like howl from him.

She scrambled to her knees. Stumbling to her feet, she headed for the front door. *Outside. Draw him away from Ethan. Hide in the woods. Please let Ethan be all right.*

Todd bellowed behind her. "You bitch!"

She heard glass breaking and furniture shifting.

Lurching forward, she found the doorknob. Locked.

Unwilling to part with the flashlight, she used her left hand to turn the deadbolt. She jerked open the door.

He was coming.

She threw herself through the doorway and dashed across the porch. As she hit the first step, she realized she was barefoot.

He'd probably check the road first. There, she'd be easy

to spot. She shut off the flashlight; then ran around the house, toward the woods.

Christ, it was dark. The ground was uneven and she was headed uphill. If she could find a hiding place...then what? No. She had to keep moving. It was her only chance—slim as it was. Todd knew how to navigate in the woods. She didn't. Hell, she couldn't even tell what direction she was headed.

What if he had a flashlight?

Stop thinking and keep running.

Chapter 30

IN THE EARLY MORNING HOURS, it wasn't truly necessary to use lights and siren to race through the deserted streets of Buckeye. Gabe took no extra chances. He used both as he crossed town at high speed.

The distance between the bridge on Settlers Road and Maddie's house was about as far as it could be and still be in the same township. Todd had made certain Ethan's walk would be a long one. Maddie had been alone in the house for over two hours.

Please don't let us be too late.

Stamping out his rising panic, Gabe drove faster.

He glanced at Ethan. The boy was stonefaced, leaning forward as if urging more speed. His hand was gripped tight on the door handle.

"Go faster!" Ethan said, keeping his own gaze on the road ahead.

They hit a chuckhole and the steering wheel jerked in Gabe's hands. He was already going too fast. He pressed on the accelerator and prayed nothing strayed into their path.

They reached the outskirts of town where the road grew more serpentine and undulating. Gabe had to decrease his speed to keep the Jeep on the road.

"What are you doing? Don't slow down!"

Gabe couldn't spare a look toward Ethan; it took all of his concentration to keep the vehicle under control.

MADISON STUBBED HER TOE AND FELL, but was back on her feet almost as swiftly as she'd gone down. Her first steps were hobbling, but she quickly found her stride, straining against the uphill grade.

Whiplike branches stung her already bruised face. The uneven ground tortured her feet and strained her ankles. Twigs poked and rocks sliced. But she kept going.

Trying to listen for Todd behind her, she couldn't hear anything except her own breathing and the slap and rattle of the underbrush as she moved.

Quiet. She had to slow down and be quiet. All he had to do was listen and she'd give her location away.

When she slowed, she did hear him—crashing like a bull and uttering vile threats. Threats she had no doubt he'd make good if he caught her.

She stopped moving and listened. He was off to her left; it didn't sound like he was headed directly toward her. That fact gave her hope.

Her best bet was to find help, not to try to outsmart him on terrain where he had the advantage. Instinct told her to keep running. She had to bet he thought she would—and she had to act opposite of what he expected.

She decided to circle around and head back toward the

road, maybe even her house. Ethan might be hurt. She could call for help on her cell phone.

Forcing herself to move smart instead of fast, she veered right first, to put more distance between her and Todd. Then she could swing the rest of the way around toward the house.

It took all of her will not to run. She picked her path as carefully as the darkness allowed, quietly making her way back toward home—at least she hoped she was pointed toward home. Why did it have to be the dark of the moon? She had nothing to guide her at all.

At least she was headed back downhill.

GABE KILLED THE EMERGENCY LIGHTS and siren as they turned onto Turnbull Road. He took the corner too quickly and the back end of the Jeep fishtailed before he got it completely around the corner.

"Why did you turn the siren off? Maybe it'll scare him away."

"Because maybe it'll scare him away," Gabe echoed. *And maybe it'll force him to complete his act quickly and run.* But Ethan didn't need to hear that. "If he takes off into the woods, it's gonna be much harder to catch him."

"But M—"

"I know." Gabe didn't want to think what precious seconds could mean. But Todd was his father's son. He could disappear into these mountains and never be caught. He would be a lingering threat against which they had little defense.

He pushed the car as fast as he dared.

Because of the S curve at the railroad overpass, Gabe

didn't see the tree lying across the road until he was almost upon it.

He slammed on the brakes. Still, the Jeep skidded into the wall of green. Branches crackled and snapped. Gabe heard the plastic lens of the headlight break. The vehicle stopped with a jerk and an explosion of airbags when the front bumper hit the main trunk.

MADISON SUDDENLY REALIZED she no longer heard Todd's rage-filled rants, or the sound of him thrashing everything around him with that bat. She couldn't tell how much farther the house or the road was; her progress was radically slower than it had been when she'd been running *into* the woods.

She held perfectly still, straining to hear movement. There was a slight breeze in the treetops; the rustle of the leaves sounded like very distant applause—Mother Nature enjoying the human hunt.

Madison didn't hear anything that sounded like Todd moving nearby.

Was he holding still, listening for her like she was listening for him? Dare she move?

She squatted down, making herself as small as possible, and waited. As she hunkered there next to a thick-trunked tree, she looked at her light gray sweatshirt. Setting the unlit flashlight down, she ripped the sweatshirt over her head and wadded it into a ball. Her black T-shirt didn't provide much protection, but it wouldn't show up against the trees, either.

Dropping the sweatshirt, she rolled it around to dirty it up so at least it didn't stand out in contrast to the ground and vegetation. She didn't want to leave a visible trail.

Then she shoved it into the underbrush, stayed low, and listened.

It seemed the more intently she listened, the more confused she became. There were hundreds of small sounds all around her...which ones could be a warning of danger?

Todd had been loud in his movements as he chased her. None of those tiny sounds could be him.

She took a deep breath and stood, ready to move again.

A twig snapped behind her.

Instinctively, she crouched as she turned.

Nothing moved toward her.

Waiting another few seconds, she didn't hear anything except the breeze and the night creatures—the four- and six-legged kind.

She had to get to the house—to her phone, or her car. But she couldn't leave until she'd searched the house for Ethan. Had he taken refuge in some hiding spot before Todd had found him?

As unlikely as that was, she could hope. In her heart, she knew Ethan would never willingly stay hidden while she was being attacked. If there was any way in his power to help, he would have.

Was he injured? Did he need medical help?

Driven by urgency to discover Ethan's condition, she took a risk and moved more quickly.

JESUS CHRIST, HAD TODD thought of everything?

Gabe blinked the stinging pain from the airbag away and reached to unfasten his seat belt. "You okay?"

"Yeah." Ethan coughed. "That wasn't here when I left."

Gabe jabbed the button turning on the emergency flashers, picked up the small flashlight from the console, then shoved open the driver's-side door. Tree branches fought him, but he finally managed to get it open far enough to get out.

Ethan put down the passenger window and slipped out that way.

His way lighted by the remaining headlight, Gabe climbed over the tree trunk, then pushed his way through the branches, breaking into a run as soon as he was free.

He hadn't gone six strides when Ethan passed him.

"Wait!"

The kid kept going.

IF ONLY TODD HADN'T CUT THE POWER, she'd at least have a light to head toward once she got close. In this pitch black, she'd have to be practically right on it before she saw the house.

Then she thought grimly, if Todd hadn't cut the power, she wouldn't have had any warning at all. She'd be dead.

She stopped and looked around her. Even if it hadn't been so bloody dark, she wasn't familiar enough with the terrain around her own house to recognize where she was.

With a leap of faith, she pressed forward.

What if she wasn't going the right direction—

There it was! The white hulk of the rented Taurus stood out against the dark side of the house. She'd angled in from the side instead of coming directly up behind the backyard.

She sprinted toward the front porch—the door she knew to be unlocked. Not only unlocked, she saw, but still open; for some reason that unsettling and vulnerable sight gave her pause. Stupid, since there was a madman chasing her with a baseball bat.

She didn't slow as she ran through the house. Luckily it was a fairly straight shot from the front door to the kitchen; it didn't matter that her vision wasn't good enough to guide her. She didn't want to risk the flashlight showing through the windows.

Her purse was on the kitchen table. Her cell phone was in her purse.

She flew through the kitchen door with the flashlight clutched in her left hand and reached toward the table with her right.

The pain in her right forearm was so sharp and so unexpected that she thought she might faint. Nausea rolled and she collapsed to her knees clutching her arm across her stomach.

"Damn, but you're making this difficult," Todd said; his cold calm voice now laced with an edge of anger.

She heard the bat tap the glass tabletop. *Tap. Tap. Tap.*

She tried to move her arm, but the lightning bolt of pain told her it was broken. She drew in deep draughts of air trying to keep from throwing up.

"Gotta give you credit. Most people wouldn't have thought to ditch the sweatshirt. Would have been faster to come in the back door, though."

He *had* been following her. How long?

What did it matter?

Focus. She had to focus.

Gritting her teeth, Madison tried to gather her thoughts, make a plan, but there was nothing in her mind but a red-hot swirl of pain.

NO MATTER HOW HARD GABE PUSHED, he couldn't gain ground on Ethan. At least he wasn't falling farther behind.

He concentrated on keeping the rhythm of his feet steady; he couldn't allow himself to slow down. His lungs felt as if someone had reached down his throat and was trying to pull them out with taloned fingers.

It was three-quarters of a mile between the S curve and Maddie's house. Thank God they were getting close.

They passed Todd's car pulled into the brush on the side of the road about thirty yards from the house—confirmation of Gabe's fears.

Ethan started to run faster.

Gabe didn't waste the breath to caution him. His shout would be a warning that he didn't want to give Todd.

Maddie's house was dark...completely dark, including the porchlight she usually left on.

Gabe reached for his gun.

Maddie screamed. Glass shattered.

Todd gave an unearthly bellow that bounced and echoed all around Gabe, turning his insides to water.

Ethan vaulted up the porch steps.

Gabe was about six strides behind. He raised his weapon, positioning the flashlight below it in his supporting hand.

Ethan was headed toward the kitchen.

A quick sweep of the light showed the living room was empty.

Returning the light to Ethan, he saw the boy launch himself through the kitchen door.

A loud crash was followed by the grinding of glass.

Todd bellowed again.

Gabe reached the door. Todd had Ethan pinned on the floor, a baseball bat pressed across Ethan's windpipe. Ethan's feet pushed helplessly against the tile.

Maddie was on her knees beside them.

Before Gabe could go for Todd, Maddie swung a flashlight, clubbing Todd on the back of the head.

Instead of going down as Gabe expected, Todd reared up on his knees. With a feral roar, he twisted, raised the bat and started to bring it down on Maddie.

Gabe didn't have time to utter a warning before he fired his gun.

ETHAN MADE HORRIBLE GASPING NOISES as he scrambled to get out from under the dead weight of Todd's legs. Madison dropped the flashlight and reached for Ethan with her good arm, moving across the broken glass on her knees.

Once she had her hand on her son, she finally heard Gabe calling to her in that beautiful voice. Then he touched her and the realization that this nightmare was finally at an end washed over her.

Chapter 31

T HE SHADOWS WERE LONG as the sun began to set. Madison could almost feel the darkness creeping closer, the damp chill of it lying like a cold hand on her skin. The air bag hanging like a deflated balloon from the Jeep's dash reminded her of how close shed come to losing everything. From the passenger seat next to Gabe, she looked at her house, lights already burning although true darkness was at least an hour away. That had been Gabe's doing, she knew. He'd made certain the power had been restored and the lights turned on before they returned.

Not that she'd confessed her dislike of darkness to him—he seemed to be particularly intuitive about her inner thoughts and feelings. She'd never had that kind of connection with anyone.

They had left this house this morning just as the sun was rising, as the promise of light kissed the morning sky. And now Gabe ensured she would not be coming home to darkness.

As she looked at the deepening purple of the evening woods, Madison realized then that she didn't dread the dark quite as much as before—before she'd faced the worst it had to deal her. Having come through last night broken and yet still whole had shifted something inside her.

That hadn't been her only epiphany. The stark realization that she needed both Ethan *and* Gabe had hit her hard. They were like air and water, so different and yet so necessary to sustain life. Funny, for a woman who never wanted protecting she drew surprising strength and pleasure from the fact that they both had been there fighting for her.

At the hospital, after it was all over, Ethan had admitted he'd been running away. When he'd said it, her heart nearly froze in mid-beat and her mouth had gone dry. Just the thought of losing him, even though the danger had passed, was a shock to her system. She'd known that if Ethan had left and hadn't wanted her to find him, she probably never would.

She wrapped that cold lump of fear and put it away in a place where she could draw it out for a perspective adjustment if the frustrations of motherhood ever grew overwhelming.

Gabe assisted her out of the car and up the front steps of her house as if she were an invalid. Ethan hovered at her other side, apparently ready in case she lost all of her strength and collapsed completely. And truthfully, at the moment it wasn't all that unlikely. Every cell in her body ached. The throb in her newly casted arm kept time with her heartbeat. The pain medication they'd given her made her head feel as if it might float away from her body—not an unwelcome prospect, considering the stiff neck and ache behind her eyes.

"I really would feel better if you two would stay at my place for a day or two," Gabe said for the tenth time.

Madison didn't bother to argue yet again; they were here.

Ethan had insisted on coming home. And Madison had agreed. She'd never seen any point in putting off the unpleasant; it usually got harder, not easier, to face things a person would rather not. The memory of what had transpired in their kitchen would only intensify if she didn't walk right back in there and deal with it. She hoped she wasn't wrong in her assumption that it was the same for Ethan. She'd be watching him closely. Before they'd left the hospital, they'd made an appointment with a counselor for next Monday.

She hesitated at the bottom step to her porch—not because of the pain, but to brace herself. Even though the crime scene had been completely processed and Todd's body removed, in her mind's eye she still held the picture of Ethan's blood-spattered face as he struggled to get out from under Todd's legs.

Ethan unlocked the front door.

The fact that it was locked seemed ludicrous, considering there was a pane broken out of the back door, which allowed anyone to stick their hand through and turn the deadbolt. Todd had been very skilled in breaking it; taping it to keep the pieces from falling to the tile floor on the inside. It made her wonder if he'd had previous experience with breaking and entering.

Not that it mattered now.

Gabe guided her toward the stairs. She resisted, looking toward the kitchen. "I need to..."

It was Ethan, not Gabe, who said, "No, M."

She looked at him, surprised.

"We need to sleep," Ethan said. "Then we'll deal."

Madison looked toward Gabe. There was something in his eyes as he looked at her son. After a moment, she recognized it...respect. That silent nod of regard gave her a deep sense of peace.

Gabe said, "He's right. I have to go to the office and take care of some things. You two get some sleep and I'll be back in the morning—you can call if you need me before then."

Madison knew the unpleasant things an officer had to do after a line-of-duty shooting. She felt sorry for Gabe. He looked every bit as exhausted as Ethan did.

With a nod, Madison allowed her two men, her two protectors, to help her up the stairs to her bedroom.

As soon as she sat down on the bed, Ethan said to Gabe, "I'll meet you downstairs."

Gabe plumped her pillows and took off the socks the hospital had put on over her bandaged feet. "Do you want to change?" he asked.

She shook her head, the action making her dizzy. She had on her flannel pants and Tennessee sweatshirt that Gabe had brought to her and was just too tired to change.

He lifted her legs onto the bed and pulled sheet and blanket over her. Then he kissed her gently, mindful of her cuts and bruises. "Get some rest."

As he stood and turned to go, she reached out and snagged his hand. "Stay and talk...just for a minute."

He sat down on the edge of the bed and held her hand in both of his.

She realized how selfish her request was and shook her head. "No. No. I'm sorry. You still have so much to do." She tried to pull her hand away, but he held tight.

"I'd welcome a quiet moment," he said, making her feel like she was doing him a favor. Instead of delving deep into emotions, he began to tell her about his house, about the trees growing in the gutters and the squirrels that kept getting into the attic, about the plans he had, and the renovations he'd already done.

Her responses were limited to tired smiles and heavy-lidded blinks. But he didn't seem to mind. He just kept talking.

His voice invaded every pore of her skin, soothed each and every frayed nerve. It was a drug more powerful than the shot they'd given her in the hospital. She wanted to say something, to tell him how much she cared for him, but could not make her lips move.

Gabe's deep lyrical voice flowed around her like a warm river as she sank into sleep.

THE NEXT MORNING Gabe walked in the front door wearing a grin and holding up a red Sharpie. "Want me to sign your cast?"

Even after the hell they'd all been through, just the sight of him brought lightness to Madison's heart. She smiled at him from the couch—where Ethan had placed her and forbidden her to move—thankful for Gabe's touch of humor.

"Sure," she said. "Then you can take me to the sock-hop after school."

He'd showered and shaved and was wearing jeans and an oxford shirt, but he still looked tired. Moving to stand in front of her, he leaned forward, bracing his hands behind her on the couch. He looked in her eyes for a long moment.

"You look beautiful," he said, then kissed her gently on the forehead.

In that sweet, smooth-talking voice of his, she could almost believe him.

Unfortunately, she'd seen herself in the mirror. The green-purple bruise on her face from her accident had been joined by welts, newly forming scabs, and what looked like a long rug burn where she'd grazed the bark of a tree. Her left arm looked equally bad, and the nurse in the ER had warned her that the scratches beneath the cast on her right were going to be itching like mad in three days.

Gabe looked up at the sounds from the kitchen. "I told him to wait for me."

Ethan had seemed more man than boy when he'd insisted that she not go into the kitchen until he had all of the glass from the broken tabletop cleaned up.

Madison pulled Gabe down on the couch next to her. "Let him do this. He needs to."

"I guess we all need some closure," he said.

"How's Kate?" she asked.

"A wreck. Bobby's with her. They're going to see Jordan and his doctors today—figure out the best way to tell him."

"That poor boy. Do you think Todd being gone will help him recover?"

Gabe sighed. "Who knows how long Todd had been

bullying and threatening Jordan. It might take a long while to undo the damage."

"If it ever can be," she added sadly.

After a moment, she said, "He admitted to me that he did it...Todd killed his mother." The cold damp hand of revulsion ran down her spine.

Gabe wrapped his arm gently around her and rubbed her shoulder. Madison leaned into his warmth, wanting to banish the chill that came with the image of a boy shoving his mother down a long flight of stairs. Had he spoken to her in that detached tone he'd used on Madison? Had his mother had a moment of recognition, known her own child was a monster?

"Why?" she asked softly. "What would make a child do such a thing? He sounded so...dispassionate when he told me."

"No one will ever know," Gabe said, resting his cheek on the top of her head. "And, unless Jordan recovers and can tell us, we won't know with certainty that he killed his father, too."

Madison sat up straight and looked at him. "You mean you have doubts?" Good God, she'd thought this nightmare was over. If Gabe still thought someone else killed—

"No. I don't have doubts. And I don't have other suspects." He gave her a pointed look. "It'd just be nice to see if we could discover what happened. I suppose we'll never understand why—not in a way that makes sense to us rational folk."

Madison might never get those low-spoken words out of her head. *My momma died falling down the stairs. She didn't need to die, either.* "He was just so...matter of fact. He even made it sound like it was her fault." She paused. "From what I saw, Todd McPherson was a text-book psychopath. We'll never understand what went on in his mind."

"That leads to the question: are psychopaths made or born?" Gabe said thoughtfully.

"I don't think I want to know the answer," Madison said, surprising herself with the truth of the statement. She, the woman who had to dig for all of the answers, fig-ure out every piece of the puzzle, didn't want to know. She wondered if Todd had broken more than her arm.

Glancing at Gabe, she could see his face was drawn with fatigue. There were deep purple circles under his eyes. "Did you sleep?"

His answer was a shrug.

"Go home," she said. "Sleep before you fall on your face."

His green eyes locked with hers. "As I plowed through the past twelve hours, the only thing that kept me going was the thought of seeing you. I'm not leaving anytime soon."

"But—"

He leaned back, put his arm around her and pulled her close. "Let me do this. I need to."

And, as the tears came, Madison realized she needed it too.

Chapter 32

"WATCH YOUR FINGERS, THERE," Gabe said, as he and Ethan carried Madison's new kitchen table in through the back door.

She squeezed one eye shut, cringing in anticipation of Ethan's yelp of pain when his fingers connected with the door jamb.

Surprisingly, the guys made it all the way into the kitchen without incident and set the table in the empty space where the old one used to be. Madison hadn't been able to bring herself to buy another glass table; even without a reminder, she would never get the sound of that bat shattering her old one out of her head.

Gabe tossed Ethan a dishtowel. "Shine that baby up for your momma."

Ethan snagged the towel out of the air and went to work on the dark wood tabletop. "M, you'll never guess who we ran into at the furniture store."

Even though Gabe had never voiced it aloud, it was obvious that he had taken every opportunity during the past two weeks to assimilate Ethan into the social fabric of Buckeye. They'd attended a high school football game and volunteered together at park cleanup day. Gabe had enlisted Ethan's help in a couple of projects at his house that included frequent trips to the hardware store. They'd even grocery shopped. (Supposedly because Madison was still in a cast; and she wasn't fool enough to turn down good help.)

Ethan's comfort level and confidence had skyrocketed. It showed in his eyes, in the way he carried himself. He finally was beginning to feel as if he *belonged*—probably for the first time in his young life.

"Who?" she asked.

"Coach Lawrence. He said this town owed you and me a lot."

"Oh, how nice." But it didn't account for the big grin on her son's face.

"That's when Gabe suggested maybe Coach could pay us back by letting me join in football practice . . . you know, see if I have any talent that could contribute to the team next year."

Madison cast a glance toward Gabe; his grin matched Ethan's. Her heart felt as if it were rolling around on a cloud.

"Is that so? Do you think that's something you'd be interested in?" she asked needlessly; excitement was written all over Ethan's face. "I mean, I don't want Gabe to push you into something—"

"Oh no! He's not pushing me." Ethan stopped wiping the table. "I told him I might want to play when we went to the game the other night—and saw the Rebels get slaughtered. I think I could be good at it." He looked at Gabe. "Gabe thinks so, too."

She put a hand on her hip, feigning disapproval. "What if you get hurt?" She lifted her cast. "I don't think we can manage with two of us wearing these."

"I won't be officially playing until next year. You'll have plenty of time to heal before I break something." The teasing tone in his voice told Madison that her son had truly come out on the other side of his trials a stronger—and yes, unbelievable as it seemed, happier—person.

The doorbell rang.

Gabe's grin widened. There was a playfully devious look in his eye when he suggested Ethan answer it.

Ethan left the kitchen and Madison asked, "What do you have up your sleeve?"

"You'll see," he whispered, then moved to the doorway to the living room and peeked around the jamb.

Madison leaned against his back and peered around his shoulder. She barely noticed what was going on at the door, lost as she was in Gabe's closeness. Was that his heartbeat against her chest, or was it her own?

They'd had precious little time alone, she and Gabe, to expand their carnal knowledge of one another. Their romantic encounters had been all too brief, leaving them both hungering for more. But at every turn, Gabe had insisted that Ethan be included in whatever they did. Madison decided that fact showed Gabe's true measure as a man—selfless and giving, a man with family as a priority.

Even so, *she* was going crazy with sexual frustration. She wanted to explore the promise of passion she saw in his eyes every time he kissed her.

As she stood there drinking in the feel of him against her, the innocent contact set off not-so-innocent physical responses. Maybe she'd passed frustrated and was sliding fast toward desperate.

Suddenly, she felt Gabe's back stiffen. He moved away from her so quickly, she nearly fell forward. His back blocked Madison's view of who was outside the door.

She moved closer and heard a woman's soft voice. "May I come in?"

"Uh, yeah, sure," Ethan stammered.

As Ethan and Gabe stepped back, Kate McPherson stepped across the threshold.

Madison shot Gabe a questioning look. He responded with a puzzled expression and a lifted shoulder. This obviously was not who he was expecting.

Kate stood with her hands buried in her jacket pockets, looking at Ethan. He shifted awkwardly in the open doorway.

Madison stepped forward, "Kate, come in, please. Sit down."

Kate appeared smaller and more colorless than ever. Since Todd's death, she'd become understandably reclusive. Madison knew firsthand how it felt to be Buckeye's pariah. Kate's sin of association would be a long time in being forgotten.

She shifted her weight from one foot to the other, finally pulling her hands out of her pockets. "Thanks, but I can't stay. I'm on my way to see Jordan. I just wanted to talk to Ethan."

Madison saw Gabe move a fraction closer to Ethan. She moved to Ethan's other side. A united front that felt entirely natural.

Kate visibly swallowed. "I won't take long." A weak, heartbreakingly pathetic smile curved her pale lips. She looked Ethan in the eye. "I...I want to apologize to you." Her hands were trembling.

Surprise colored Ethan's expression. "You didn't...I mean, it's not necessary—"

"It is," Kate cut him off. "An apology isn't nearly enough, but it's all I can offer. And I want to ask you not to hold my mistakes against Jordan. You're his friend—a *good* friend."

"Thank you." He paused and then asked softly, "Is... is he any better?"

This time a real smile graced Kate's face. "He's making progress. I've made sure the staff at Pleasant Hill knows you're welcome to visit any time. He's asked for you."

"Really?" Ethan broke into a grin. "I can't wait to see him."

Madison said, "We'll go next weekend." She was glad that although Ethan's life was branching out and moving forward, he wasn't leaving his first friend behind.

Kate looked over her shoulder and Madison noticed that Bobby was sitting in his car waiting for her. "I'd better go."

"Don't forget to tell Jordan I'll be there next week," Ethan called as she walked down the steps.

"I won't." Before she got in the car, she turned and said, "Thank you."

Ethan raised a hand to wave, a more graceful gesture

of forgiveness than Madison managed. She felt impossibly sad for Kate, and yet she could not forget what the woman had tried to do to her son.

Gabe closed the front door.

Madison grabbed Ethan around the neck with her good arm and brought him into a hug. "I'm so proud of you."

He pulled away. "Sheesh, M. Did you think I was gonna hit her or something?"

Gabe said, "You accepted that apology like a gentleman. It's not an easy thing to do."

"No big deal," Ethan said as he moved away.

Madison watched Gabe watching Ethan. She liked what she saw; kindness, respect, caring. It struck her then that Gabe Wyatt would be a good father when his time came.

Before Ethan reached the kitchen, there was another knock at the door.

Gabe's face lit up as he called, "Ethan, can you get that?"

Ethan turned around, wearing a dubious scowl. "You're standing right there."

"I don't live here."

Ethan pointed to Madison, who was still standing within four feet of the door. "M—"

"Has a broken arm," Gabe finished for him.

Ethan rolled his eyes, walked past both of them, and yanked open the front door.

When Madison saw the puppy, she looked at Gabe. "I know I said I'd think about it—"

"A dog! I've always wanted a dog." Ethan reached out, asking Mr. Whetzel, "Can I?"

The old man passed the brown ball of fluff to Ethan.

"This little'un here was dumped out t'the house. The missus is allergic. Sheriff said maybe y'all could take her in."

"She's just here for a visit," Gabe said quickly. But his excitement outshone the sun. "You know, to meet everyone and see how y'all get along."

Madison said, "She is awfully cute." Then she raised a brow toward Gabe. "And you don't play fair."

Gabe leaned close to Madison's ear and whispered, "Every boy needs a dog." There was enough enthusiasm in his voice to make Madison wonder who really wanted the dog. Gabe added, "You know, to learn responsibility and all."

"Oh yeah," she muttered behind her smile, "Ethan really needs a lesson in personal responsibility." She touched Gabe's cheek. "You're so transparent. Sweet, but transparent."

"Can we keep her, M?"

"How big do you think she'll get?" Madison reached out and stroked the dog's soft head.

"Reckon nobody'll know 'til she's done growin'," Mr. Whetzel said.

Gabe whispered, "Does it matter?"

A quick pink tongue darted out and kissed Ethan's cheek.

"She loves me already," Ethan said. Then he turned his clear blue eyes Madison's way. "She needs us. She's a street kid, just like I used to be."

Who could argue with that?

MADISON SAT CURLED AGAINST Gabe's side, watching the flames flicker in his fireplace. They'd just finished carry-out pizza and were drinking grocery store wine out of plastic glasses. The couch was lumpy, the wallpaper was water-stained, the wind whistled through the cracks around the windows, and occasionally there was a downdraft that backed smoke up into the room—it was the most beautifully romantic setting she'd ever experienced.

While they'd been eating, Gabe had told her how he'd come to purchase this house, looking upon it as an act of pity, taking on something that was too dilapidated to attract a family. His compassion was so pure, so kind that she'd nearly cried.

Man, she thought, she *was* getting sentimental in her old age.

Gabe kissed the top of her head. "I'm glad Ethan's social life is branching out."

She chuckled. "You mean you're glad he's finally got someone to do stuff with so we can be alone."

He pulled away, looking truly hurt. "No. I mean I'm glad he's finally getting to live the life he deserves. He's a good kid."

She felt like a heel. "Yes, he is." She nodded and gave him a contrite smile. "And I apologize for thinking you had a self-serving reason for your—"

He moved so quickly Madison was pinned beneath him before she could react. He even managed to do it and keep her cast safely out of the way. "Oh, don't apologize." He grinned, his eyes sparking with mischief. "I'm happy for him"—he dipped his head and nibbled at her lower lip—"but I'm ecstatic for me."

His fingers worked the buttons of her blouse as his mouth pushed aside the fabric. Everywhere his lips grazed her skin, it was set afire.

"Mmmmmm." She shifted beneath him, urging him

toward her breast. "Me, too." Ecstatic was the understatement of the century. Her body had hungered for his; her dreams had foreshadowed this moment. Now it was finally here and she wished time would stand still.

After a teasing encounter with her still-clad nipple, he covered her body with his own again. Framing her face with his hands, he looked at her. The cool humor had left the depths of his eyes; now they were hot, suggestive, and filled with tenderness. A lightning bolt shot through her, striking in the pit of her stomach.

She pulled him close and whispered, "I was beginning to think we were going to have to wait for Ethan to go to college before we'd get around to this."

His warm breath caressed her lips when he groaned. "Dear Lord, woman, you can't be serious. I'm only human."

She shifted so her thigh slipped between his legs. As she moved it against him, she said, "Oh yeah, I can see that now."

Burying his face against her neck, his mouth did things that completely shut down her brain and turbo-charged her senses. He slowly peeled her clothes away. Agonizingly slowly. So slow as to border on cruelty. She had to bite her tongue to keep from shouting for him to just rip them away, and had to still her own hands to keep from doing the same to his.

She could feel him trembling with restraint. His torment was no less than hers. Following his lead, she savored each deliciously torturous moment, realizing that it was the care with which he made love to her that gave the act its full sweetness.

Gabe's hands and body thrilled her, but it was what she saw in his eyes that ripped her apart.

"Maddie, my love." He kissed her and finally brought them together in the union they'd both so long desired.

His love erased the outside world and invaded every fragment of Madison's body and soul. She became so lost in him, she couldn't remember her own name, but whispered his as if it were a prayer.

Epilogue

Madison waited in the lobby of the stress center. Jordan was finally ready to make his statement to the police about his stepfather's death. He'd requested that Ethan be there with him. Which wasn't surprising; the doctor had repeatedly said how instrumental Ethan's visits had been in Jordan's recovery.

Madison felt a little like the odd man out; Gabe, the district attorney, Kate, Bobby, Dr. Brinegar, Ethan, and Jordan had all ensconced themselves in the conference room an hour ago.

Getting up, Madison moved around the lobby, too restless to sit any longer.

The door to the hallway that led to the conference room opened and Gabe appeared. His face was unreadable.

Her heart beat faster as she walked over to him.

He took her elbow and moved her toward the exit. "Ethan wants to spend some time with Jordan. Let's go get some coffee."

Even though it had been four months since that horrible weekend on the mountain, the need to know what
had really happened suddenly became urgent. But she
held her questions; it was obvious Gabe didn't want to discuss it here.

They walked in silence a half-block to a Starbucks and
ordered coffees.

It was a freakishly warm day—nearly fifty. They sat
outside in the watery late-January sunshine.

Gabe leaned back in the metal chair, looking tense and
frustrated. "I tell you, Maddie, after hearing the mental
torture Todd put that boy through, I'd shoot him again
given the chance."

"That bad?"

He nodded, taking in a deep breath, and blew it out.
"It's a wonder Jordan didn't try to commit suicide years
ago." His face grew more grim. "Apparently, he didn't
try four months ago, either. Todd had stood over him,
demanding he take those sedatives, using threats to Kate
as a motivator."

"Dear God." The image of a hulking Todd holding out
a handful of pills, standing over poor Jordan, who reluctantly took them one after the other, brought tears to her
eyes. She was suddenly so cold she wished they'd sat
inside.

"Todd did kill Steve," Gabe said. "But I don't think he
planned to."

Madison couldn't imagine how that could be...he
went up on that mountain and as much as hunted the man
down.

Gabe continued, "Right before they left on that camping trip, Jordan had discovered Todd's steroid stash. Todd

caught him. Of course this was right after the Gilbert kid's death—making the implications much more serious. Todd must have felt he hadn't sufficiently ensured Jordan's silence before Kate had interrupted them. Todd made a trip up the mountain to "remind" Jordan of the consequences of telling what he knew.

"Jordan said Todd had been crazy—wound up. He had Jordan by the neck with one hand and was holding a rock over his head with the other when Steve showed up. When Steve went to pull Todd away, Todd swung blindly and hit him.

"After that, Todd totally lost control. Jordan said it was like watching a wild animal."

She recalled the look on Todd's face when he'd swung the bat at her head. "I can believe that." She paused and tried to banish the image. Good God, if it was this difficult for her, what must it be like for poor Jordan to deal with his memories? "Between Todd's psychological problems and the steroids, he wasn't much short of *being* a wild animal."

Madison clutched her coffee with both hands, her chest aching for Jordan. How horrified he must have been, how terrified.

Gabe leaned forward and wrapped his own hands around hers. "If he had taken you from Ethan…from me…I . . ." He dropped his gaze and shook his head.

Madison got up and walked around behind him. She leaned forward, draping her arms across his chest and pressed her cheek to his temple. "I know."

Over the past months, her need for Gabe had grown to match her need for air and water. She never would have predicted she could be this completely, insanely, irrationally in love. The trials they'd been through early on had tempered their relationship, making it stronger than time alone would have.

Gabe and Ethan had found solid ground, creating their own special relationship—one that seemed to be nearly independent of her.

She held him tighter. "I want to ask you something."

He put his hand over hers where it rested over his heart. "Anything."

"It's not something I want you to answer right now. I want you to really think, because it's a biggie."

He pulled her around to sit in front of him again. "Okay." His eyes searched hers.

"I'd like for you to be Ethan's guardian...if anything should happen to me." Having stared her own mortality in the eye made her realize how vulnerable her son would be if she died or was incapacitated.

At a moment when she expected Gabe to put a little more distance between them, he took her hands and leaned closer. "I don't need to think about it. It would make me happy to be a permanent part of his life. But"— he squeezed her hands—"I have a request of my own."

As hard as she studied him, she couldn't tell where he was headed. She knew what she'd like to hear...but reason said it was too soon. They'd just come off a raw, emotional time.

That time, for her, had crystallized many things, however. Had made her see what a sin it was to waste precious days, how fleeting a chance at happiness could be.

He said, "We're not kids without experience. We both know our own hearts and minds." He paused and her heart sped up. "I want us to be a real family...you, me, and Ethan. Will you marry me?"

His words stole her breath. She looked into his eyes, so green in the sunlight, and saw her future. Her heart leaped at the prospect. She'd known for weeks that she wanted to build a life with him.

She reminded herself, too soon. Much too soon.

Say no...not yet. Be the voice of reason.

She shook her head slowly. "Yes."

His face clouded. "Which is it, yes or no?" he asked.

"What?"

"You shook your head no and said yes. Which is it?" Before she could answer, he said, "No. Too late. I choose the verbal answer. Yes, your answer is yes."

Leaning forward, she kissed him. "Of course it is."

About the Author

Susan's novels have garnered numerous awards. She is a three-time RITA award finalist and winner. PITCH BLACK is her seventh novel. She lives in her native Indiana hometown with her husband and a menagerie of critters.

Visit her on the Web: www.susancrandall.net
Contact: P.O. Box 1092, Noblesville, IN 46061

THE DISH

Where authors give you the inside scoop!

♥ ♥ ♥ ♥ ♥ ♥ ♥ ♥ ♥ ♥ ♥ ♥ ♥

From the desk of Susan Crandall

Dear Reader,

I'd like to share with you a little secret. It's one of those crazy writer things—you know, like making sure you have the right music playing, or just the right scented candle burning, or spinning around in a circle three times before you sit down to write. The kind of thing you simply cannot write without.

Superstitious, you say? Perhaps. A mind game? A crutch? Maybe. Doesn't really matter. As writers, we believe. And when your entire product comes out of your mind, you have to believe.

During those last grueling weeks before a book deadline, I indulge in a special writing snack. This snack is something I like to eat in mass quantities. Something I wouldn't normally allow myself to consume in such ridiculous amounts. But after seven novels, it's become obvious that the writing snack is integral in the process, necessary in order to properly tie off all of the plot threads, to make certain the villain gets his due, and the good guys get their happy endings.

And yes, I do require a serious diet and exercise

program when all is said and done. But I do it for you, my dear reader. So the story is satisfying. So when you read that last page, you're glad you opened the first.

Like all of my books, PITCH BLACK (on sale now) had its very own writing snack. This novel is my first romantic suspense, so the choice was critical. I lost count of the number of boxes of Cheese Nips I went through as I wrote this story about a single-mother journalist whose adoptive son is the main suspect in a brutal crime.

Who knew romantic suspense required even more snacking than women's fiction? At the rare moment when I didn't have a backup box, I panicked. Luckily, I live close to the store.

I'd like to invite you to visit my Web site, www.susancrandall.net, to see the snack that accompanied each book. I have them listed on each book's description page.

While you're there, you can read an excerpt of my upcoming novel of romantic suspense, SEEING RED, which is slated for release in early 2009. Also, please stop by my message board and say hello. I always love hearing from readers, and it's a good place to connect with other book lovers.

Enjoy!

Susan Crandall

From the desk of Jane Graves

Dear Reader,

Did you know that over three hundred weddings are performed in Las Vegas every day? I learned that while researching my latest book, TALL TALES AND WEDDING VEILS (on sale now). So why is Sin City such a popular place to tie the knot?

Top Five Reasons to Get Married in Vegas

1. You've always loved Elvis, so having him perform your wedding ceremony is a dream come true, even if the Vegas version is fat and fifty and can't carry a tune in a bucket.
2. You figure marriage is a gamble anyway, so thematically speaking, it works.
3. It's between that and a New Orleans graveyard wedding performed by a voodoo priestess. The graveyard has spirits, but Vegas has martinis.
4. You can't resist the Austin Powers "1967 Summer of Love Groovy Baby Love Scene Wedding Package."
5. A woman you've just met helps you win a big jackpot, and after a champagne-soaked celebration in a stretch limousine, heading for a drive-through wedding chapel suddenly seems like a *fabulous* idea.

Now, how about that annulment?

Okay, that's not quite as easy. At least it isn't for Tony McCaffrey and Heather Montgomery, the hero and heroine, who spend the first morning of their married lives wondering how fast they can get *un*-married.

When they made the drunken decision to marry in haste, they overlooked an obvious truth: No two people on earth were more incompatible. Tony's a handsome, sexy charmer who spends his life surrounded by women, and Heather's a serious-minded plain Jane whose idea of a good time is balancing her checkbook. But when an unexpected turn of events forces them to stay married for a month, slowly they begin to see each other in a whole new light. What started out as a drunken mistake just might turn out to be the best decision of their lives.

Hope you enjoy TALL TALES AND WEDDING VEILS!

Jane Graves

www.janegraves.com

*Want to know more about romances at
Grand Central Publishing and Forever?
Get the scoop online!*

GRAND CENTRAL PUBLISHING'S
ROMANCE HOMEPAGE

Visit us at www.hachettebookgroupusa.com/romance
for all the latest news, reviews, and chapter excerpts!

NEW AND UPCOMING TITLES

Each month we feature our new titles
and reader favorites.

CONTESTS AND GIVEAWAYS

We give away galleys, autographed copies,
and all kinds of fun stuff.

AUTHOR INFO

You'll find bios, articles, and links to personal
websites for all your favorite authors—and
so much more!

THE BUZZ

Sign up for our monthly romance newsletter,
and be the first to read all about it!